The MANAGER'S DESK REFERENCE

SECOND EDITION

The MANAGER'S DESK REFERENCE

SECOND EDITION

*Cynthia Berryman-Fink
and Charles B. Fink*

amacom
American Management Association

New York · Atlanta · Boston · Chicago · Kansas City · San Francisco · Washington, D.C.
Brussels · Mexico City · Tokyo · Toronto

Library of Congress Cataloging-in-Publication Data

Berryman-Fink, Cynthia, 1952–
    The manager's desk reference / Cynthia Berryman-Fink & Charles B.
Fink. — 2nd ed.
      p.   cm.
    Includes bibliographical references and index.
    ISBN 0-8144-0342-5
    1. Management—Handbooks, manuals, etc.   2. Personnel management—
Handbooks, manuals, etc.   I. Fink, Charles B.   II. Title.
HD38.15.B47   1996
658.3—dc20   96-12325
                                                                  CIP

Printing number

10   9   8   7   6   5   4   3   2   1

Contents

Preface

Organizations of all types need good supervisors, managers, administrators, and executives in order to survive and thrive in a competitive world. Even though management is a vital function in any organization, many people holding management positions have little or no formal training in managing others. Even those with degrees in management or human behavior have difficulty obtaining all of the information and skills needed to manage effectively in today's complex organizations. Because organizations are changing so rapidly, it is increasingly difficult for managers to stay abreast of the latest developments in information technology, human resources, legal mandates, globalization, and specialized issues affecting the workplace. The role of the manager is a diverse and demanding one, requiring skills of communication, counseling, advocacy, diplomacy, sensitivity, judgment, integrity, organization, risk taking, and insight, to name a few.

The business-information industry has responded to the need for management advice. Indeed, managers are bombarded with information and advice on a variety of management issues, presented in current best-sellers, popular magazines, professional and trade journals, newsletters, newspapers, seminars, audio and video tapes, on-line formats, and television and radio talk shows. Busy managers may be overwhelmed and find it difficult to digest the massive amounts of information on new issues and methods of managing people.

The Manager's Desk Reference was written to provide managers with a concise yet comprehensive source of management information. The first edition was published in 1989. This new edition updates the earlier material and adds sections on vital, contemporary topics such as AIDS; change management; managing disabled employees; substance abuse; preventing and responding to workplace violence; managing part-time, temporary, and contingent workers; organizational diversity; and family-friendly management. It offers new information and discusses new management practices related to teams, quality, innovation, and ethics. And it provides selected resources for additional reading on relevant management topics.

This book has grown out of our experiences as management consultants in manufacturing and service organizations. For over fifteen years, clients have asked for practical yet substantive sources of information that they could consult on numerous management issues. We have sorted through the massive management literature; culled from it the most important theories, concepts, strategies, and advice; and presented that information in an easy and practical format.

The Manager's Desk Reference is limited to information on managing people. You will not find information on accounting, budgeting, planning, forecasting, computer programming, or other tasks that managers may encounter. What you will find is information on most aspects of human behavior to help you deal with peers, subordinates, supervisors, customers, the public, the press, and others with whom you may interact as a manager. In most cases you will find all the information you will need on a topic, but you can also use the cross-references and additional sources listed at the end of each section for further information related to that topic.

This book can be used as a starting point for new managers becoming acquainted with the management arena; as a reference source for supervisors, managers, executives, or administrators who want to update their knowledge of management issues; or as a sourcebook of strategies for any manager handling problems or embarking on new people-management projects. Managers at all levels, in the full spectrum of organizations, in the private and public sector should find this book useful. In addition, the book may serve as a valuable tool for students of management or management trainees.

We are indebted to several people and organizations for assistance, insights, and support related to this project. First, without the invaluable interaction with hundreds of client organizations, we would not have been able to fully develop our theories, perspectives, and practices of management. The second author extends special thanks to Gilbert Richards for his mentoring and wise demonstration of theoretical and applied management practices. Jim McCarty's unique brand of leadership modeled for us a style of management that proves good managers excel by meeting the needs of both the organization and its people. Michael Hawkins, a respected attorney specializing in employment law, provided the authors with valuable assistance in legal matters. The University of Cincinnati has given the first author countless opportunities to formulate and test leadership and administrative management ideas and practices. Kristin Shelt and Traci Anderson are acknowledged for their help with background research. Adrienne Hickey and others at AMACOM have advocated for the project and provided editorial assistance.

Finally, the impact of family members on one's identity, values, and vision cannot be overlooked. This is a book about human behavior in a particular context. Our parents and our children have shaped our views of human behavior so deeply and so pervasively that their teachings are woven into this volume. Thank you Elmer for your emphasis on learning, Gertie for your common sense, Joe for your ethical practices, Ella for your resolve, Drew for your youthful wisdom and sense of fairness, and Greg for sharing, by example, your enthusiasm and philosophy that work must be fun! Managers would do well to acquire this wonderful combination of assets of human behavior.

Cynthia Berryman-Fink
Charles B. Fink

The
Manager's
Desk
Reference

SECOND EDITION

AIDS in the Workplace

All indications suggest that acquired immune deficiency syndrome (AIDS) will become a prevalent issue in the workplace. The Centers for Disease Control states that about one in every 250 people is infected with human immunodeficiency virus (HIV), the virus that produces AIDS. AIDS can be considered the health epidemic of the 1990s and beyond.

Relatively few workplace organizations have faced the problem of AIDS. An American Management Association report in 1993 revealed that 36 percent of the companies surveyed had an employee afflicted with HIV or AIDS. Surveys have shown that as few as 10 percent and as many as 30 percent of U.S. companies have developed policies on AIDS. Clearly, this is an issue that organizations of all types cannot avoid. An attitude of "it can't happen here" can cost a company thousands of dollars in lost productivity and lawsuits. Predictive models calculate the average expected medical, disability, employee replacement, life insurance, and pension costs to a business for one HIV-infected employee at $17,000.

It is important to have an AIDS policy in place before the first case occurs. Such a policy can help a company manage AIDS-related workplace issues and can reduce exposure to discrimination claims. In this section, we discuss legal issues for employers regarding AIDS, present the elements that should be included in an organizational policy on AIDS, and describe the nature and role of workplace educational programs about AIDS.

Legal Issues

There are at least six potential legal issues that can be raised concerning AIDS in the workplace.

1

1. *Reasonable accommodation.* Currently, there is no federal legislation specifically related to AIDS and employment. However, employees with HIV or AIDS are protected by federal, state, and local legislation governing discrimination against handicapped workers. The Americans with Disabilities Act (ADA) of 1990 prohibits discrimination against qualified individuals on the basis of disability in terms, conditions, and privileges of employment. This includes all aspects of employment, such as hiring, firing, discipline, promotions, work assignments, and compensation and benefits. HIV and AIDS are considered conditions or disabilities covered under the act.

The ADA mandates that employers provide "reasonable accommodation" that would enable qualified individuals with disabilities to perform their jobs. This might include renovations that make buildings and offices accessible to the physically handicapped, auxiliary aids such as interpreters for the deaf, job restructuring or work schedule adjustments, placement of telephones at a height to be used by people in wheelchairs, and modifications to restrooms. Specific definitions of "reasonable accommodation" do not exist. Judgments are made on a case-by-case basis. Reasonable accommodations should not cause undue financial or administrative hardship to an organization, however.

2. *Health and safety risks.* In addition to legally protected status for AIDS employees, potential legal issue concerns health and safety risks to coworkers of persons with AIDS. Employers must determine if AIDS employees present any health and safety risks in the work environment that could result in liability against the employer. They must assess potential harm to coworkers and customers, especially if the business is in a health-care field. Because AIDS is carried by body fluids and not by casual contact, the risk of transmission is very low in most work environments, so employers who claim a health risk to employees and/or the public must present substantial evidence of potential harm and resulting potential liability. If there is no risk of transmission, an employer cannot terminate an employee with AIDS. Nor can an employer isolate or quarantine an AIDS-afflicted worker. The employee cannot be restricted from using workplace equipment and facilities. Other employees cannot refuse to work with an AIDS-afflicted coworker.

3. *Continuation of work.* Employers must determine if, with reasonable accommodations, employees with AIDS can adequately perform their jobs. Employees with AIDS cannot be terminated if they are meeting the standards for job performance. If the employee can no longer perform up to standard, then the employer may terminate the person. In such a case, the employer should be prepared to substantiate the below-standard performance and the provisions of reasonable accommodation.

4. *Routine medical screening.* Employers may give medical exams, but only after a job offer has been made and only if all employees are given the same exam. An employer cannot rescind a job offer to a potential employee if a medical screening shows that person to be HIV-positive.

5. *Medical benefits coverage.* Some health plans may cap AIDS-related benefits. Recent case law stipulates that an employer decision to limit health-care benefits for AIDS-related illnesses violates the Americans with Disabilities Act.

6. *Record keeping.* The ADA mandates that medical records and health insurance data be kept separate from other personnel data and that access to such records is limited.

Organizational Policies

Because of the legal complexities involved, organizations are advised to seek legal counsel in formulating an AIDS policy. There are some basic elements that should be included in any organizational policy about AIDS. Company policy statements about AIDS should address issues of hiring, retention, employee education, benefits, confidentiality, and employee-assistance program options.

The organizational policy should state that usual hiring procedures will apply regarding job applicants who have AIDS or who are suspected of having AIDS, and that such individuals will continue to be employed as long as they demonstrate the ability to perform their jobs to standard levels.

The policy should also state a commitment to educating employees about the nature of the disease, the forms of transmission, and the negligible possibilities of their contracting AIDS from fellow employees. Further, the policy should affirm that AIDS-afflicted employees will receive the same levels of medical and insurance coverage as any other employee with a life-threatening disease. Employees should receive a written guarantee of medical confidentiality, and records management personnel should be instructed to keep medical and health insurance data separate from other personnel data.

Finally, the policy should communicate the availability of employee assistance programs or counseling services through the workplace. Such a comprehensive statement will show compassion on the part of the company, will articulate the rights of AIDS-afflicted employees, will dispel myths on the part of employees, and will help to protect the organization from legal liability.

AIDS Education Programs

To be fully effective in dealing with workplace issues related to AIDS, companies are advised to have some form of employee education. Such education will go a long way in dispelling employees' fears, which can undermine productivity, and help reduce turnover of employees who fear working with AIDS-afflicted colleagues. Additionally, educating employees will demonstrate an organization's compliance with the Americans with Disabilities Act, and thereby reduce liability in discrimination complaints.

Education programs have five goals:

1. Provide information about the causes and transmission of AIDS.
2. Dispel fears about working with AIDS-afflicted coworkers.
3. Discuss the employer's position and responsibilities in hiring and retaining AIDS-afflicted workers.
4. Identify community resources available for afflicted employees and their families.
5. Answer common questions about AIDS.

Such programs should have clear objectives and should use qualified trainers. It is best to provide information through a variety of forms, such as brochures, posters, newsletter articles, and workshops.

There are many resources to help organizations conduct AIDS-related education programs. In addition to what might be available locally through medical organizations and community health agencies, the American Red Cross distributes public education materials and the National Centers for Disease Control has a centralized information and referral service linking businesses to local, state, and national programs and educational materials.

Though employers may want to avoid dealing with the problem of AIDS, the burgeoning number of cases makes it likely that every company will soon face this challenge. Understanding the legal constraints, examining the benefits issues, establishing policies, and informing the workforce are hallmarks of a progressive organization dealing with contemporary workplace issues.

[*See also* Employee Assistance Programs; Ethics in the Workplace; Family-Friendly Management]

For Additional Information

Bohl, Don L., ed. *AIDS: The New Workplace Issues*. New York: American Management Association, 1988.

Brown, Darrell, and George R. Gray. "Designing an Appropriate AIDS Policy." *Employment Relations Today*, Summer 1991, pp. 149–55.

Ormsby, Joseph G., Geralyn McClure Franklin, Robert K. Robinson, and Alicia B. Gresham. "AIDS in the Workplace: Implications for Human Resource Managers." *SAM Advanced Management Journal*, Spring 1990, pp. 23–27.

Assertiveness

Assertiveness means standing up for yourself without anxiety and without denying the rights of others. You must communicate assertively when you present and defend positions, negotiate on behalf of a department or work team, and give or receive performance feedback. Many other workplace situations require assertiveness skills, such as dealing with colleagues, subordinates, supervisors, customers, suppliers, competitors, or the media. The ability to communicate assertively distinguishes the powerful, effective manager whom others respect from the manager whom others take advantage of.

Distinguishing Nonassertive From Assertive and Aggressive Behavior

Some people think they are being assertive when, in fact, they are being indirect, subtle, and vague. Other people are brutally direct and inconsiderate while claiming to be assertive. Thus, not only shy people need to develop assertiveness skills. Aggressive or domineering individuals can also benefit by replacing an aggressive communication style with an assertive one. Assertiveness is behavior that falls midway between nonassertive and aggressive behavior. To better understand assertive behavior, compare it with nonassertiveness and aggressiveness in the following way:

Nonassertive Behavior

- Uses indirect communication.
- Communicates the opposite of what you really feel.
- Lacks honesty.

- Denies your own rights and feelings.
- Makes you feel negative.

Assertive Behavior

- Uses direct communication coupled with tact.
- Communicates exactly what you feel.
- Is honest.
- Balances your own and other's rights and feelings.
- Lets you and others feel positive.

Aggressive Behavior

- Uses direct but tactless communication.
- Goes overboard in communicating what you feel.
- Is brutally or offensively honest.
- Denies others' rights and feelings.
- Makes others feel negative.

Elements of Assertive Communication

To be optimally assertive, the visual, vocal and verbal elements of a manager's message must be synchronized. You must look assertive, sound assertive, and use assertive language. The following are guidelines for behavior in each of those areas:

Visual Elements of Assertiveness

- *Eye contact*—should be direct and steady. Do not look away when making a point; do not stare.
- *Facial expressions*—should be relaxed but serious. Do not frown angrily; do not smile or giggle.
- *Gestures*—should be natural and relaxed. Do not pound fists or point fingers; do not fidget or wring hands.
- *Posture*—should be businesslike. Do not intimidate or slouch.

Vocal Elements of Assertiveness

- *Voice volume*—should be moderate. Do not shout or mumble.

- *Speaking rate*—should be moderate. Do not show uncertainty by speaking too slowly; do not show nervousness or aggressiveness by speaking too rapidly.
- *Tone of voice*—should be firm, direct, sincere, and calm. Do not use voice tones of anger, sarcasm, excitement, or disinterest.
- *Fluency*—should be such that you speak in complete sentences without fillers such as "um," "ah," "ok," "like," and "you know."

Verbal Elements of Assertiveness

- Statements should be direct, clear, and concise.
- Sentences should be complete.
- Avoid intensifying words, such as "extremely," "very," and "incredibly."
- Avoid qualifying words, such as "sort of," "kind of," "somewhat," and "it's just my opinion."
- Avoid evaluative labels and name-calling, such as "stupid," "lazy," "inconsiderate," and "selfish."

Common Situations Requiring Assertive Behavior

Specific situations requiring assertive communication are numerous and diverse. However, most assertive situations you face will fall into one of these four categories:

1. Making requests
2. Saying no
3. Giving criticism
4. Accepting criticism

While the guidelines for maintaining consistency among visual, vocal, and verbal parts of an assertiveness message apply to all four categories of assertive situations, the following are specific suggestions for managers in dealing with each type of situation.

Making Requests

The best way to make a request is to ask, rather than hint, demand, or manipulate. Hints are usually ineffective. Because they are vague or subtle, they are often not perceived. Or, if perceived, they can be easily ignored. Requests disguised as hints are not likely to be taken seriously. On the other hand, ordering someone to do something often leads to resistance. When you phrase a request as a demand, others will resent having to comply. And resentment frequently translates into anger, hostility, and sabotage. Manipulation tricks others into doing something. It takes away the other person's choice and, in the long run, will earn you the reputation of being devious and underhanded.

The assertive style of making a request is to ask specifically and directly for what you want. By asking directly, you take responsibility for your requests and allow others the choice to grant or refuse them. The clear, direct style is most likely to be effective. Assertively making a request means stating a need, asking for action, and giving a reason for the request. For example, an employee who requests a coworker to switch a workday says: "Joan, I'm scheduled to work next Saturday morning. Would you be willing to switch with me since you're scheduled for the following Saturday? My niece is getting married and I'd like to be able to attend the wedding." If the request is honored, it is important to express gratitude and to follow through on the negotiated arrangement. If the request is denied, be a gracious loser. Show no resentment and refrain from guilt-producing remarks.

Saying No

An essential element of assertiveness involves the ability to turn down others' requests. Some people have much difficulty saying no. As a result, they find themselves doing favors and resenting it, or feeling trapped in obligations. Some people nonassertively say no by hinting, whining, deceiving, complaining, or blaming others. Aggressive people become outraged or abusive when faced with another's request. Assertive individuals directly say no without hesitation and without giving lengthy excuses or apologies. They do not fall into the trap of feeling guilty, being manipulated, or being coaxed into granting the request. As assertive response to a request to switch work schedules could be worded like this: "No, Ellen, I can't work next Saturday for you. I'm having out-of-town guests. Maybe I can help you out some other time."

Giving Criticism

Frequently, managers have to give negative feedback on the behavior or performance of others. The capacity to be firm but fair when giving criticism is the hallmark of an optimally assertive individual. It is important to be direct, clear, and honest while showing tact and compassion for the person receiving the criticism. Because giving criticism is awkward for many managers, it is seldom handled properly. Weak managers postpone or avoid giving the feedback, use hints or sarcasm, or absolve themselves of responsibility by attributing the message to others. Aggressive managers belittle the target of criticism in front of others, angrily attack the target without getting to specifics, or allow the recipient of the criticism little opportunity to save face.

The constructive communication of criticism entails describing a specific problem, indicating why it is a problem, requesting a concrete change, and conversing nondefensively to work out an agreement for accomplishing that change. For example, an assertive manager delivers the following message: "Rich, this report you wrote doesn't have enough detail on the marketing plan. There's not enough information to prepare a marketing budget that will be approved. Can you redo that section to include all your marketing strategies with a time schedule?" Then a question to create a dialogue should follow. The manager can ask, "Do you understand what I need? Can you get it to me by Friday?"

Giving criticism in such a straightforward, assertive style has many advantages. It is specific, making change easier. It avoids evaluations and name-calling. It deals with work-related behavior rather than people's egos. It encourages two-way communication to ensure understanding and to promote change. Both parties can come away from the criticism feeling positive, and the problem that engendered the criticism is likely to be solved.

Accepting Criticism

Realizing that everybody makes mistakes, accepting your own mistakes, and trying to improve as a result of criticism are essential ingredients of assertiveness. An assertive individual can listen to criticism without becoming defensive, objectively examine that feedback, and then use the information constructively. The nonassertive recipient of criticism whines, cries, pleads, makes excuses, or engages in self-pity. Aggressively handling criticism entails being defensive, making counterattacks, resenting the critic, and stubbornly refusing to change.

The assertive approach to receiving criticism involves patiently listening to and paraphrasing the feedback, asking for specifics or examples to ensure understanding, acknowledging the parts of the message with which you agree, stating your position or needs without becoming defensive, and engaging in a dialogue with your critic. For example, a manager gives this response to criticism about the quality of output from his department: "You're saying that our parts aren't meeting specification. Can you tell me which shipments haven't met your specifications and what percentage of error occurred in each batch?" On receiving an answer, the manager continues, "OK, I can see where Batch 103 had problems. I should have had more people on the line since that was a rush order. We're less likely to make mistakes if we have at least two days to prepare an order. We'll replace this shipment. Can you give us at least forty-eight hours' notice on future orders?" Assertively dealing with criticism solves problems and maintains good working relationships.

[*See also* Feedback]

For Additional Information

"Assertiveness: More Than a Forceful Attitude." *Supervisory Management*, 39, No. 2 (February 1994), p. 3.

Graham, Roderick S., and Shan Rees. *Assertion Training: How To Be Who You Really Are.* London: Routledge, 1991.

Tingley, Judith. *Say What You Mean, Get What You Want.* New York: AMACOM, 1996.

Zucker, E. *Assertive Manager.* New York: AMACOM, 1989.

Business Writing

All managers, regardless of their function, level, or type of organization, must be effective writers. Workplace organizations produce large amounts of written information in the form of memos, letters, short reports, formal reports, and specialized documents such as employee handbooks, company newsletters, and annual reports for stockholders. While most managers may not be involved in creating these specialized documents, they surely will write memos, letters, and reports on a regular basis. Indeed, a large portion of a manager's time involves writing.

Workplace organizations need information to function. A manager's job is to seek and provide information so that decisions can be made, problems can be solved, work can be coordinated, and results can be evaluated. In this information age, with its explosion of knowledge, written communication is even more important. The number of organizations whose purpose is to provide information is increasing in our society.

Writing ability is also an important component of an employee's credibility and success in an organization. Individuals who are competent in specialized fields such as engineering, personnel, or accounting, for example, are passed over for promotions if they cannot communicate effectively. They will not be given managerial responsibility unless their oral and written communication skills allow them to be understood. Successful managers accomplish their goals by being able to communicate in clear and powerful ways. They may also have to edit their subordinates' written work. Knowing and applying the principles of business writing, therefore, makes a manager's job easier, affects individual and company credibility, and advances careers.

Stages in the Writing Process

All business writing, whether it be for memos, letters, or reports, follows the same stages. The three stages in the writing process are prewriting, writing, and editing.

Prewriting

Prewriting is the preparation stage that precedes actual writing. Typically, you should plan to spend more time in this stage than in the other two stages, especially when writing long reports. Attention devoted to prewriting will make writing easier and will increase the quality of your written material. Prewriting includes determining your objective, analyzing the audience, gathering information, and outlining.

1. *Determining your objective.* Deciding on the purpose of a written document is the key to getting organized. All other planning decisions relate to the purpose or objective of the written communication. Knowing the purpose even helps you decide whether to write a memo, letter, short report, or long report. Just as a builder uses blueprints or a traveler consults a map to guide actions, a writer should develop a plan to follow when writing.

In determining the objective of your written document, analyze the one main idea you are trying to communicate. If you do not identify, ahead of time, the overall purpose of the document, then you are likely to ramble and confuse the reader. You should write out the objective as specifically and as concisely as possible. Then review it often while writing and editing the document. Objectives that are too general provide little direction. For example, writing a letter to a customer to "follow up on a complaint about service" gives little direction about the information, tone, or outcome of the letter. A more specific objective might be to "explain the company's service policy in a way that will retain the customer." Likewise, writing a report to "explore the possibility of drug testing of employees" probably would result in a disorganized, vague document. A more specific objective would be to "examine the legal, financial, and psychological implications of employee drug testing at Company X."

2. *Analyze the audience.* Another aspect of prewriting involves analyzing the audience so that your document meets their needs. Determine who will read this communication. Are they internal or external to your organization? If internal, what are their job titles or areas of responsibility? If they are external, what is their relationship to the writer and the company? How familiar are the readers with the topic of your communication, or with the field of specialization embodied in the document? What is their attitude to your communication? What do you want readers to do after reading your document?

These are just some of the questions that provide a reader profile. There will be other audience-analysis questions related to specific forms and objectives of written communication. By creating a reader profile, you can select what information to provide, what writing style to use, and what language to include.

The steps of determining the objective and analyzing the audience go hand in hand. They have been separated into two distinct steps here for the sake of clarity. Obviously, the objective of a document must be based on the nature of the reader. For instance, a letter to employees about anticipated layoffs would have a different objective than a letter about layoffs written to the head of personnel.

3. *Gathering information.* After determining both the objective of the communication and the nature of the readers, it is time to gather information to be included in the document. The extent of this step will vary according to the type of document being written. A minimal amount of information may be needed for a memo to announce an upcoming meeting, for example. A substantial amount of information, on the other hand, may be necessary for a formal report on sales volume or minority recruitment.

Whether you are writing a short memo or a detailed report, you will have to gather information and check its accuracy before including it in the written communication. If you are writing a memo to announce a meeting, you will need accurate information about the date, time, place, and the purpose of the meeting. It may take only a few minutes to gather this information, but you still have completed this step of the prewriting process.

Gathering information for a formal report can take many months. You will need published material from libraries, data from company records, or specialized information from professional associations. You may need to commission market research studies, interview employees or clients, or distribute questionnaires. Depending on the purpose and scope of the report, the manager as writer may launch a comprehensive research investigation before writing the report. Managers who write formal reports must be skilled researchers as well as skilled writers.

One additional point should be made about the information-gathering step. There comes a point where information gathering should stop and writing should begin. This is important because some writers use information gathering as an excuse not to write. You can easily delay writing because of the need to collect more information. Productive writers make sure that their information is thorough and timely, but they do not get caught in the trap of an endless search for complete information. If a report deadline is not imposed on you, make sure that you impose a realistic deadline for the completion and cut off information gathering at an appropriate point.

4. *Outlining.* The next step is to arrange the information into an order appropriate for communicating it. You must decide what the best sequencing of information would be, given the nature of the information and the document's purpose and audience. Again, the extent of outlining will vary from one type of written communication to the next. Some reflection on the order of points suffices for a letter. But the writer of a formal report should spend considerable time writing and rearranging an outline to achieve the best organization of information.

For example, a report on increases in the cost of employee benefits may lend itself to a chronological pattern of organization. You could present information on a year-by-year basis. Or, if the information revealed that certain types of benefits were more costly than others, then a topical pattern of organization might be preferable. You could subdivide the information according to medical, dental, child-care, insurance, and vacation benefits.

Other common approaches to organizing ideas include arrangement by place, quantity, problem solution, and comparison. An example of organization by place is a nonprofit organization's report on fund-raising, divided into eastern, midwestern, southern, and western regional concerns. A report evaluating the success of a quality circles program in a hospital could be divided into sections that deal, in turn, with the medical, nursing, dietary, housekeeping, maintenance, security, and administrative departments.

Examples of the organization of ideas by quantity are a market research report showing consumer purchases by income levels from under $5,000 to over $50,000 and a report from a pharmaceutical company to physicians about a new drug, with research data broken down according to the age of patient. Organization according to a problem-solution pattern would be, for example, a report calling for building renovation that shows the problems (maintenance costs and safety violations) stemming from lack of renovation and the solutions (tax savings and expansion possibilities) stemming from renovation. A comparison method of organization could be used in a report showing the sales of paperback versus hardback books for a publishing company.

Regardless of the method of organizing and sequencing information, there should be a comparable amount of material written for each main idea. When outlines are included with reports, use proper outline symbols and parallel construction of terms. Consult style manuals for conventional outline symbols. Parallel constructions means that you use either complete sentences or noun phrases throughout, but do not mix the two. Finally, writers often create outlines that are too skimpy or too detailed. A good rule is to make the total number of words in an outline less than one-third the number of words in the report.

Writing

Two issues must be considered when writing business documents. They must attract attention and be readable.

Creating Attention-Getting Material

Managers and executives in organizations usually receive large amounts of written information. They read some documents in great detail, skim some, and give others little more than a cursory glance. This means that your document, if it is to compete with all the others in the organization, must grab the reader's attention. There are several ways to create attention-getting documents.

First, the *format and appearance* of the document will create an overall impression. If readers obtain a favorable first impression of the material, then they are more likely to read it. The impression comes not from what the document says but from how it is packaged. The quality of the paper, the neatness of the typing, the amount of white space, and the visual appeal of charts and graphs all contribute to the reader's impression of the document. The graphics and desktop publishing software packages available today allow managers to easily produce visually appealing documents. A long letter packed with words, with narrow margins and few paragraphs, will seem intimidating. A report without subheadings, summaries, or professional-looking visuals may be impossible to comprehend. Writers of internal memos and electronic mail should devote care even to these brief, informal documents. A sloppy memo without visual appeal or an E-mail message laden with errors may not be taken seriously.

Another way to produce attention-getting documents is to have *a powerful opening*. The first few sentences of a letter, for example, should immediately convey the document's purpose. Within the first minute of scanning the document, readers should see how the material relates to them. If the first few lines are confusing, vague, rambling, or irritating, readers may toss the material aside. The opening should compel them to continue.

A final suggestion for producing attention-getting written material is to make the document *easy to read*. The reader should not have to struggle to process the information in your documents. Of course, ease of reading depends very much on the quality of the writing. But there are devices that can make your documents easy to read. In a memo, you can highlight information in a letter by placing it in a list form with bullets next to each entry in the list. A report ought to have an outline or executive summary to highlight major points.

Creating Readable Material

While there are general guidelines for creating readable material, the question of readability depends on the nature of the audience. A highly technical report that uses specialized jargon, for example, will be readable to experts in that specialty but not to a layperson. What is readable to college graduates may not be readable to people who have not completed high school. Writers must adapt their writing level to fit the identity, education, experience, and knowledge of the readers. When the audience is diverse, it is best to aim for the lowest-level reader.

A major factor in producing readable material is to simplify your writing. *Simple sentences* with familiar words are always more readable than complex sentences replete with impressive vocabulary. In business writing, sentences should be short and powerful. Aim for an average sentence length of fifteen words. This does not mean that all sentences should be fewer than fifteen words. An occasional longer sentence provides variety and interest to a document. But a document containing only long sentences with dependent clauses and multiple ideas will be tedious even for the most advanced reader. If you tend to produce long sentences when writing, then try to break each of them into two sentences. After a while, the shorter sentences will come to you more naturally.

Another way to simplify writing is to select the *simplest words*. In conversation, most people select simple, familiar words. But for some reason, many writers fall into the trap of using stilted, awkward words. If we wrote more similarly to the way we talked, documents would be clearer. Consider the following list of less familiar words found often in business documents and their more familiar counterparts:

Unfamiliar Word	Familiar Word
utilize	use
furnish	give

ascertain	find
accomplish	do
transmit	send
attributable	due
correspondence	letter

You can also improve the readability of material by using the *active voice* rather than the passive voice. Active voice means that the subject of the sentence comes before the object of the sentence. The following sentences show the difference between active and passive voice:

Passive: "The meeting was arranged by Jane Smith."
Active: "Jane Smith arranged the meeting."

Passive: "Sales reports must be distributed by sales managers each Friday."
Active: "Sales managers must distribute sales reports each Friday."

Sentences using the active voice tend to be more interesting, shorter, and clearer. They immediately call attention to the subject performing the action. By converting sentences from the passive to the active voice, you will eventually learn to compose originally in the active voice.

Next, watch your *grammar, spelling, and punctuation.* It is impossible to cover all the relevant rules here. You can familiarize yourself with common problems in these areas by consulting reference books on writing style. Today's spell check and grammar check computer software programs make writing easier than ever before. Despite these tools, managers may also seek the skills of competent editors and proofreaders.

Using transitions is another way to increase readability. Transitions are words that help the reader make a shift from one idea to another. They can be words, phrases, or sentences that signal a movement in information. Transitions help readers follow the progression of ideas and connect points in a document. For example, the word "conversely" signals a contrast of ideas.

The word "thus" signals a conclusion. "In addition" suggests movement to a similar point.

A final suggestion for increasing readability is to eliminate *trite, cluttered phrases.* Over the years, the conventions of business writing have led us to overuse some of these phrases. Writers should remove the following expressions from their material:

Enclosed, please find
Deem it advisable
As per your instructions
In accordance with your request
Kindly advise
Thanking you in advance
Pending receipt
Agreeable to your wishes in this matter
Under separate cover
Regarding the aforementioned

Writing readable copy becomes easier with practice. However, you will see immediate improvement in the readability of your documents if you follow the six guidelines discussed:

1. Keep sentences short.
2. Use familiar words.
3. Convert sentences from passive to active voice.
4. Use correct grammar, punctuation, and spelling.
5. Use transitions.
6. Avoid cluttered phrases.

Editing

The final phase of the writing process involves editing. Under no circumstances should a writer consider the first draft of a document to be the final draft. Even experienced business writers cannot produce letters and reports in their complete and final form on the first try. All writers should expect to edit and revise written material. The number of drafts for a document will vary according to the writer's skill and the nature and importance of the document. A short letter may need only one rewrite to become excellent copy. When writing a formal report, you may need five or six crafts before it is in excellent shape.

Editing is a skill that improves with practice. The following suggestions can guide the editing process and help writers become skillful editors:

1. *Let the material sit a while before revising it.* You are less likely to catch errors or to notice confusing information if you are very familiar with the writing. Reading the material cold will enable you to look at it from the reader's perspective.

2. *Do not become wedded to the written material.* Some writers have trouble revising their material or accepting editorial suggestions from others because they attach their egos to their writing. They feel the need to defend every idea, sentence, or word; or they reread their copy to bask in the pride of their eloquence. Editing should mean rereading with the goal of changing and improving your writing.

3. *Review the document four separate times with the goals of editing content, organization, style, and appearance.* Editing content means examining the information to see if it is correct, thorough, and understandable. When examining your organization, ask yourself if the order of information makes sense, if the ideas progress logically, if the information rambles, and if your reader could outline the information. Stylistic revisions involve enhancing the readability of the material. Finally, examine the physical appearance of the document for spelling, punctuation, and typographical errors.

Only after all these areas have been examined and revised, and the document is as good as it can get, should it be sent to the reader. Clear and credible written communication is imperative in workplace organizations.

When to Use the Written Form

Some managers and some organizations opt for written communication when oral communication would be better. Writing a memo rather than talking to someone can be the cowardly or the ineffective choice. Managers who are unsure about the efficacy of written communication should follow these guidelines:

1. Put information in writing if you want a verifiable record. Often managers need to document actions or need a written record for later use.
2. Put complex or detailed information in writing. Some information cannot be grasped orally or remembered if it is not written down.
3. Create a written document if you want to convey the same information to several people. It is easier and quicker to distribute a written document to many people than to communicate with each one of them individually. You can be sure they each get identical information if it is written, whereas individual conversations inevitably differ.
4. Use the written form if it is too costly or too inconvenient to meet in person or to talk on the telephone. Sending a letter to someone in another state is usually more logical than traveling to talk. Written communication may be necessary if your repeated attempts to reach a person by telephone have failed.

For Additional Information

Berger, Arthur Asa. *Improving Writing Skills: Memos, Letters, Reports, and Proposals.* Newbury Park, Calif.: Sage Publications, 1993.

Blake, Gary. *The Elements of Business Writing.* New York: Macmillan, 1991.

Brill, Laura. *Business Writing Quick & Easy, Second Edition.* New York: AMACOM, 1989.

Ober, Scot. *Contemporary Business Communication.* Boston: Houghton Mifflin Company, 1992.

Soden, Garrett. *Looking Good on Paper: How to Create Eye-Catching Reports, Proposals, Memos, and Other Business Documents.* New York: AMACOM, 1995.

Career Development

A career can be defined as an evolving sequence of work experiences over time. Managers deal with career issues at two levels: First, you must be concerned with your own career—that is, make choices, accept opportunities, and develop strategies for dealing with it. Second, you must think about the careers of your subordinates; develop, coach, and act as mentors to them; and delight in the career successes that result.

Many organizations are concerned about how employees move through their structure of roles and responsibilities. Their forecasting and long-range planning efforts often involve projecting personnel needs relevant to human resources development activities. Consequently, career-development issues are important to managers whatever their level, function, or organizational type.

The Need for Career Development

Career-development issues are taking on greater importance for individuals and organizations alike. From the individual perspective, people are no longer spending a lifetime in one career or at one job. The day of the loyal employee affiliating with one company and allowing that company to dictate career decisions is clearly over. Employees are also bringing different motivations to the workplace. Increasingly, they want challenging work and a sense of contribution to the organization. Salary and promotions as motivators compete with other job features such as meaningful, flexible schedules and input into decision making. Nor is the workforce as homogeneous as it used to be. Women, minorities, people with disabilities, foreign-born workers, and older employees add diversity to the workplace. A different composition of employees means different work attitudes and career patterns. Moreover, family and leisure concerns have taken on more importance to today's workers at all levels. Career decisions may be affected by family needs and a vocational interests more than by promotional opportunities.

Burgeoning changes in technology, business activity made volatile by mergers and acquisitions, downsizing, and the global business community have all caused workplaces to become more dynamic. Employees in some industries have found that the job they performed yesterday is not there today. Certain job skills and knowledge are rapidly becoming obsolete. Employees are often forced into an awareness of the dynamics of their careers.

In short, individuals are making explicit career decisions and want more control over their careers. Compared to previous generations, they are willing to take more risks, are more geographically mobile, and want to be more self-directed in career matters. And because of societal forces and business activity outside of their control, employees must face more career decisions than they ever had to before. Since the life span is increasing, many individuals take early retirement from one organization and seek a new type of work challenge in their early retirement years.

From the organizational perspective, career-development issues are equally important. Increasingly, companies are realizing the costs associated with low productivity and high turnover. Thus, they see career development as a way to retain talented employees and to motivate them to reach organizational goals. It is more cost-effective to develop existing employees than to recruit, hire, and train new ones. Organizations also emphasize career development as a way of meeting affirmative action and equal employment opportunity (EEO) goals. By providing career-development assistance, they retain and develop the potential of certain underutilized categories of employees.

Finally, companies turn to career development to ensure that personnel will be qualified for future staffing requirements. By assisting current employees with career-development concerns, progressive organizations can match career goals with future organizational needs. Thus, career-development programs become an important human resources planning tool.

Individual Strategies for Career Development

There are many ways that you can plan your own management career, whether your goal is to stay with one organization or to switch organizations. Managers often turn to career-development strategies when they are dissatisfied with the current job situation or are facing a job loss. But strategizing your career should be an ongoing activity and not be neglected until a time of crisis. By being aware of career-development issues as they relate to individual career goals, you can develop a sense of direction and control over your career. Successful managers who are attuned to their career dynamics practice many of these strategies.

Clarifying Your Values

It is important to know how work fits into your life priorities. Is career success your top goal? How do career goals fit in with personal, family, leisure, or spiritual goals? In order to be satisfied and successful, a job must fit your needs and must not contradict your fundamental values. Some people, for example, may find themselves in highly competitive work situations, although collaboration or helping others is more important to them than competition. Other people with high need for affiliation may have jobs that isolate them from others. What do you find important in a job—challenge, excitement, stability, responsibility, freedom, money, titles, or chances for advancement?

Obviously, the first step in planning a career path is determining the kind of work or job you would like. A variety of values clarification books, workshop, or counselors are available to assist with this self-assessment activity.

Determining Your Occupational Aptitudes and Interests

In addition to clarifying values, it is important to know what kinds of jobs you would be good at and interested in. There are numerous standardized tests for measuring vocational aptitudes and interests. These are best administered, scored, and interpreted by qualified career counselors. High school and college guidance counselors often administer these tests before prospective graduates enter the world of work. Industrial psychologists and assessment center evaluators also use these tests relative to hiring and promotion decisions.

Realizing Your Options

The number of career options that any manager has is enormous. There may be many directions you can take within a particular organization. Probably there are numerous employers within a particular industry for whom you could work. Then there are an infinite number of possible job types that you could hold. Indeed, for each of us, career options are more expansive than we realize.

Realizing options means being aware of the opportunities within a company and identifying the market for your skills. Managers should have well-developed networks of company colleagues in order to receive advance information about opportunities, trends, and projects. They should discuss career interests and goals with their superiors and stay abreast of options through job posting, reorganization, relocation, job redesign, or project management.

Most successful managers stay aware of the job opportunities in their fields even if they are completely satisfied with their current position and current employer. For the sake of career development, it is important to "keep your eyes open." In order to practice self-determination in your career, you should continually, but subtly, job hunt. Network to learn of opportunities at other firms, join placement bureaus of professional associations, circulate your credentials to recruiting firms, and check the classified advertisements.

Creating a Career-Development Plan

It is wise to have both a short-term and a long-range plan for your career. What would you like to be doing one year from now, five years from now, ten years into the future? What skills, experiences, education, or training accomplished now would pave the way for reaching future career goals?

A career-development plan is like a blueprint for putting the pieces of a career together. Of course, it is tentative and will be altered as unexpected opportunities or exigencies occur. It seems ironic that while most adults spend at least two-thirds of their lives in a career, few adopt a systematic plan for charting the course of that career.

Using Career-Development Resources

A variety of resources are available to assist managers in their career-development activities. You can look to mentor and networking relationships, the human resources department of your company, professional associations, educational institutions, the public library, and on-line resources for career-development assistance. Mentors provide career information and opportunities for protégés. Developing mentor relationships can provide both immediate and long-term career benefits. Likewise, developing a network of professional contacts is a positive career-development strategy.

The human resources function in organizations exists to develop personnel to meet organizational needs. Some have career-development specialists or provide workshops on career dynamics. But even those human resources departments that do not have explicit career-development functions can help you advance your career. Take advantage of all training workshops that could help you develop the skills necessary for reaching your career goals.

Attending seminars or conferences of professional associations is a great way to develop knowledge, to learn trends, and to meet influential people in your field. Many managers have developed leadership, communication, and planning skills by holding office in professional associations. Participation in professional associations can lead to career advantages later.

Local vocational schools, colleges, and universities offer a wealth of courses, materials, and experts to help you plan and advance your career. There you can learn the technical skills, obtain the knowledge, and find career counselors for developing your career in the direction you want it to take. Finally, public libraries and on-line services offer substantial information about occupational opportunities and outlooks, job hunting, vocational aptitude and preference testing, and values clarification.

Being Realistic About Career Development

It is important to realize that career goals are not reached overnight. Setting unrealistic aspirations or being impatient about career progress will only create dissatisfaction. Careers take years to build. They require nurturing.

Career-Development Strategies for Organizations

There are many ways in which companies assist their employees with career development that will ultimately benefit the companies themselves. Of course, there must be a match between the employees' career goals and organizational needs. While it is important to retain valuable employees and to reduce turnover, it is counterproductive to try to keep an employee whose career goals would be better served elsewhere. One casualty of career-development assistance is that some employees leave. Nevertheless, the advantages of developing satisfied and productive employees for future personnel needs far outweigh the risk. Some strategies to achieve this include the following:

1. *Encouraging management-employee discussions of career pathing.* One of the responsibilities of a manager is to help subordinates with career development. Help them develop realistic career plans by sharing information about organizational career opportunities and help them attain career goals. Managers and executives at all levels should have career-development meetings with their employees. This activity reduces the number of bored, unproductive or plateaued employees and channels employees into paths that meet organizational needs.

2. *Practicing job enrichment.* Typically, there are not enough higher-level positions for all qualified employees who would like

to be promoted. This means that some careers must develop other ways. One way to encourage growth and development in employees is to expand or to enrich job responsibilities. By adding new responsibilities that the employees find appealing or by increasing authority, you are helping them to develop their careers without abandoning their current positions. The keys to successful job enrichment are sensing when employees need more challenge and adding duties that are challenging, not just time-consuming. Job enrichment is best negotiated between the manager and subordinates.

3. *Practicing job rotation.* Another avenue for career development is horizontal. Moving to another function or department without a vertical change in position can provide career-development opportunities. Such horizontal moves can offer new challenge, develop new skills, and help meet career goals. In some organizations, managerial candidates work in various departments to get a perspective on the whole organization and to develop generalist skills. Job rotation implies a series of lateral moves over time. For the organization, such movement can be a way of testing employees in certain jobs. For the employees, job rotation can be an unthreatening way of experimenting with job moves.

4. *Providing opportunities for project management.* All organizations have ongoing projects as a way of bringing about change in systems and procedures or as a way to implement new programs. Putting key organizational personnel in charge of such projects represents another career-development strategy. By heading a temporary project, a manager can develop technical knowledge, enhance planning and problem-solving abilities, and practice leadership and communication skills. The opportunity to lead or to participate in an exciting, innovative project may be just the catalyst to stimulate an employee whose job has become routine and who was considering leaving the organization.

5. *Providing education and training for career development.* Progressive organizations develop their people so they will stay with the company. Providing employees opportunities to learn about new developments in their field, to retool, to master a new skill, or to branch into a new area keeps the organization vital and

competitive. Companies can enhance the careers of their employees by offering tuition assistance for education and by sponsoring training on relevant topics.

6. *Offering career-planning workshops.* Besides offering training on technical and managerial topics, organizations can sponsor career-planning workshops. A sample workshop can help participants clarify their values and goals, pinpoint their aptitudes and interest, and identify organizational options for career development. In addition to teaching individual employees about career dynamics, career planning can help them understand organizational decision making in such areas as personnel selection, appraisal, promotion, and termination.

7. *Providing access to career-counseling specialists.* Managers can assist with career-development issues, but they are not career-development specialists. The training department can provide self-assessment and information resources, but career development is just one of many topics training must address. Organizations that are dedicated to the career development of their staffs will provide them with access to career-development specialists. If organizational size and financial resources cannot justify a full-time career counselor, consider using consultants or providing career counseling in conjunction with an employee-assistance program.

[*See also* Mentoring; Project Management; Training]

For Additional Information

Barner, Robert. *Lifeboat Strategies: How to Keep Your Career Above Water During Tough Times—or Any Time.* New York: AMACOM, 1993.

Harriot, Peter. *Career Management Challenge: Balancing Individual and Organizational Needs.* Newbury Park, Calif.: Sage Publications, 1992.

Koonce, Richard H. *Career Power: 12 Winning Habits to Get You From Where You Are to Where You Want to Be.* New York: AMACOM, 1994.

Krannich, Ronald L. *Careering and Re-Careering for the 1990's.* Manassas Park, Va.: Impact Publications, 1993.

McCanna, Walter F., Robert F. Pearse, and Donald A. Zrebiec. "Career Strategies for the 1990's Manager." *Business Horizons* 37, No. 3 (May/June 1994), pp. 27–31.

Otte, Fred L., and William M. Kahnweiler. "Long-range Career Planning During Turbulent Times." *Business Horizons* 38, No. 1 (Jan./Feb. 1995), pp. 2–7.

Change Management

Change has become a constant in today's organizations. Indeed, the rate of change is accelerating in the workplace, whatever the industry type or size. Thus, today's managers must be adept at managing change. This chapter defines the concept of change management, discusses the reasons for organizational change, indicates the importance of managing change, and provides strategies for managing change in the organization. By developing procedures for planning and directing change rather than merely reacting to change, managers can help organizations thrive in an increasingly competitive marketplace.

What Is Change Management?

Change management is a process by which organizations understand, anticipate, and communicate the impact of changes in company structures, processes, procedures, products, or services. No organization is static. Since change is continuous rather than a single event, managers must understand the dynamics of change and human reactions to change so that they can successfully effect change. To manage change is to make change a planned, strategic activity rather than a random phenomenon.

Reasons for Change

There are many factors accounting for rapid and pervasive change in the workplace. In most organizations, numerous change factors operate together to create a dynamic quality in an organization.

1. *Competition.* One strong force creating change is the increasingly competitive and global marketplace. Even in medical, governmental, and educational organizations, which in the past did not face the competitiveness typical of private-sector corporations, notions of competition and survival are paramount. To be competitive, most organizations are introducing programs to contain costs and improve quality.

2. *Reorganization strategies.* Many companies are introducing different structures because of mergers, downsizing, or decentralization. Creating new structures in an organization means establishing a different configuration of personnel, adjusting to different reporting relationships, and adopting altered job responsibilities.

3. *Rapidly improving technology.* The revolution in information technology is altering the very ways we communicate and do business. New management style create force for change, as well. Many organizations are moving from leader-directed styles to self-managing teams. Such changes in management philosophy and style create new policies and procedures in the workplace.

4. *New products and services.* This type of change has been recurrent throughout history, as products and services evolve and organizations alter their products and service lines.

The Importance of Managing Change

To anticipate the external forces that impinge on an organization is to have foresight as a manager. To develop plans for introducing change into an organization is to have strategic vision as a manager. An effective manager needs both foresight and strategic vision. To have neither is to be a mere caretaker, not a leader.

Since change is the norm in most organizations, leaders must be able to manage change so they are not at the mercy of unplanned change. Unplanned change is chaotic and stressful, and it forces the organization into a reactive rather than a proactive position. An organization routinely coping with the chaos and stress of haphazard change may not survive in today's competitive marketplace.

Strategies for Managing Change

Understand the Phases of Change

Various organizational theorists have outlined the phases by which change occurs and how people deal with such change. One model proposes five phases of resistance to change. In this model, the first phase of any change encounters massive resistance, as only a handful of individuals see any need for change. In the second phase, the factions for and against change become readily identifiable. Third, there is direct conflict between the factions for and those against change. If the proponents of change win the conflict, then the fourth phase occurs when the resisters are seen as a nuisance. Finally, the change gets implemented and any remaining resisters are few and are alienated.

Another model of change delineates three phases. First, there is a letting-go phase, when people relinquish former attitudes, behaviors, styles, and strategies. Next comes a transition phase, when people relinquish the old way of doing things but do not fully embrace a new way of doing things. A third phase is the new beginning, when people psychologically accept and behaviorally embrace change.

If managers understand that these phases are likely to occur with the introduction of any change, they can cope with employee resistance and develop strategies for obtaining acceptance and commitment to change.

Plan for Change

Managers need to give sufficient thought as to how to introduce and implement change. They must analyze why the organization is changing, where the organization is headed, what each person must do to get there, what the timetable is for change, and what the consequences are of the new initiatives.

Organizations anticipating a major change in structure or systems may benefit from the services of expert change agents. External consultants in the area of organizational change can provide unique perspectives and valuable experience to help create planned and effective change. The planning aspect of change also involves identifying key issues to be addressed and anticipating the impact of each element of change on people and on the system.

Communicate During Change

When people are in transition, communication is paramount. A major factor accounting for people's resistance to change is their lack of involvement in the change. Employees who will be affected by an organizational change should be informed of the purpose and nature of that change. They should have the opportunity to provide their opinions about the change and to ask questions about the process. They need to understand why the change is necessary and how it will benefit them and the organization as a whole. Most important, employees want to know how the change will affect them, immediately and in the future.

Educate the Employees

During periods of change, employees should receive training to help them deal with their fears of change, to create understanding about the phases of change, and to equip them with new information and skills to function in the dynamic organization. The introduction of new technology certainly must be accompanied by training in the use of that technology. Likewise, new structures, management styles, and products or services must be supported with training such as quality, teambuilding, communication, and customer service programs.

Understand the Facets of Change

There are some fundamental aspects of any change. Part of managing change is being able to accept these situations.

In any change effort there is a basic dilemma in needing to both focus on the future and deal with immediate tasks. That is, daily business must be conducted via old systems and procedures while simultaneously those systems and procedures are being dismantled. To focus too much on the status quo or too much on the future at this point is to cripple the change process.

Additionally, any change effort inevitably involves a paradigm shift. That is, change involves new ways of thinking and new frames of reference as well as new behaviors. Getting employees to change involves more than just encouraging them to do some things differently. It also entails urging them to think differently.

Managers skilled in guiding dynamic organizations will be competent agents of change. Given the prevalence of change of today's workplace, leaders who can manage change will be an asset to any organization.

[*See also* Career Development; Consultants; Innovation and Creativity; Organizational Culture]

For Additional Information

Berger, Lance A., Martin J. Sikore, and Dorothy R. Berger. *The Change Management Handbook: A Road Map to Corporate Transformation.* New York: Irwin, 1994.

Bridges, William. *Managing Transitions: Making the Most of Change.* Reading, Mass.: Addison-Wesley, 1991.

Carr, Clay. *Choice, Chance & Organizational Change.* New York: AMACOM, 1996.

Felkin, Patricia K., B. J. Chakiris, and Kenneth N. Chakiris. *Change Management: A Model for Effective Organizational Performance.* White Plains, N.J.: Quality Resources, 1993.

Pasmore, William A. *Creating Strategic Change: Designing the Flexible, High-Performing Organization.* New York: Wiley, 1994.

Thompson, LeRoy. *Mastering the Challenges of Change.* New York: AMACOM, 1994.

Coaching Employees

Since the success of an organization depends on the performance of its people, the development of human resources is an essential management task. The job should not be left solely to the company's human resources specialists. Rather, all managers should be committed to this endeavor. Indeed, many specific managerial job requirements entail coaching—specifically, face-to-face techniques for solving employee performance problems and for helping employees develop on the job to their fullest potential. You must employ coaching techniques when giving job instructions, correcting performance problems, delegating, developing work teams, and encouraging career development.

Managers who are good coaches benefit in two ways: They receive quality work from employees, and they look good in the process. As a consequence, they are recognized and rewarded by their supervisors. Being a good manager-coach means knowing whom to coach, when to coach, and how to coach. It also involves being aware of common coaching problems and developing the characteristics of a good coach.

Deciding to Coach

Ask yourself several questions before selecting coaching to solve a performance problem.

1. *Is there actually a performance problem?* In other words, is the employee *not* meeting some objective performance standard? Some mangers assume there is a performance problem because they do not like the employee or because the employee is not performing as well as someone else. Coaching involves the devel-

opment of specific behaviors, and it should not be used to change attitudes or to foster competition in a work group.

2. *Is the problem correctable?* This may entail judgment about the subordinate's motivation, past performance, and ability to change, as well as assessment of available time and resources for bringing about a change. If the performance is not correctable, then coaching is not the answer. Other options might be transfer or termination.

3. *Are there any external obstacles to performance?* Are there circumstances beyond the employee's control that are leading to the poor performance or are impeding employee development? If so, no amount of coaching will solve the problem or promote career development. Instead, you must remove the obstacles. Many factors can be involved. Faulty material, late deliveries, deadlines missed by others, lack of information, equipment failures, confusing instructions, and unrealistic schedules are just a few reasons why employee job performance may fall short. Nor will coaching help an employee develop if growth opportunities are unavailable or if there are political or economic deterrents to advancement.

4. *Are there any rewards or costs associated with job-related behavior?* Ironically, in many organizations poor performance is rewarded. How many times are poor performers relieved of important tasks and those tasks given to ore competent workers? Many employees realize that the less they do, the less they are asked to do. Unless the reinforcements of poor performance are removed, no amount of coaching will improve performance.

5. *Is the timing right?* It is not necessary to wait until there is a performance problem. While coaching is often associated with performance problems, you can use it to bring about change in behavior. For example, when you delegate an important project to a competent worker, you may want to coach that person on strategies for successful performance. If you give new job instructions, you should coach the employee on how to follow those instructions. Training involves not only introducing job skills but also helping employees develop those skills through observation, feedback, and advice. Any manager who acts as mentor coaches that person to develop professionally. Thus, you

should think of coaching as a tool to develop employees as well as a device for correcting performance.

Preparing for a Coaching Session

Before beginning a coaching session, do some advance planning: collect necessary information, structure your message for the particular person, anticipate possible reactions, and choose a suitable time and location for the session. If the coaching concerns a performance problem, gather the relevant written materials, such as job descriptions, policy statements, performance records, training history, and prior disciplinary actions or grievances. If the session involves employee development, have together all the details of the project or opportunity to be offered. As in all formal supervisor-employee communication, you should have enough documentation to be thorough, specific, and objective.

As manager-coach, analyze the best strategy for dealing with each individual in light of that employee's personality, intelligence, competence, motivation, work experience, and career goals. Then structure the message and communicate in a style that is most likely to be effective with that given individual. One person may respond to a tough coaching style characterized by challenges, demands, and timetables. Another may need praise, encouragement, and instruction to produce a new behavior. Adapting your coaching style to each employee means identifying when that person is ready to be developed, knowing how to motivate the individual, or anticipating the best way to discuss a performance problem. Managers who treat each employee as a unique individual get the best results.

Likewise, you should anticipate how the employee might react to the performance feedback, delegated assignment, or career-advancement opportunity. Examine your message from the receiver's point of view. Has the individual responded angrily to prior discussions of performance problems? Does this person underestimate his or her capabilities for handling new projects? Will the worker welcome or feel burdened by your attempts to coach?

Finally, in preparing for a coaching session, select an appropriate time and location. The session should be private and the physical surroundings comfortable. Allow yourself enough time to accomplish your coaching objectives.

Conducting a Coaching Session

Because coaching is frequently used to correct performance problems, we emphasize that aspect of the technique. The steps can be altered slightly for coaching employees while delegating, giving job instructions, or building teams.

Basically, there are five steps in the coaching process:

1. *Seek agreement about the need for change.* Presumably, there is a problem or a deficiency in the employee's behavior that makes coaching necessary. You must get the employee to agree that a problem exists. That means discussing the exact nature of the problem, how often the problem occurs, possible causes of the problem, and consequences of the problem. Both you and the employee must perceive the problem similarly if you are to agree on a change. Typically, managers speak in generalities about work-related problems. Employees, who naturally want to end an uncomfortable discussion about their poor performance, may agree to a problem without really understanding it. Then both manager and employee become frustrated when subsequent progress does not occur.

Getting agreement on a specific problem versus vaguely hinting at a problem can be illustrated by the example of a sales manager who says to a subordinate, "You're slipping in customer service." A better approach is to give specific examples of what "slipping in customer service" means. You might say, "four of your customers this month complained that you didn't return their calls after you closed the sale." Then you can identify the customers and ask whether your subordinate returned the calls. If the employee agrees to the problem by indicating a failure to return the calls, then you can ask for reasons for the behavior. Such discussion will reveal whether there was a valid reason for not returning the calls. You should also indicate the consequences of unreturned calls in terms of a loss of customers and profits.

2. *Discuss alternative solutions to the problem.* Being specific is important. You and your employee should consider several specific options for solving the problem, not merely agree to the most obvious solution. In our example, the simple solution is for the subordinate to return customers' calls. More specific solutions, however, might be: (1) the employee could reserve the last hour of each day for returning customer calls, (2) the customer service department could handle the routine calls, or (3) a pamphlet for handling common customer questions could be prepared. All feasible options should be considered for dealing with the problem.

3. *Agree on the specific action to be taken.* It is not sufficient to get the employee to agree to try harder or to do a better job. That promise, no matter how well intentioned, is an empty commitment. You and your employee should agree on one action, as well as a target date by which the problem should be solved. Further, you should agree on how success will be evaluated. In this example, the problem could be considered solved when no more customer complaints about unreturned calls are received.

4. *Follow up to make sure the action was taken.* This might entail checking with the employee to assess progress or calling customers to see that their requests have been handled promptly.

5. *Recognize accomplishments.* Praising a good behavior helps reinforce that behavior. You should recognize progress that contributes to the solution of a problem, as well as the employee's successful accomplishment of a behavioral change. This motivates the employee in difficult areas of change and makes the person more amenable to similar coaching in the future.

If your goal is to develop an individual or a team to succeed at a project, you can alter the five steps in this way:

1. Obtain agreement that a task needs to be accomplished.
2. Make sure the employee knows the exact nature of the job.
3. Discuss possible approaches to the task.
4. Agree on what constitutes successful completion of the project (this includes a discussion of how the project outcome will be evaluated).

5. Follow up to make sure the tasks are accomplished, and then reward the employee for the accomplishment.

Common Coaching Problems

The manager as coach should be aware of and try to avoid these four common pitfalls:

1. *Coaching only when there is a problem.* If coaching is to be your tool for developing employees, then it cannot be associated only with correction or discipline. If you coach only to correct poor performance, then employees will be resentful and not respond to your attempts. Employees should regard coaching as an opportunity for growth, not as a punitive measure.

2. *Lecturing the employee instead of coaching.* Coaching should involve dialogue and mutual decision making. It is teamwork between supervisors and subordinates. Telling or directing an employee to engage in a certain behavior is not coaching.

3. *Dealing in generalities.* Probably the hardest part of coaching involves being specific. We often think that labeling a behavior is the same as giving a specific description of that behavior. To avoid generalities, you should provide examples, documentation, quotations, statistics, and dates to illustrate a point.

4. *Making assumptions.* To avoid assumptions, you should explicitly communicate every step of the coaching process to your employee. Do not assume that employees realize performance needs or problems, know how to perform competently, will perform appropriately even when they promise to, or know when they have done a good job.

Characteristics of a Good Coach

Studies of good coaching practices, regardless of the coaching context, reveal some common characteristics of successful coaches. The manager who wants to succeed in developing employees:

- Is interested in people
- Is predictable
- Is straightforward
- Lets you know where you stand
- Gives credit to others
- Builds confidence
- Has high standards
- Is objective
- Is firm but fair
- Is a good teacher
- Makes employees want to do their best

[*See also* Feedback; Mentoring]

For Additional Information

Deeprose, Donna. *The Team Coach: Vital New Skills for Managers and Supervisors in a Team Environment.* New York: AMACOM, 1995.

Jacobs, Dorri. "Coaching Employees to Perform Better." *Management World* 18, No. 4 (July/Aug. 1989), pp. 6–9.

Kinlaw, Dennis C. *Coaching for Commitment: Managerial Strategies for Obtaining Superior Performance.* San Diego: University Associates, 1989.

Kirkpatrick, D. L. *How to Improve Performance through Appraisals and Coaching.* New York: AMACOM, 1982.

Mink, Oscar, Keith Q. Owen, and Barbara P. Mink. *Developing High-Performance People: The Art of Coaching.* Reading, Mass.: Addison-Wesley, 1993.

Conflict Management

Interpersonal conflict is inevitable in the workplace. Because organizations consist of numerous individuals who must coordinate their activities to get work done, there are many opportunities for conflict. Whenever two people or two groups have opposite goals, they are likely to find themselves in conflict. Hardly a day goes by when the activities of one person or group are not at odds with others. The sales department may be in conflict with the advertising department, supervisors of different shifts may be at odds, executive officers may disagree with trustees, management and unions may have conflicting goals, customers' needs may oppose company policies, or coworkers may have personality clashes.

Dealing with conflict is a part of every manager's job. You will find yourself in conflict with others and will be called on to settle the disputes of employees. Never shy away from conflict; the effective handling of conflict is a necessary part of your managerial duties. Effectively handling conflict means understanding what causes disputes, promoting positive effects of conflict in organizations, encouraging the use of productive styles of communicating, and following guidelines for managing conflict.

Reasons for Conflict in the Workplace

There are many reasons why conflicts develop on the job. Causes can range from basic human nature to workplace structure and policies. A common cause of workplace conflicts is scarce resources. Because resources are needed to get jobs done and because resources are limited, we often compete for them. For example, managers from two departments may compete for budgetary resources. The larger one manager's budget, the smaller the other's. Other resources are office space, equipment, personnel, and decision-making power.

Conflicts also occur because of basic differences in beliefs. A conflict can develop, for example, if one member of a planning team believes in expanding the company's product line and another team member doesn't agree. The personnel specialists in an organization may believe in the value of employee-assistance programs while upper management does not. Just as there will never be enough resources in an organization to satisfy everybody, there can never be total agreement of beliefs.

Competition or rivalry between individuals or groups in an organization also leads to conflicts. Disputes are likely between two people who must work together when both are in line for one promotion. Two divisions of a company may refuse to cooperate with each other if both are competing for leadership of a key project. Two research colleagues may argue because of their long-standing rivalry over equipment and facilities.

Some conflicts arise because lines of authority are not clearly delineated. Power struggles are particularly difficult, because the power issues usually are not openly discussed. A secretary who has been with a company longer than a junior executive may feel justified in telling the executive how to do things. A consultant to an organization may make decisions that the client organization did not authorize. One department may make changes that affect another department without checking, in advance, with those who will be affected. Anytime that people or groups feel that their power has been usurped or that their authority has been questioned, disputes are likely to result.

Sometimes conflicts occur because people simply cannot get along. People with aggressive, insecure, or defensive personalities frequently clash with others. In some cases, there are no valid reasons for arguments other than the fact that two people do not like each other.

Conflicts Can Be Positive

Some managers are very uncomfortable with interpersonal conflict. As a result, they try to avoid or suppress disagreements. The wise manager, however, realizes that it is futile to try to eliminate conflict from the workplace. Suppressed conflicts fester below the surface and erupt sooner or later. Inevitable and even a necessary aspect of organizations, conflicts are not necessarily bad but can be challenging and enjoyable. Employees who disagree with each other and debate issues care enough about the job to fight for their positions. Where there is no conflict, there usually is apathy. Better decisions often result from a real give-and-take of ideas. Challenging decisions rather than rubber-stamping them makes for better decisions.

Conflicts can stimulate creativity and prevent stagnation. Differences of opinion challenge the manager who may have become complacent or dogmatic. And rivalry between groups can stimulate motivation and performance. Two departments with opposing goals may work cooperatively to find creative solutions to problems between them.

When conflicts are resolved, the conflicting parties feel more respect for each other. The ability to work together to resolve differences builds a sense of cohesiveness. Working through disputes brings individuals closer together, increases loyalty, and enhances solidarity.

Styles of Communicating in Conflicts

People display many different kinds of behaviors in conflict situations. Some people use a predominant style of dealing with conflict regardless of the nature of the dispute. Other individuals vary their conflict-management style based on the context, the issues, or the conflict partner. Common styles of dealing with conflicts include aggression, withdrawal, surrender, compromise, problem solving, and third-party intervention.

The *aggressive* style of dealing with conflict involves threats, ultimatums, defensiveness, name calling, and coercion. Rarely does it result in a resolution of the dispute. Through aggression, one person may force the other to "give in." The aggressor has seemingly won, but the conflict usually continues below the surface and will erupt again later.

Most managers would agree that there is no place for the aggressive style of dealing with conflicts. Organizations may tolerate a rare and mildly aggressive outburst from a valuable employee, but most consider an aggressive style of communication as grounds for dismissal. Some companies offer psychological counseling to employees who demonstrate aggression in interpersonal conflicts on the job.

Withdrawal as a style of behavior in conflicts means physically or psychologically removing yourself from the situation. It is an attempt to avoid or ignore the conflict altogether. "Looking the other way" can be an effective approach if used infrequently. It may be wise to avoid a conflict if the issue is minor or if the potential conflict partner is a formidable opponent, for example. But you should not routinely withdraw from conflicts. The manager who uses withdrawal as a predominant conflict-handling style will appear weak, will have to give up resources, and will get little respect from others.

People who *surrender* in conflicts are willing to get involved in them but give in prematurely. Rather than trying to fully represent their own position, they accommodate to the partner's position too quickly. When you surrender, you do not actually see the merit of the other position. You merely give in because you are uncomfortable with the conflict. A disadvantage of this style is that good ideas can get lost when you throw in the towel. Like withdrawers, managers who surrender sacrifice their positions and their reputations.

Compromise represents a rational and effective way to deal with conflicts. With this style, the parties agree to partial victory and partial defeat for each. Each person is willing to concede minor points in order to preserve higher-priority goals. By trading concessions, both parties win a little and lose a little. The conflict partners stick with the issues, care about an equitable outcome, and are willing to take the time needed to reach a compromise.

Being skilled at the bargaining or negotiating process involved in reaching a compromise is the hallmark of a good manager. Compromise through bargaining is a part of many managerial functions, including hiring, salary or contract settlement, budget allocations, purchasing, selling customer service, and handling grievances or complaints.

The *problem-solving* approach to conflict means cooperatively and objectively examining the issues in a dispute to arrive at a solution that represents the best interests of all conflict parties. Rather than examining the positions advocated by the conflicting parties as a starting point for compromise, the approach seeks innovative, creative options not yet considered by the people in conflict. If a new option fully satisfactory to everyone involved can be generated, then trading concessions need not occur. The problem-solving style involves collaboration and mutual decision making.

While true collaborative problem solving may be difficult to apply to workplace conflicts, this style probably best meets organizational goals. It forces people to work together as allies rather than to argue as adversaries. There are no sides in a dispute, but only mutual problem solvers.

When all other approaches to conflict resolution fail, conflicting parties can seek the help of a third party or have a mediator intervene. Basically, there are two types of external intervention in conflict situations: mediators and arbitrators. A mediator is a *third party* who assists with the conflict process. Mediators have no power to make decisions, but they can help clarify the issues, urge participants to cooperate, establish ground rules for rational interaction, and serve as impartial aides to help the conflicting parties settle their own dispute.

An arbitrator, by contrast, is a third party who intervenes to make a decision. The conflicting parties agree on an arbitrator, who will decide on the issues. The arbitrator hears both sides, evaluates the evidence, and makes a decision to settle the dispute. The conflict participants agree to abide by the arbitrator's decision.

It is preferable for conflicting parties to settle their own disputes rather than resort to third-party intervention. However, in many instances, managers will be called on to serve as mediators or arbitrators of others' conflicts. To maintain the trust and credibility of conflicting participants, arbitrators and mediators must treat each side fairly and equitably. By intervening, the manager not only seeks to help resolve the conflict but attempts to develop rational, effective conflict-management skills in others.

Guidelines for Managing Conflict

Following these guidelines will help make conflict constructive, rational, challenging, and manageable activities with positive outcomes for both individuals and organizations:

1. *Take your time in conflicts.* It takes patience to listen, to weigh issues, and to reach equitable outcomes. When you slow down the communication and avoid interruption, real discussion can occur. It may take several sessions or many months to settle a disagreement

2. *Avoid defensiveness.* Try to remain objective and cooperative. This means being open-minded and not forcing predetermined positions or solutions. Avoid manipulations, put-downs, know-it-all attitudes, and stubbornness. Rather than blindly defending your position in the hopes of winning, be willing to consider the merit in others' positions.

3. *Avoid deception.* In an attempt to inflate a position or enhance bargaining power in conflicts, deception is sometimes used. This can impede conflict resolution and destroy credibility. Effective managers of conflict are ethical, straightforward, and honest. Deal directly and assertively with issues rather than is representing or distorting facts.

4. *Be willing to admit mistakes and allow others to graciously admit mistakes.* Dealing effectively with conflict means having a willingness to give and take. When presented with opposing evidence, rarely can a conflict participant hold steadfast to all original points. Be willing to accept valid reasoning and evidence. Refrain from ridicule, gloating, or blame if a conflicting party accepts your valid points.

5. *Avoid assumptions.* When situations get heated, we sometimes fail to communicate explicitly. We jump to conclusions, make faulty assumptions, and try to second-guess our partner. It

is important to spell out all details, to ask questions, to put agreements in writing, to summarize progress, and to list agenda items for discussion. The more rational, specific, and direct the communication, the more likely the conflict will be resolved fairly.

[*See also* Negotiation]

For Additional Information

Donohue, William A. *Managing Interpersonal Conflict.* Newbury Park, Calif.: Sage Publications, 1992.

Kaye, Kenneth. *Workplace Wars and How to End Them.* New York: AMACOM, 1994.

Rahim, M. Afzalur. *Managing Conflict in Organizations.* Westport, Conn.: Praeger, 1992.

Consultants

The term *consultant* has come to refer to a broad range of roles, activities, or functions that people perform. Consultants may solve problems, give advice, disseminate information, perform specialized services, or intervene in other ways in organizations. They may be self-employed, may affiliate with large consulting organizations, may be on the payroll of the organization for which they consult, or may be professors, lawyers, doctors, engineers, psychologists, or other professional specialists. Consultants play an essential role in many organizations. By understanding the role of consultants, the reasons organizations use them, the process of selecting consultants, and the nature of the consultant-client relationship, you can utilize consultants effectively.

What Is a Consultant?

Typically a consultant is a person with specialized knowledge or skills who establishes a temporary relationship with a client to help that client in some way. For internal consultants, the client may be another division, department, or unit in the same organization, and the transfer of money for services may not take place. External consultants provide services to an organization of which they are not a member and receive compensation in return.

In either case, there are some key points in defining the term consultant. The relationship is voluntary, temporary, and helping. The nature of the client, the nature of the help, and the duration of the relationship are variable elements. The arenas in which consultants perform are also quite diverse, including accounting, personnel, information systems, law, engineering, finance, safety and health, recruiting, public relations, sales and marketing, labor relations, organization development, and research. There are many consulting specialties within each of these areas as well.

Why Use Consultants?

There are many reasons why the need for consultants has accelerated in the workplace. Our society, and the workplace in particular, is becoming increasingly complex and technological. Economic and social forces are rapidly changing. Information and technology is expanding at such a rate that many managers can no longer keep pace with the change. Managers can no longer be generalists, possessing the information and skills to handle all problems. Some industries are so dynamic that managers in certain areas need specialists to advise them. Burgeoning technology and information in the engineering, computer, and communication fields, for example, can make the proficiencies of even the most conscientious managers outdated. Rather than restaffing the organization to acquire people with state-of-the-art skills, the organization can hire consultants on a project basis.

There are several issues to consider when deciding whether your organization should use the services of a consultant. First, you should question whether someone in the organization has the expertise or could easily acquire the expertise to handle the project. Many organizations overlook their internal talent and assume that a consultant is the only option.

Second, cost must always be a consideration in hiring a consultant. Can your organization afford the services of a consultant, or would it be more cost-effective to recruit and hire a specialist as a permanent employee? Perhaps your organization could underwrite the education or training to help existing staff stay current in their fields.

A third reason why organizations use consultants is the credibility factor. While inside people may be able to do the tasks, the external person might have more credibility with employees. Information provided by an outsider may be seen as more valid, or a change recommended by a consultant may be more readily accepted. Situations addressed by outsiders are sometimes taken more seriously than if handled by insiders.

Fourth, organization may prefer a consultant for certain sensitive tasks that are more difficult for an insider to accomplish or for unpopular tasks that could destroy the insider's career. For example, a consultant will get more honest responses to an employee-opinion survey than an insider would. It is also less awkward for consultants to handle reorganization or downsizing decisions, since they can leave the organization after unpopular decisions are implemented.

The Process of Selecting a Consultant

Once the decision has been made to hire a consultant, there are certain steps to follow in selecting the right one. In choosing consultants, you must identify your needs, locate consultant possibilities, and screen applicants to make a selection decision.

Identifying Needs

Someone in the organization must perceive a problem or realize a need in order for the question of a consultant to arise in the first place. The more specifically you can define your need or problem, the greater the chances of selecting a qualified consultant to address it. There is a dilemma, though, in the attempt to match your needs with a consultant's services. Your organization may not be able to accurately or objectively perceive its own needs or problems. In the process of identifying the need for a consultant, your organization can also fall into the trap of dictating a solution to the consultant.

Locating Possible Consultants

Once key people in your organization identify the type of consultant they need and the goal the consultant is to accomplish, it is time to search for possible specialists to assume the consultant role. This step involves detective work. If the need is quite specialized, it may mean a national or international search for the handful of qualified people who are capable of meeting your needs. If the task is somewhat routine, there may be plenty of talent in your local area.

There are various sources to check to locate potential consultants. The professional associations affiliated with the specialty area are a good place to start. Libraries have directories of associations. Professional and technical associations can serve as clearinghouses for information and will be able to recommend specialists within their fields. The faculty of your local university represents another pool of talent that is abreast of the latest developments in many fields. There are also directories of consulting organizations and associations for consultants in various specialties. Other sources for consultants include the business-to-business yellow pages, the chamber of commerce, and colleagues in your industry or profession.

Screening Potential Consultants

Specialists who are capable of and interested in doing the job usually submit proposals. After meeting with their organizational contacts, and in some cases doing some needs-assessment research, consultants prepare a proposal outlining the proposed project, their qualifications, a tentative schedule, and expected costs. The proposal is an important device for evaluating a consultant. It allows the client organization to see sample work of the consultant and to make some judgments about a consultant's problem-solving style, writing ability, fee structure, and professionalism.

Consultant proposals serve another function in addition to being a screening device; they allow organizations to see the various approaches to their problem that different consultants would take. Through proposals, you obtain information about your problem from different perspectives. Submitting proposals without compensation to apply for a consulting project is a standard and legitimate practice in the profession.

One aspect of a proposal that is often difficult to evaluate is the fee structure. There are no standard rates for consulting services. Even within a particular consulting specialty, rates vary.

Some relatively standard practices can serve as guidelines, however. Most consultants charge daily fees ranging from $500 to $1,500 per day. The more sophisticated the project, the more unique your need, and the fewer specialists there are capable of performing the service, the higher the rate will be. Most consultants will negotiate their fee downward for long-range projects, and some will adjust rates according to the size (and budget) of the client.

Some consultants charge by the project and not by the day. Whatever the fee structure, it is advisable to know what can be billed and what cannot. Some consultants will not charge for preliminary or follow-up work, and others will charge for telephone calls. You should determine the maximum amount that a project can exceed cost estimates and realize that almost all proposals are negotiable.

Proposals represent just one, albeit important, source of information for screening consultants. Other sources include recommendations, testimonials, work samples, and trial projects. Whatever the consulting specialty and nature of the prior work experience, consultants should be able to provide pictures, models, diagrams, slides, manuals, or workbooks to document their work quality. A good way to evaluate potential consultants is to hire them for small projects. Allowing them to do a pilot project or some small aspect of the job will allow them to demonstrate their skills and will permit you to make an objective decision about their capabilities. This trial project also provides information to both parties about the nature of their working relationship.

Though it will take time, it is wise to get as much information as possible in screening consultants. Information from proposals, recommendations, background qualifications, work samples, or trial projects will help you make the best decision.

The Client-Consultant Relationship

After evaluating possible consultants and hiring one for your project, you still have some important roles to perform. Three areas of concern in the initial client-consultant relationship include the working agreement or contract, the identity of the client, and the nature of the client-consultant relationship.

The Working Agreement or Contract

The working agreement or contract is a written statement that specifies the expectations of both parties: who will do what, for whom, how, by when, and for how much. The written agreement varies in detail and explicitness, but early dealings between consultants and organizations should probably be characterized by explicit statements. Long-term relationships between clients and consultants may involve no more than oral agreements.

But whether the agreement involves a formal contract or an oral understanding, both parties must agree to the objectives of the project, their roles and responsibilities, the physical and personnel resources devoted to the project, the tentative schedule, and the costs of the project.

Identity of the Client

While this seems like an obvious point, the actual identity of the client can be elusive. Is the consultant working for the contact person in your organization, the unit or department that perceives the problem or need for the consultant, top management of your organization, your entire organization, the larger social system such as the customers of your organization, or its stockholders or financial supporters?

Anyone who has served as a consultant knows how difficult it is to identify the client. This question is important because it determines who the consultant reports to, who has decision-making authority, who the consultant has access to, and who evaluates the success of the project. There may be many clients with different perspectives about the project making simultaneous demands on a consultant. The client and consultant should try to reach agreements about the client's identity before the project begins.

Nature of the Relationship

Organizations usually put more effort into selecting a consultant than into building the client-consultant relationship. Several relationship factors, such as power, collaboration, trust, and integrity, should be considered.

Some consulting projects fail because of the perceived power differences in the relationship. The best client-consultant relationship is a partnership. Neither party makes all the decisions or is totally dependent on the other. You should know enough about the project specialty area to participate in the project. Decisions should be mutual. However, in many consulting projects, one party feels superior to the other and tries to take charge.

Before the project begins, the parties should discuss the nature of authority and decision-making power in the relationship. While power is not an easy issue to discuss in initial interactions, it is important to bring the underlying power issues to the surface so that both parties can determine if they can work with each other.

The client and the consultant may want to include mechanisms for collaboration in the working agreement. Perhaps an individual from the consulting organization should work with someone from the client organization as project co-directors. At the very least, both parties should realize the collaborative nature of their relationship. They should get in the habit of exchanging information and opinions and making mutual decisions.

The factors of trust and integrity are essential to the success of the client-consultant relationship. Neither party should withhold information from the other. Sometimes an organization will distort information to present itself in a good light to the consultant. Likewise, consultants may be reluctant to disclose their shortcomings or uncertainties. Each party must have confidence in the other. You and your consultant are a team working together to solve a problem. Following are some guidelines for using consultants:

1. *Avoid consultants who do more selling than helping.* While consultants must market their services, their primary role is to be consultants. Be wary of consultants who spend more time pushing their services than listening to your needs.

2. *Beware of crippling the consultant's effectiveness.* Some organizations hire competent consultants and then put too many re-

straints on them. As sensitive as some information can be, the consultant needs access to all people and all information in the organization to be effective.

3. *The client should not become dependent on the consultant.* Some consultants create procedures or systems to foster client dependency on them. Some organizations cling to consultants.

4. *Beware of consultants who apply the same solution to all problems.* Some consultants rely on one mode or approach for all clients, all needs, and all situations. Consultants who push certain solutions or approaches during initial meetings are likely to have canned answers before they even know your needs. Solutions should emerge in collaborations between clients and consultants over time after the problem or need has been fully identified.

5. *Do not put unrealistic expectations on consultants.* Consultants help organizations solve problems. They do not work miracles. Most organizations would be well advised to set their expectations a bit lower when working with consultants. Realize that change in organizations comes slowly.

6. *Do not make decisions on the basis of cost alone.* Cost should be just one consideration in selecting consultants. Some organizations opt for the lowest bid and get nothing more than a quick fix. Most organizational problems are complex and multifaceted, requiring interventions from several perspectives. Good solutions take time. Some problems are never completely solved. Your organization may have to spend more money than it anticipated to obtain the results it expects.

For Additional Information

How To Negotiate With Consultants: A Step-By-Step Guide. Baltimore, Md.: Project Management Publications, 1990.

Idol, Lorna, Ann Nevin, and Phyllis Paolucci-Whitcomb. *Collaborative Consultation.* Austin, Tex.: Pro-Ed, 1993.

Shenson, Howard L. *How to Select and Manage Consultants: A Guide To Getting What You Pay For.* Lexington, Mass.: Lexington Books, 1990.

Customer Service

All organizations, not just sales-oriented businesses, have customers. Increasingly, medical, educational, and governmental organizations also are focusing on their customer service functions. While customer service used to be narrowly defined as handling customer complaints, it is now regarded as a philosophy as well as an activity. That is, progressive organizations of any type make sure that concern for the customer, or end user of their product or service, permeates the culture of the organization. When the whole organization is customer-oriented, fewer customer complaints occur. And when they do occur, they are handled swiftly and appropriately.

How often you deal directly with customers obviously depends on the particular function or the nature of your organization. Nevertheless, all managers should be aware of the basics of customer service. We are in an era when customer service is seen as a way to enhance productivity and profits. Perhaps because the quality of service has deteriorated to abysmal levels in some spheres, customers are demanding better service. Stiff levels of competition in many industries are forcing managers to pay more attention to service. Indeed, you may find yourself immersed in customer service issues, which the business environment will no longer allow you to ignore.

What Is Customer Service?

There are various views of customer service, ranging from all-encompassing philosophies to specific actions. Which definition best reflects your organization's view of customer service?

- Meeting customers' expectations
- Providing customers with what they want, when they want it, in good condition, at a fair price
- A philosophy that affects every organizational decision and policy
- An opportunity to retain and build business
- Behavior to ensure a long-term vendor-customer relationship
- Handling customer complaints satisfactorily
- Sacrificing short-term costs for long-term customer loyalty
- Providing consistent, quality products or service
- All events related to keeping customers
- All communication between an organization and its customers, both internal and external

Why Emphasize Customer Service?

There are many reasons, besides the current popularity of the concept, to emphasize customer service in organizations. It makes good business sense to give high priority to customer needs. The many advantages of a customer-focused orientation include:

1. *Customers are the livelihood of any business.* They are the very reason why organizations exist. Whether they are patrons of the arts, patients in a hospital, students in a school, guests in a hotel, residents using city services, wholesale distributors, industrial clients, or retail shoppers, people using products and services keep organizations alive. Employees who do not come into regular contact with customers may forget the pivotal role customers play. We must all remind ourselves that our jobs and our livelihood depend on someone else's using the services we perform or purchasing the products we make. For some managers in advertising or industrial organizations, for example, losing an important account may mean losing their job. Even people in support functions in organizations should realize that they contribute to the organization's production of goods and services and that they have jobs only as long as there are users of those goods and services. Sam Walton, founder of Wal-Mart, was once

heard to say, "I never lay off anyone . . . my customers do by shopping elsewhere."

2. *Customer service gives organizations a competitive edge.* Often there are negligible differences between the products or services that organizations provide. Some carry identical stock. Department Store A carries the same five brands of lawn mowers as Department Store B. Airline X has the same number of flights to the same cities at the same prices as Airlines Y or Z. So on what basis does the customer select between vendors? One company will be favored over another on the basis of the nature and quality of the service provided by each. Some customers will go out of their way and will pay higher process to obtain better service. That is how important service is to customers!

3. *Losing customers costs a company money.* Not only is revenue lost, but finding a new customer to replace the former one is costly. Some companies project that it costs at least five times the annual business of the original customer to find a new customer. Therefore, on average, an accounting company that loses a corporate client of $50,000 per year not only loses that revenue but will have to spend at least $250,000 to woo a replacement customer. The costs of sales, advertising, and marketing to attract new customers far exceed the costs of good service to maintain that customer.

Calculating the lost revenue from just one angry customer who decides to boycott your business should convince you of the financial importance of customer service. A person who spends $60 a month on gasoline and defects to a competitor will give that competitor over $7,000 in business over a ten-year period. Imagine the staggering amounts of lost revenue from industrial and corporate customers.

4. *Quality of service may be what the customer is buying.* In some situations, the customer is purchasing a relationship with an organization rather than a specific product or service. A patient may be loyal to a physician or a customer may use a certain dry cleaner, not because of the competence of the physician or the quality of the cleaning but because of the nature of the relationships each provides. Customers may care more whether the service providers know them by name and make them feel special

than they do about the actual service provided. Managers and organizations should determine just what their customers are buying. It may be that customers select you over a competitor because of the personal relationships or reliable service you provide.

5. *Customers remember poor service.* A customer is more likely to remember one incident of poor service than 100 incidents of good service. Organizations receive little feedback about what they do well, but their problems are noticed. Indeed, organizations should provide ways for customers to communicate problems to the organization. A customer who complains always is preferable to the customer who silently disappears. In either case, dissatisfied customers will tell their friends about the poor service they received from a particular organization. So one incident of poor service can have a multiplying negative effect. Some customers have long memories and are quite unforgiving. If mistreated, they may refuse to do business with an organization for the rest of their lives!

6. *Customers provide information about product or service operations and improvements.* Customers' future needs pave the way for new product development. Customers are the major source of information about the quality of a company's products of service. If one location is losing customers or receiving more complaints, this tells something about the operation of that location. If one product needs more repair than another product in a particular line, the company may eliminate or redesign that product. Customers who complain or praise one employee more than they do others provide valuable feedback about employee performance.

Some organizations solicit customer reactions before they encounter customer complaints. At the very least, they should regard customer complaints as valid sources of feedback. Information from customers can help organizations improve products, develop new products, or enhance services.

Who Are Your Customers?

When we think of customers, we envision people external to the organization who interact with the organization and provide money either directly or indirectly to it. In addition, groups of employees within an organization serve as suppliers and customers to each other. For example, Production may need the services of Research and Development, physicians need the services of laboratory technicians to make diagnoses, educators need the maintenance staff for the upkeep of classrooms, and salespeople need warehouse personnel to supply merchandise. The list is endless.

The service that a company provides to external customers will be a direct reflection of the service that various departments within an organization provide to each other. We can carry the analogy even further. The way that employees treat each other and the way they treat customers is directly associated with the way they are treated by their supervisors and managers. So for good customer service to exist, there must be quality relationships throughout the organization. Consider anyone who interacts in or with the organization (employees, vendors, suppliers, distributors, contractors, etc.) as customers. They do not have to provide money to your organization to be considered a customer. If you depend on them in any way for the existence or success of your business, they should be treated as valuable customers. Also, they must treat you in a like manner.

It may be overwhelming to think that all aspects of the workplace affect the organization's ability to provide customer service, but a mistreated, underpaid, stressed, or underappreciated employee cannot be responsive to customers' needs. An employee who gets little cooperation from supervisors, coworkers, or other departments in the company is not likely to cooperate with others.

Caring about internal customers as well as external customers affects all organizational decisions and systems, including hiring practices, orientation and training, compensation and benefits, working conditions, job security, supervisory and management styles, performance-review practices, motivation and reward systems, and career-development opportunities.

Providing Customer Service

Attention to every detail of organizational life is necessary for maintaining high standards of customer service. A step-by-step process for developing or enhancing customer service in an organization follows:

1. *Hire the right people.* If you want to develop a customer service focus, then you must remember, when hiring employees, that some people are more pleasant, more motivated, more cooperative, and better communicators than others. Even if a job description does not involve customer contact, an employee who is skilled at interacting with others will contribute to the overall customer service philosophy.

2. *Provide orientation and training.* The employee should receive information about the company, its history, its mission, its leaders, and its policies. It is important that employees know how their jobs both fit into the overall mission and coordinate with other jobs. Training can equip employees with customer-relations skills and can emphasize the importance of customers to the organization.

3. *Set standards for customer service.* For each job, there should be clear standards for performance. What is the maximum allowable time between receiving an order and shipping the goods? How long should a restaurant patron wait before placing an order and receiving the food? What is the maximum number of rings before the telephone is answered? Such standards enable you to establish, monitor, and control quality. Jobholders benefit from knowing what is expected of them, supervisors know when to intervene to develop improved performance, and customers know what to expect in terms of quality and consistency.

4. *Improve communication throughout the organization.* Good customer service depends on several basic communication skills. Whether it is for dealing with client departments internally or for retaining paying customers externally, employees need to listen, be patient, coordinate information, ask and answer questions, avoid being defensive, and handle conflicts.

5. *Develop shared accountability.* A sign of poor customer service in an organization is passing the buck. Nothing angers a customer more than hearing such remarks as "It's not my job," "I just work here," or "I don't know what to do." Shared accountability means several things. The organization must de-

velop in its employees a sense of shared responsibility for customers. Customers are not the concern of just sales, service, or delivery personnel. Everyone in the company from the board room to the shop floor must keep customer service in mind.

Organizations must also empower their employees at all levels to make decisions that benefit the customer. Customers with a problem do not want to hear that the person dealing with them does not have any authority to act. Making them wait until a supervisor or manager can intervene is not good customer service. Organizations that encourage their employees to make decisions, bend rules, or act immediately to satisfy customers' needs are well on their way to having exemplary customer service.

6. *Audit customer service.* Organizations with excellent customer service records collect information about their performance in this area. Ways to collect such information include the full range of research and evaluation methods. Some companies use computer systems to record all information about product movement, such as order entry, processing, shipping, billing, and repair. Other companies use customer service questionnaires to measure satisfaction with such transaction elements as pricing, convenience, reliability, friendliness, and quality. At the very least, organizations should log and track customer complaints to identify and solve problems.

7. *Put as many employees as possible in contact with customers.* Some progressive companies have a system of job rotation so noncustomer-contact employees can interact with customers from time to time. Perhaps employees from various functions can rotate through the customer service department and deal with customers' questions in person or by telephone. Engineers, quality-control experts, or operations people can accompany the sales staff on customer calls. Educational administrators can teach courses occasionally, and the management staff of a hospital can visit patients. Whatever the method, organizations can improve their service to customers by putting more of their people in contact with more of their customers more often.

8. *Recognize and reward quality service.* Organizations can develop creative ways to foster customer service. Incentive programs, contests, awards, banquets, recognition letters, bonuses,

publicity, or something as simple as verbal praise can recognize and reward excellence in customer service. Such devices can motivate employees and reinforce the organization's customer service goals.

[*See also* Quality]

For Additional Information

Anderson, Kristin, and Ron Zemke. *Delivering Knock Your Socks Off Service*. New York: AMACOM, 1991.

——. *Knock Your Socks Off Answers*. New York: AMACOM, 1995.

Bell, Chip R., and Ron Zemke. *Managing Knock Your Socks Off Service*. New York: AMACOM, 1992.

Cannie, Joan Koob. *Turning Lost Customers Into Gold*. New York: AMACOM, 1993.

Desatnick, Robert L. "Managing Customer Service for the 21st Century." *Journal for Quality and Participation* 17, No. 3 (June 1994), pp. 30–35.

Donnelly, James H. *Close to the Customer: 25 Management Tips From the Other Side of the Counter*. Homewood, Ill.: Business One Irwin, 1992.

Griffin, Jill. *Customer Loyalty: How To Earn It, How To Keep It*. New York: Lexington Books, 1995.

Mahfood, Phillip E. *Customer Crisis: Turning an Unhappy Customer Into a Lifelong Client*. Chicago: Probus, 1993.

Zemke, Ron, and Thomas K. Connellan. *Sustaining Knock Your Socks Off Service*. New York: AMACOM, 1993.

Delegation and Empowerment

Delegation involves the assignment of a job, as well as the accompanying authority and responsibility for doing that job, to an employee who is held accountable for the performance of the job. Quite simply, it is getting things done through others. Effective delegation means clearly communicating the specific results expected, then empowering and motivating the subordinate to achieve the results, monitoring the person's progress, and evaluating performance upon completion of the task. Delegation and empowerment are essential parts of any manager's job. Understanding the advantages, process, problems and ground rules of delegation and empowerment can make this role more comfortable and more effective for you.

Why Delegate and Empower?

There are many reasons why you should delegate and empower. A major advantage is that delegation makes the job of managing easier. It frees you from some time-consuming, repetitive, or detailed tasks and allows you to concentrate on other important activities, such as long-range planning or new-project development. Managers who try to do everything themselves are burdened unnecessarily and fail to make effective use of their human resources. Some management experts believe that delegation and empowerment are the key factors distinguishing good from bad managers.

Delegation, or developing people, is a primary duty of managers. Empowering and delegating are the best ways to develop employees. While employees can learn from observing managers as role models, as well as from training and coaching, delegated assignments give them hands-on experience. You can develop your employees by initially giving them challenging, but not too difficult assignments and the authority to make decisions about those assignments. With employee success comes increasing challenges and increasing authority. Through effective delegation and empowerment, employees have the opportunity for guided practice of their own management skills. Managing this process thus allows the manager to empower directly reporting employees.

Empowerment is a process that combines training, education, on-the-job application, defined employee authority, and trust. The empowering manager does not *bestow* anything upon employees. Rather, the empowering manager unleashes abilities and skills already possessed, or those skills capable of being developed by the employee. By sharing control, authority, information, and influence among employees, the empowering manager frees up in employees their untapped or underutilized skills and abilities. The manager works hard to prepare and to develop employees. Then the manager stays in the background while the employees perform tasks, make decisions, and solve problems that are task related. This benefits employees, managers, and the organization as a whole.

Delegation and empowerment allow for the best use of human resources in an organization. Employees at lower levels who are closer to a work unit are often in a better position to perform tasks and make decisions related to the unit. Many of these people have good ideas and would welcome the responsibility and power to implement them. Besides utilizing employees fully, delegation and empowerment free your own time for more efficient use of your managerial talents. The organization benefits by challenging more of its people and using more of its human resources.

When done properly, delegation motivates employees. Most employees enjoy greater responsibility. Surely there are exceptions, and you must identify those individuals who fear or resent additional responsibility. But for employees who like to be challenged, being empowered to make decisions and to complete assignments can be a real boost to morale.

Delegating Effectively by Empowering People

Empowerment is not management abdication of authority and responsibility. In fact, empowerment requires more hard work and patience than other management styles. There are several key elements of empowerment that result in successful delegation:

1. *Select appropriate employees for a task.* A good manager is keenly aware of employees' strengths and limitations, and delegates projects accordingly. Work cannot be effectively delegated unless the person is capable of handling the task and accepting empowering authority and responsibility. Managers who do their jobs of selecting, training, coaching, and developing people will know when employees are ready to handle certain kinds of projects. This is the first step in promoting successful delegation.

2. *Trust the subordinate.* The empowering manager must believe in, support, and help the worker succeed with the delegated task. Effective managers realize that they look good when their employees succeed. You must trust employees to select them for delegated projects in the first place. That trust then enables you to share authority and allows the employee enough freedom to make independent decisions.

3. *Clearly communicate the task to be accomplished.* You must fully understand all that is involved in the work to be assigned. Only then can you communicate the objectives and anticipated outcomes of the project to the empowered employee. Too often, managers make general and vague delegations. When the employee is not given enough direction, especially on initial delegations, work performance rarely meets your expectations. A personnel manager, for example, who asks a benefits specialist to "work on finding a new benefits plan for employees" has omitted much essential information. A more thorough communication would be "We'd like to find a new insurer that is customer-

oriented but provides comprehensive coverage at a lower rate. See if you can get at least three bids on benefits packages that would reduce our cost by at least 3 percent from last year's budget while maintaining the same level of courage in all areas."

4. *Indicate the responsibilities of the employee in accomplishing the task and how performance will be judged.* Frequently, employees accept a delegated task without clearly understanding what exactly they are expected to do or what criteria will be used to evaluate their performance. It is your responsibility to make these issues clear, to encourage the person to ask questions, and to check the individual's understanding of the delegated project.

5. *Empower the employee with enough authority to complete the task.* The employee must have free rein on the task. That means defining an approach to the project, obtaining information, utilizing other people, solving problems, and making decisions. An essential element of delegation is empowering employees with broad authority to match their responsibilities. Employees or team members must have the resources necessary to complete their tasks and the freedom to operate fairly independently. If you ask a team member to seek your permission for small details of a project, you are violating the principle of delegation and empowerment.

6. *Establish a schedule for progress reports and task completion.* The manager who delegates must maintain some control over the project in terms of periodic checks to see progress and detect problems. Delegation does not mean abdication. A good delegator gives employees freedom while establishing a system to determine whether satisfactory progress is being made toward accomplishment of the objective. This reduces some risk for the delegator. The team member benefits also by having a clear schedule and the opportunity for periodic feedback on performance.

7. *Be accessible but not meddlesome.* You should let the employee know that you are available if the employee wants to consult with you. This is not to encourage dependence, but to promote dialogue and teamwork. Nor does this mean that the employee has to check with you. A confident, competent employee working on an assignment that develops no snags will not

consult with you except for prearranged progress reports. An accessible delegator provides some security to employees on new projects. On the other hand, you should refrain from repeatedly asking about the project or needing to be familiar with all details. Accessibility means letting employees come to you.

8. *Give credit for tasks well done.* An effective delegator acknowledges the employee's success and gives public recognition as well as private praise. You always look good when a delegated project turns out well. Thus, it is not necessary to take any of the credit. By letting employees shine, everyone benefits.

Why Managers Fail to Delegate

There are many reasons why managers are reluctant to delegate tasks to employees. Being aware of some of the common excuses for the failure to delegate and empower may help reluctant managers feel more comfortable with the process.

- *Perfectionism.* The perfectionist has the attitude that "no one can do the job as well as I can." Included in this excuse is the view that "I want the job done my way."
- *Fear.* This excuse includes fear of looking bad if the empowered employee performs badly, as well as a fear that the team member might do too well and outshine the manager.
- *Lack of trust.* Some managers do not have enough trust in employees to delegate projects to them. These managers may not perceive that any team member is qualified to assume the project, or perhaps they have suffered in the past because of an irresponsible employee.
- *Workaholism.* Some managers want to do every task themselves. They thrive on hectic schedules and working around the clock, and need to have their personal stamp on all projects—no matter the cost to their work groups.
- *Need for control.* A fear of losing control or giving up power keeps some managers from delegating or empowering employees. The manager does have to give up some authority and control when delegating to employees. Managers who cannot tolerate any loss of power or control avoid delegat-

ing and despise the concept of empowering others. Yet ironically it is the sharing of power and control with employees that leads to the ultimate power and control—success.

- *Guilt.* Some managers feel that they should do all the work rather than burden employees with it. This excuse also involves a fear of being caught with nothing to do or guilt about accepting a salary without working hard enough for it.
- *Waste of time.* The view that delegation takes more time than it saves keeps some managers from delegating. Some reluctant managers claim that "the project is too complicated to explain to someone else," "I don't have enough time to train an assistant," or "I can do it more quickly myself." This reason actually is closely tied to the previous reasons.
- *Organizational norm of nondelegation.* Some companies have a "do it yourself" philosophy. In this setting delegation is neither encouraged nor supported. Instead, managers are expected to "roll up their sleeves and get their hands dirty."

Why Delegation May Fail

It is rare that all delegated assignments turn out well. Mistakes do occur. Managers just beginning the process of delegation should be aware of these common mistakes:

- The employee did not understand the task.
- Too much was expected of the empowered person.
- The schedule for the project was unrealistic.
- The empowered person did not feel free or comfortable to ask questions.
- The employee did not have enough authority on the task.
- The manager did not monitor progress on the task.
- Problems were not anticipated

Guidelines for Effective Delegation

Experienced delegators offer these additional five tips to make the process of delegation smooth and effective:

1. *Make sure that managers function as role models.* Employees learn how to organize, manage time, and make decisions by observing their managers.
2. *Delegate total projects, not parts of projects.* Employees learn better when they can handle entire tasks themselves rather than merely doing detail work. Also, it is too difficult for you to coordinate a project when several people are in charge of many small pieces of the project.
3. *Allow employees to make mistakes.* An effective way to develop employees is to let them make mistakes on their own. You must resist the temptation to jump in to keep them from making a mistake.
4. *Realize there is no best way to handle a project.* You must allow workers to use methods different from your own. Resist the tendency to become upset if things aren't done "your way." By allowing employees significant freedom, you will discover better ways to solve old problems.
5. *Delegate good and bad projects.* Resist the tendency to keep exciting projects for yourself while delegating boring or distasteful projects. A motivated person will soon turn sour if given only "grunt work" to do.

[*See also* Coaching Employees; Feedback; Motivation; Time Management]

For Additional Information

Alster, Judith, and Holly Gallo, eds. "Leadership and Empowerment for Total Quality." *Conference Board Report* No. 992, 1994, p. 25.

Baslie, Frank. "Old Style Management Doesn't Work Any More." *Journal of Property Management* 60, No. 1 (Jan./Feb. 1995), pp. 14–15.

Belasco, James A. *Teaching the Elephant to Dance: The Manager's Guide to Empowering Change.* New York: Penguin Books, 1991.

Boyett, Joseph H., and Henry P. Conn. *Workplace 2000: The Revolution Reshaping American Business.* New York: Penguin Books, 1991.

McConkey, Dale D. *No-Nonsense Delegation.* New York: AMACOM, 1986.

Nelson, Robert B. *Empowering Employees Through Delegation.* Burr Ridge, Ill.: Irwin Professional Publishers, 1994.

Disabled Employees

The Americans with Disabilities Act (ADA) of 1990 prohibits discrimination in the areas of private employment, public accommodation and services, transportation, and telecommunications against those individuals with disabilities. This chapter addresses the law's impact on employment practices.

What ADA Covers

The ADA defines a disability as any physical or mental impairment that substantially limits a major life activity, such as seeing, hearing, caring for oneself, performing manual functions, walking, speaking, breathing, learning, and working. A wide range of conditions are covered by the ADA, including life-threatening diseases, physical handicaps, learning disabilities, mental illnesses, and substance abuse. ADA also covers family members and friends who are caretakers of those with covered disabilities.

The philosophy behind the ADA is that all individuals, whatever the disability, should have equal access to employment based on merit. The law requires employers to determine whether current employees or job applicants can perform the essential functions of a job with or without reasonable accommodation. Employers are not required to hire or retain disabled workers if they cannot perform the job. Likewise, employers cannot automatically assume that a disabled person is incapable of performing a job. Employers cannot discriminate against qualified individuals with disabilities in the areas of hiring, job placement, transfer, training, promotion, or termination.

Further, there are benefits implications to the ADA. An employer cannot make a hiring decision about a disabled individual based on the potential impact that hiring will have on the company's health plan. Disabled employees must have equal access to benefits provided to nondisabled employees. Let us examine the nature and types of reasonable accommodations to be provided by employers, the concept of essential functions of a job, and appropriate organizational policies and procedures related to the employment of disabled individuals.

Reasonable Accommodation

The ADA mandates that employers provide "reasonable accommodation" that would enable qualified individuals with disabilities to perform their jobs. Such accommodations may take the form of barrier-free access to the employment premises, technology to assist in job performance, or flexibility in employment practices. Changes that provide access might include specially adapted computer software and hardware, wheelchair access ramps, renovated restroom facilities, handicapped parking spaces, wider doors, lower telephones and drinking fountains, and door handles rather than knobs. Assistive technology might include equipment to enhance sight or hearing. Flexible employment practices may include altered work schedules, job redesign, or job sharing.

While the costs of providing such accommodations would seem prohibitive for many businesses, research shows that about 50 percent of disabled employees require no accommodations at all. And many of the necessary accommodations cost very little. Where there is cost in providing the ADA's reasonable accommodation, businesses can deduct up to $15,000 of that cost. It should be noted that the ADA does not require an employer to accommodate a disabled employee if, to do so, would constitute a major hardship for the employer's business.

Determining what is a major hardship the reasonableness of an accommodation is complex. Many factors are considered, such as the cost and nature of accommodation, the financial resources available to the company, the impact of accommodation expenses on the operation of the company, the number of persons employed, and the overall size of the business. In most cases, the costs of noncompliance with the ADA far outweigh the cost of

compliance. Noncompliance may result in the hiring, reinstate-
ment, or promotion of the disabled worker, payment of back
wages or damage payments to the employee, mandated accommodations, and civil penalties.

Essential Job Functions

Organizations should create job descriptions that list the essential
functions, marginal functions, and physical requirements of each
job. *Essential functions* are the necessary, central, or critically
important aspects of the job. *Marginal functions* are the supplementary aspects that an employer might desire but that are not
necessary for minimal performance. *Physical requirements* could
involve the amount of weight to be lifted or the number of words
to be typed in a job. By specifically defining, and in many cases
quantifying, the aspects of a job, it is easier to evaluate whether
any employee—disabled or not—is adequately performing that
job. Disabled employees who can satisfactorily perform the essential functions of a job, with or without accommodations, must
receive the same employment opportunities as able-bodied employees. Employers may discipline or even terminate a disabled
employee who, with reasonable accommodations, is not performing the essential job functions at a satisfactory level.

Employment Practices

Employing disabled workers and complying with the ADA means
that organizations must examine their interviewing, supervision,
and human resources practices with regard to sensitivity and
legality. When interviewing job applicants, a company representative cannot ask questions about disabilities. Instead, questions
must address the applicant's ability to perform job-specific functions. For example, an interviewer could not ask, "Do you have
total or partial blindness?" Instead, the question could be
phrased, "Can you analyze data from computer printouts or
when displayed on a computer screen, with or without reasonable accommodation?" Only job-related questions can be asked

of any applicant, and the same questions must be asked of all applicants to avoid discrimination. Organizations must educate everyone involved in interviewing job applicants so that they are knowledgeable about the sensitivities and legalities of interviewing disabled individuals.

Supervisors of disabled employees likewise cannot refer to disabling conditions during work discussions, performance reviews, or disciplinary meetings. Such communication should focus only on standards of performance and not on disabilities that may or may not affect job performance. Supervisors and managers should receive training about appropriate and legal behaviors in supervising all employees, including those with disabilities.

According to the ADA, medical records of employees cannot be retained by supervisors, as was past practice. Now medical records must be kept either by the human resources department or the company medical officer. Finally, a company's human resource specialists should be well acquainted with the requirements of the Americans with Disabilities Act. These human resource specialists should work with legal counsel to ensure that the organization's policy statements, benefits plans, job descriptions, interviewing practices, supervision practices, and physical facilities are conducive to the full employment of disabled individuals. It is advisable to appoint an ADA officer in an organization. This individual can assist the organization in its ongoing review and evaluation of ADA compliance.

By understanding the provisions of the ADA, by providing equal employment opportunity to individuals with disabilities, and by creating a work environment free of stereotypes and discrimination, companies may find that disabled employees are excellent, productive workers.

[*See also* AIDS in the Workplace; Employee Assistance Programs; Family-Friendly Management; Feedback; Mentoring]

For Additional Information

Abrams, Andrew L. "Americans with Disabilities Act." *Business and Economic Review,* July–Sept. 1992, pp. 27–31.

Akabas, S. H., L. B. Gates, and D. E. Galvin. *Disability Management*, New York: AMACOM, 1992.

Bennett, Linda. "The First Step in Complying with the ADA." *Supervisory Management*, April 1993, p. 8.

Ledman, Robert, and Darrel Brown. "The Americans with Disabilities Act: The Cutting Edge of Managing Diversity." *SAM Advanced Management Journal*, Spring 1993, pp. 17–20.

Tracey, William R. *Training Employees with Disabilities*, New York: AMACOM, 1994.

Vernon-Oehmke, Arlene. *Effective Hiring and ADA Compliance*, New York: AMACOM, 1994.

Disciplining Employees

Employees find it comfortable to be part of a disciplined workforce where expectations are clear, behavior is predictable, and supervisors are fair and consistent in their treatment of employees. Certainly employers benefit from developing a disciplined workforce. There are fewer performance and behavior problems; there is higher morale and productivity; and the rate of discharge, with its associated financial and psychological costs, is reduced.

While discipline often carries a negative connotation, a disciplined workforce is an organizational asset. Managers should reexamine their attitudes toward employee discipline and strive for corrective rather than punitive discipline. Developing employee discipline means training, coaching, and molding employees to exhibit appropriate behavior on the job. An effective and equitable system of employee discipline should include a set of clear rules, a set of progressive actions for rule infractions, well-trained supervisors, and an understanding of documentation procedures, legal constraints, and employee rights of appeal.

Communicating Workplace Rules

If employees are to meet organizational standards of behavior and performance, they must know the standards. It is ironic that in some organizations employees learn that a rule exists only by being punished for violating it!

All new employees should receive an employment handbook that includes, among other things, the rules they are to follow. Orientation training should explain the rules, the reasons for them, and the specific consequences of rule violations. There should be no surprises about how employees are expected to act. By providing a written statement of expectations for conduct, by explaining the rules, and by answering employees' questions about rules, managers can help employees meet organizational expectations. Most employees are reasonable and will gladly comply with rules, if they know what the rules are. By making expectations clear, you need not accept ignorance as an excuse for breaking a rule.

Policy statements about appropriate behavior often include specific requirements in the areas of attendance, use of sick leave, tardiness, leaving the work area without permission, adhering to work schedules, unauthorized visitors, insubordination, use of alcohol or drugs, fighting, disruptive behavior, safety regulations, smoking, theft or destruction of property, sabotage, failure to meet job performance standards, and falsification of records. Include all rules that are relevant and reasonable. In each area, there should be an explanation of what is expected, what constitutes a violation of the rule, and what disciplinary action occurs with each successive violation of the rule.

For example, how is tardiness defined? Is the employee considered late after one minute, five minutes, or ten minutes? What action will be taken the first time the employee is late? The second time? The third time? Some employee-conduct statements are quite detailed in defining the nature and severity of rule violations and quantifying how violations result in certain disciplinary actions.

Establishing Progressive Discipline

Progressive discipline is a series of disciplinary actions that progress in severity as rule violations increase in frequency or seriousness. A system of progressive discipline gives employees plenty of time and assistance in correcting their behavior. It becomes punitive only after various approaches to correction have been used and the employee still refuses to follow a rule. A system of progressive discipline increases communication between you and your employees and ensures that they are treated fairly. Likewise, progressive discipline helps you solve problems, retain employees, and develop documentation necessary to justify personnel decisions.

Typically, the sequence of disciplinary actions in a progressive system of discipline includes counseling, oral warning, written warning, reprimand, suspension, and discharge. This means that for minor or first offenses, the immediate supervisor begins by counseling and coaching the employee to help alter problem behavior. In many cases, this is successful in bringing the employee's behavior into compliance with workplace rules. If the particular problem continues, however, the supervisor goes to the next step in the disciplinary sequence—an oral warning. Here, the supervisor indicates that the employee has failed to correct the problem, reiterates the specific change required, and warns the employee that noncompliance will result in a more severe disciplinary action. Finally, the supervisor maintains a written record of the interaction.

If the misconduct continues or if the initial transgression was severe, the next step in the progressive discipline process is a written warning, which provides the employee with a written statement of the rule violation, the desired change in behavior, and the next consequence for noncompliance. The employee receives a copy, the supervisor retains a copy, and a third copy is placed in the employee's file.

A reprimand is an official notification produced by a higher level of management, such as a department head. Again, the employee receives written notification of the problem and desired change of behavior, as well as a warning that termination may occur if the problem is not corrected.

If the problem persists, suspension may be necessary. This means that the employee is relieved of job duties for a certain length of time without pay. A written notice of suspension, authorized by the department head or higher authority, is provided to the employee, maintained by the supervisor and manager, and placed in the employee's file. At this point, the employee is notified, in writing, that the next step for noncompliance is termination.

Should discharge need to be used as the final step in the

progressive-discipline process, the manager must adhere to various personnel and legal guidelines for conducting a termination.

The progressive-discipline system is fair in that it encourages supervisors and managers to work with employees to help them correct problems. It gives employees ample opportunity to change problematic behavior and plenty of warning about ensuing disciplinary actions. Indeed, in this system, the employee is included in at least five separate communications about the problem. The employer has accumulated a thorough record of documentation and can demonstrate just cause for a discharge.

Training Supervisors in Corrective-Discipline Methods

The key to developing a disciplined workforce is the supervisor, who has the most contact with employees and is the first line of authority in the organizational structure. The supervisor is the person aware of the rule violations who administers the steps in the progressive discipline sequence. How the supervisor handles problems affects whether the discipline is corrective or punitive. Well-trained supervisors are essential for progressive discipline to be effective. It is the responsibility of management to develop supervisors' skills in the area of employee discipline.

1. *Supervisors should be helpful.* Supervisors should be collaborative, not anagonistic, with employees. The goal is to help the employee correct problem behavior. By noticing the problem early and bringing it to the person's attention immediately, the chances for solving a problem are improved. Effective supervisors are direct and specific with feedback, and coach the employee toward improvement.

2. *Supervisors should be objective.* It is important to view employee behavior in an unbiased way. Supervisors should not jump to conclusions or let attitudes toward employees prejudice perceptions of situations.

3. *Supervisors should show consistent behavior.* The same behavior should receive the same response no matter who violates the

rule. Showing favoritism is a sure way to destroy morale and expose yourself to legal liability. Employees become confused and resentful when discipline is applied selectively. The consequence for violating a particular rule should be clear and predictable throughout the workplace.

4. *Supervisors should be good communicators.* Supervisors must give feedback, coach for improved performance, ask questions, and listen. Supervisors must be able to remain calm and avoid being defensive when dealing with the emotional behavior of subordinates.

Developing Adequate Documentation

Thorough record keeping is an essential ingredient in an effective employee-discipline system. Written records serve to maintain objectivity and to protect the rights of both employers and employees. They eliminate problems of recall and distortion of information. Whenever you communicate with an employee about a performance or a behavior problem, document the discussion. The elements of the discussion to be documented include the following:

- *The nature of the rule violation or performance problem.* Indicate the specific rule or performance standard and the way(s) that the employee's behavior fell short. Use quantifiable terms whenever possible.
- *The date, time, and location of the problem.* When and where did the problem incident occur?
- *The nature of the discussion with the employee about the problem.* Indicate what you said to the employee about the performance or behavior problem.
- *The nature of the employee's reaction to the indication of a problem.* Did the employee agree that a problem exists? What reasons were given for the problem? What was said during the discussion?
- *The date, time, and location of the discussion about the problem.* When and where did the disciplinary discussion between you and your employee occur?

- *The nature of any agreements reached.* What did the employee promise to do in the future? What did you promise to do in the future? What did you indicate would be the next consequence for noncompliance? Were any time frames for behavior change indicated?
- *The tone of the discussion.* Was the atmosphere of discussion rational, emotional, professional, hostile, or defensive? Did the employee cry, shout, or threaten?

In addition to recording these areas of content, be aware of the process of maintaining documentation. Document the incident immediately after it occurs. Recall is most accurate at this point. Waiting even a few hours will mean losing valuable information.

You should be as objective as possible when keeping written records. Record only facts and clearly observable behavior. Refrain from indicating motives, assumption, or personal impressions of the employee. Maintaining objectivity may be difficult if you dislike the employee or if the discussion was heated. Nevertheless, for documentation to be credible, it must be factual and not emotional.

It is important to document the positive and negative performance and behavior of all employees. Recording the problems of one employee and ignoring the problems of another is tantamount to discrimination. Selective record keeping is perceived as building a case against an individual rather than letting the facts speak for themselves. While it is time-consuming, maintaining documentation (good and bad) for all employees allows you to make objective assessments of your staff.

Legal Constraints

Employers should be aware of laws regulating employee discipline and employ personnel specialists who are knowledgeable about current guidelines affecting personnel decisions. Additionally, retain legal counsel for advice and representation in areas of personnel record keeping, discipline, and discharge.

There are a host of restrictions affecting actions regarding employee discipline and discharge. Some of these include state laws, union contracts, civil service regulations, federal discrimination laws, case law, and statements in employee handbooks.

Rights of Appeal

Where there is a system of employee discipline, there must be a system of appeals to protect the rights of employees. The right of appeal is a way for employees who believe they have been disciplined without just cause to have their case heard.

There are various ways to provide employee rights of appeal. Many organizations set up mediation teams where employees and management listen to the facts of a disciplinary case and make a judgment about its fairness and adherence to organizational procedures. Union contracts specify grievance procedures for employees to follow when they believe they have been disciplined without just cause. Civil service boards, arbitration proceedings, and court hearings are other vehicles for employees to appeal disciplinary actions.

Whatever the process of appeal, the manager should be prepared to answer the following questions about the employee-discipline process:

- *Was the employment rule or performance standard reasonable?* As part of the examination about the employee's alleged infraction, the original rule will be scrutinized. You cannot hold employees accountable for unreasonable of harmful rules, standards, or procedures.
- *Was the employee aware of the rule or standard?* Employees cannot be held accountable for rules of which they are unaware. It is management's responsibility to provide written statements of rules and performance standards, to explain those rules, and to make sure that employees understand the consequences of noncompliance.
- *Was the employee confronted in a timely and specific manner about the rule violation?* It is your responsibility to discuss the problem with the employee immediately after its occurrence and to explain the problem in a direct and specific

manner. The employee must understand the nature of the problem and the consequences of noncompliance.

- *Was the employee given sufficient opportunity to solve the problem?* This means that you should have indicated ways the employee could solve the problem, assisted the employee in solving the problem, and provided a reasonable time frame for change.
- *Was a system of progressive discipline followed?* The employee should have been given several warnings with progressively more severe disciplinary actions along the way.
- *Were the disciplinary actions appropriate to the offense?* The nature of the disciplinary action must be commensurate with the severity or frequency of the problem.
- *Was the rule or standard applied consistently to all employees?* It must be clear that this one employee was not singled out for disciplinary action.
- *Is the documentation complete?* There should be thorough, objective, and convincing documentation to show that the employee committed an offense and that the disciplinary procedures were followed appropriately.

[*See also* Coaching Employees; Feedback; Terminating Employees and Downsizing]

For Additional Information

Frierson, James G. *Preventing Employment Lawsuits: An Employer's Guide to Hiring, Discipline, and Discharge.* Washington, D.C.: Bureau of National Affairs, 1994.

Grote, Dick. *Discipline Without Punishment.* New York: AMA-COM, 1995.

McAfee, R. Bruce, and Paul J. Champagne. *Effectively Managing Troublesome Employees.* Westport, Conn.: Quorum Books, 1994.

Diversity in Organizations

Most workplaces are becoming more diverse in terms of their employee populations. And various types of diversity characterize these contemporary organizations. Employees bring to an organization differing sex, race, ethnicity, age, sexual orientation, and physical ability, among other factors. Such heterogeneity should be appreciated by managers and the organization as a whole, for a diverse organization has many advantages over a homogeneous workforce.

Yet such organizational diversity can present challenges to managers and employees alike. This chapter discusses some reasons for the increasing attention being paid to diversity in the workplace, the advantages of a diverse organization, common pitfalls in dealing with diversity, and recommendations for effectively managing diversity.

Aspects of Diversity

Organizational diversity is an increasingly important issue because of demographic trends. Today white males constitute a smaller percentage of the labor force than in times past. Increasingly, new entrants into the workforce are women, minorities, and immigrants. Since the average U.S. life span is increasing and mandatory retirement no longer exists, more older workers are in the workforce as well. While gay men and lesbians have always been a part of the workforce, their increasing political visibility makes the issue of sexual orientation more salient today. Changes emanating from the Americans with Disabilities Act (ADA) make employing physically challenged individuals more relevant. We are also seeing more diversity in the ranks of management. Thus, to be successful, managers must understand how to interact with people who are different in a number of ways.

Advantages of a Diverse Organization

Managers must understand the diversity issues because people applying for jobs will run the spectrum. Even if an organization wanted a homogeneous workforce, it would not be able to find such an employee base! But besides the inevitability of a diverse labor force, there are many compelling business reasons for seeking diversity in organizations.

1. *Greater ability to meet customer needs.* Companies benefit from diversity in employees because their customers and clients likewise represent diversity. Having a workforce that mirrors the customer base allows an organization to better understand its customers. Heterogeneous employees bring varied perspectives, assumptions, cultural paradigms, and problem-solving styles to a job. They can anticipate the needs and values of a multifaceted customer base.

For example, women and minority employees would likely have relevant ideas for marketing products or services to women and minorities. An organization without a varied employee workforce, or one that fails to utilize the added value stemming from such diversity, may not succeed with a marketing plan developed by white males yet aimed at women and minority customers. With increased global competition, all organizations will need to deal with wider and more diverse audiences for their goods and services.

2. *A more contented, effective workforce.* Organizations that successfully manage diversity have lower costs owing to absenteeism and turnover. If an organization functions under a dominant heterosexual, white male culture, other employees will experience the stress, job frustration, lower morale, and lower productivity that come from being excluded. Insensitivity, harassment, and discrimination against employees because they are "differ-

ent" results in indirect costs to productivity as well as the possibility of real costs from litigation. Employees who feel that they cannot behave authentically in an organization are likely to leave the organization in search of one that values their identity, perspectives, and talents.

3. *A public relations advantage.* Increasingly, professional organizations and popular media are "rating" companies in terms of their favorable working conditions for women, minority members, the disabled, older employees, or gay people. While the good press alone is difficult to measure in terms of concrete benefits, organizations that value diversity are better able to attract and retain good employees. Being known as an inclusive organization can only benefit a company. Seeking minority applicants helps expand employers' choices, especially in light of the declining pools of qualified candidates for many jobs.

4. *Better teamwork.* The increased emphasis on teamwork in many organizations makes the ability of employees to interact with diverse people a crucial workplace skill. Diversity on a team means that there is a variety of perspectives on an issue and groupthink is less likely to occur, with better decisions made. Thus, employees today need to know how to interact with people who are quite different from them in a number of ways. They need to tolerate differences that they might initially find objectionable. Indeed, employees and the organization as a whole need to value diversity, not only as a humanitarian goal but as good business practice.

Pitfalls and Problems in Dealing With Diversity

When an organization moves from a homogeneous to a diversified workforce, a number of problems can occur.

1. *Token dynamics.* When a minority group constitutes a higher percentage of the population than is found in the workplace, that situation is considered tokenism. Being the only disabled employee in a department or organization, for example,

means greater visibility, more performance pressure, and stereotyping. Also, it is common for organizations to place their "tokens" in highly visible positions as a way to publicly demonstrate their commitment to diversity. But being in the spotlight because of your "difference" can be very stressful in the workplace.

Women or minority employees often feel greater pressure to perform because they are taken to represent their entire social category. Their failures are seen not only as personal failures but as a setback for the entire group! When only small numbers of women, minorities, gay men, or lesbians are on the job, for example, stereotyping is bound to occur. The majority overemphasizes its similarities and exaggerates its differences from these "other people." Employees are seen as the typical *woman* manager, the typical *black* executive, the typical *gay* supervisor, or the typical *disabled* worker rather than as unique individuals who also happen to be female, black, gay, or disabled.

2. *Institutional racism or sexism.* When there is wholesale advantaging or disadvantaging of a segment of employees without the organization even realizing it, this situation is termed institutional racism or institutional sexism. Privilege for the majority viewpoint is so ingrained as to be invisible to those holding power.

For example, if emotional reactions in managers are perceived as a liability and rationality is rewarded, then the white male style of management is probably dominant in the organization. Yet for many women and minority employees, to display emotion is to be authentic, direct, and competent as a manager. By privileging one management style over another, the company automatically puts some people at a disadvantage. Perhaps the preference for rational—as opposed to emotional—decision making is an organizational norm, a carryover from when the organization was strictly white male. Indeed, institutionalized sexism or racism may not even be perceived as a diversity issue.

3. *Hidden discrimination.* A type of institutional discrimination appears when company plans extend medical benefits to spouses but not to same-sex domestic partners. Such benefit plans privilege heterosexual over homosexual employees. Likewise, holding major organizational events during sacred Jewish

holidays may inadvertently tell some employees that they are less valued than other employees. These are but a few of the ways that organizational policies and practices often value the dominant culture while offending less dominant cultures in the workplace.

4. *Prejudice and harassment.* Employees frequently bring their cultural biases to the workplace. Thus, ethnic jokes, racial slurs, sexist remarks, homophobic comments, and generally insensitive statements can cause conflicts that result in disrupted teamwork, missed deadlines, and formal complaints. In their most serious form, such behavior can result in legal charges of discrimination or harassment.

5. *Reality testing.* It is not uncommon for employees who represent diversity to experience prejudice in the workplace, to confront it, and to be told that it does not exist. When your perceptions are different from most everyone else's on your job, it is easy to begin questioning your own sense of reality. Likewise, employees representing the dominant culture experience reality testing when the rules of the game seem to change without their awareness. A behavior or remark that was once acceptable and commonplace on the job now is grounds for a reprimand or lawsuit. Many employees and managers alike, be they members of a primary or a secondary culture in an organization, express confusion about traditional assumptions, changing rules, and evolving cultures in organizations. Everyone's reality is being tested as we make the transition from homogeneous to multifaceted perspectives in the workplace.

6. *Assumption of assimilation.* Many organizations expect a conformity of behavior, including similar styles of professional attire, similar communication modes, and one preferred style of management. In many organizations, minority group members are expected to blend into the majority culture, ethnicity is subordinated to ethnocentrism, women are expected to behave like the men, and the wisdom of older employees goes untapped. Even organizations that recruit for diversity in employees may inadvertently expect cultural assimilation as employees are subtly absorbed into the dominant culture.

Recommendations for Managing Diversity

1. *Replace ethnocentricity with multiculturalism.* Organizations must realize it is counterproductive to business goals to perpetuate a workplace culture that reflects only a traditional perspective. Organizations must embrace the values, communication patterns, and behavior of all groups. The previously dominant workplace culture, which is probably based on white male norms, has to adjust to, accept, and make room for other perspectives.

This may mean examining the subtle and not so subtle ways that your organization privileges one group of employees while disadvantaging another group. Until managers realize the ways in which preferred styles are based upon the views of a few, they will not be open to embracing the views of many.

2. *Actively recruit a diverse group of new employees.* Keep in touch with minority caucuses of professional associations. Communicate with religious and civic leaders representing diverse employees. Actively seek employees from a range of backgrounds and orientations by using the Internet and tapping into minority educational and professional groups.

3. *Use and reward diversity.* It is not enough to have a diversity of employees if that diversity is not used in planning, managing, and decision making. Companies should seek diversity in workgroups, teams, and projects and then seriously consider the varying perspectives that diversity brings to those discussions. Organizations should purposefully shake up old ways of doing things and solicit innovative approaches. The recognition of different viewpoints should lead to a greater openness of new ideas in general. Thus, appreciating diversity leads to more organizational flexibility.

4. *Provide equal career opportunities.* In many cases, organizations that have recruited a diverse workforce have not successfully retained those employees because the culture of opportunity still privileges one segment over another. Organizations must examine who gets promoted, who gets placed on key projects, who has the training opportunities, and whose leadership is encouraged. If one category of employee is routinely selected for such opportunities, then the organization is not effectively managing diversity.

5. *Provide diversity training.* Increasingly, organizations are offering training that creates awareness of diversity and improves intercultural communication skills. Some companies have social events related to multicultural issues, such as ethnic picnics and the celebration of nontraditional holidays. Even just contacts between people who are different from each other can reduce stereotypes and prejudice. For example, African-American, Caucasian, Hispanic, and Asian employees working together on a meaningful project will, in and of itself, improve racial understandings and interactions. In addition to formal training programs, then, companies might think of ways to create diversity on all projects.

6. *Include accountability for diversity.* For a company to effectively promote diversity, all managers should be held accountable for meeting diversity goals. A change in culture from resenting or tolerating diversity to truly valuing and using diversity will occur only if the organization provides incentives and rewards for change. The management of diversity can be incorporated into goal-setting, team-building, and performance appraisal activities.

7. *Find common ground.* The management of diversity, by necessity, overemphasizes the differences between people. Obviously, not all women in a workplace think alike. Nor are the needs of one disabled employee identical to those of another. There can be many common bonds among employees who, on the surface, appear quite diverse.

While group differences should be respected and appreciated, we must not lose sight of our common interests and goals. Thus, the management of diversity need not factionalize the workplace. Instead, it should provide a level playing field by which all employees, whatever their age, gender, color, religion, physical ability, or sexual orientation, can succeed. Employee success always means organizational success.

[*See also* Disabled Employees; Family-Friendly Management; Intercultural Communication; Organizational Culture

For Additional Information

Blank, Renee, and Sandra Slipp. *Voices of Diversity.* New York: AMACOM, 1994.

Thomas, R. Roosevelt, Jr. *Beyond Race and Gender: Unleashing the Power of Your Total Workforce by Managing Diversity.* New York: AMACOM, 1992.

Tingley, Judith. *GenderFlex: Men and Women Speaking Each Other's Language at Work.* New York: AMACOM, 1994.

Winfeld, Liz, and Susan Spielman. *Straight Talk About Gays in the Workplace.* New York: AMACOM, 1995.

Employee Assistance Programs

An employee assistance program (EAP) is a method of intervention in the workplace that focuses on a decline in an employee's job performance to restore to full productivity. The EAP provides for early identification of performance problems and is a positive mechanism rather than a punitive measure for the solution of those problems. EAPs are designed to deal with a variety of problems affecting productivity, including alcohol and drug dependency, emotional or psychological health, and marital, family financial, medical, legal, and career problems. The EAP concept stems from occupational alcoholism programs begun in the workplace in the 1940s and is based on the assumptions that workers' personal problems affect job performance.

Employers face substantial costs for impaired employees, including higher rates of absenteeism, sick leave, accidents, workers' compensation, and health-benefit claims. In addition, there are the hidden costs of poor decisions, morale of coworkers, threats to public safety, corporate theft, turnover, and training of replacements.

Developing and Implementing an EAP

Clearly, it is both cost-effective and humanitarian for companies to identify employees with performance problems resulting from personal difficulties and to offer qualified assistance for solving those problems rather than prematurely or routinely terminating troubled workers. The following sections discuss some of the key ingredients in developing and implementing an EAP in any type of organization.

Planning

Before an EAP can be developed, the concept must have top-level support shown by commitments in attitude, funding, personnel, and time. Conceptually, there are two models of EAPs: in house and out of house. The in-house approach uses an EAP staff employed by the organization. In the out-of-house approach, the company contracts with an outside provider of EAP services. Some programs use a combination of these two methods.

Management at all levels, as well as union representatives, should coordinate the development of the EAP. Input from a variety of internal people in the planning process will help ensure widespread company support of the EAP. Make sure current personnel policies and practices as well as union contracts and benefits do not adversely affect the EAP. Small companies should decide whether to set up an independent program or to join an EAP consortium available in the community.

At this stage, the planning group should assess the organization's needs, formulate program objectives, and examine options for program type, staffing, and physical location. One way to see the program options is to visit other organizations with established EAPs to learn from their models. Companies without an EAP specialist on staff may want to hire an EAP consultant to assist the project from the planning phase through the program evaluation.

Companies can also elect to use an EAP-provider organization, which establishes and maintains all aspects of the EAP for a company on a contract basis. When investigating EAP-provider organizations, you should assess their philosophies, delivery systems, costs, and capabilities in meeting the specific needs of your company.

Assessment and Referral

The organization must provide a qualified counselor who diagnoses the nature of an employee's problem, gives the employee short-term guidance, and makes a referral to an accessible and effective treatment resource. Assessment-and-referral positions are best staffed with mental health professionals who have industrial-counseling experience, strong administrative skills, and the ability to work with managers, supervisors, and unions. To make an appropriate recommendation for treatment, the assessment-and-referral counselor must be part of a well-developed community network of human services professionals and agencies. In addition, the assessment-and-referral counselor must keep thorough confidential records, coordinate the company's benefits package, provide follow-up care to troubled employees, help educate employees and their families about the EAP, and help train managers, supervisors, and union representatives for their roles in the referral of workers. Companies typically place the assessment-and-referral counselor in an inconspicuous office in the personnel, medical, or industrial-relations department.

The Community Resource Network

A successful EAP depends on a diverse network of community treatment resources. Because it is a rare treatment agency that can handle all types of problems, a range of treatment resources is necessary. The EAP staff should be familiar with the major care-giving agencies in the community, their philosophies, the specialized populations they serve, and their effectiveness. A company's EAP staff should establish a liaison with the key personnel at each agency to ensure smooth coordination of referrals and follow-up activities. All treatment resources should be located near the workplace and be available at no cost to the employee.

Employee Education

Publicizing the EAP effectively means making employees and their families aware of the program, allaying fears and stigmas about the program, and encouraging its use. The first step is to develop a written policy statement that spells out such issues as the purpose of the program, the relationship of the program to the organizational structure, who is eligible for participation (for example, employees and their families), the confidentiality for participants, the locations of the program, staff responsibilities, and step-by-step procedures for using the EAP. Notify all employees directly about the program through a letter, brochure, or copy of the policy statement. Inform families about the program, emphasizing their eligibility, indicating that they may refer other family members, and explaining methods for easy access to the program.

The EAP can be explained in a special orientation and should be part of all new-employee orientation training. Use posters, films, videotapes, memos, electronic mail, and articles in house organs or union periodicals to announce, explain, and offer reminders about the program. To encourage full use of EAP services by all employees who need help, you should emphasize that (1) the company is concerned about poor job performance caused by personal problems, (2) personal problems can hinder anyone's job performance, and (3) use of the EAP is confidential and will not hinder the employee's future with the company.

Companies with EAPs sometimes provide, as a related component, ongoing education for employees and their families on preventive topics such as wellness, nutrition, exercise, stress management, financial management, and communication. This can be done through speakers, workshops, or flyers.

The Role of Supervisors and Managers

Supervisors and managers play a crucial role in identifying job performance difficulties caused by personal problems. You must be skilled in identifying such problems without diagnosing them or counseling the employee in any way about them. Familiarize yourself thoroughly with EAP policies and procedures and work closely with the EAP staff to learn how to identify performance problems, refer an employee to the EAP, and document each step of the process.

Essentially, your role is to discuss and document unsatisfactory job performance, recommend use of EAP services in the event of personal problems, advise the union representative of this action (if applicable), and stress concern, open-mindedness, confidentiality, and the goal of performance improvement to the employee. Even in programs where self-, peer, union, and family referrals are common, managers still play the primary role in referring employees to the EAP. You are, after all, the key individual evaluating job performance. It is important that managers at all levels, not just first-line supervisors, monitor performance of their staff and make referrals to the EAP when employees' personal problems affect productivity. Successful EAP's are used by all employees, from executive to hourly level. When referrals come from many sources and employees throughout the hierarchy use the EAP, the fears and stigmas initially associated with the program will disappear.

Confidentiality and Legal Issues

Confidentiality is an important factor in the legality, acceptance, and use of the EAP. Federal confidentiality regulations and data-privacy acts of various states set forth guidelines that a company's EAP and legal staff should consult. Most companies with in-house EAPs locate the EAP staff within a larger personnel or medical function to maintain privacy and confidentiality. All EAP files should be coded rather than identified with an employee's name or social security number. Both to encourage use and to maintain confidentiality, most companies opt for a flat-fee arrangement with community treatment agencies. For the same reasons, most EAP-provider organizations charge a set monthly fee for companies using their services. With a fee-for-service approach, the company receives separate billings for employees who use treatment services and confidentiality is very difficult to maintain.

There are a number of legal issues affecting EAPs, such as malpractice and employee and company liability, in addition to questions of disclosure of records and rights of privacy. Therefore, all EAPs should have legal counsel as early as the planning phase and on a continuing basis.

Cost Analysis

Companies planning an EAP must consider both the cost of implementing a new program and the cost of operating the program over a period of years. While there is no universal formula, the following factors should be considered:

- Salary of an assessment-and-referral counselor
- Materials for publicizing the EAP to employees and families
- Orientation sessions to introduce the program
- Training for supervisors and managers
- Costs of counseling and treatment (beyond health insurance coverage limitations)
- Program evaluation costs
- EAP specialist and legal consultant fees (optional)
- Ongoing wellness education for employees (optional)

Not all of these aspects require new allocations of funds. Salaries to supervisors, for example, are paid whether or not they participate in EAP referrals. The EAP can be publicized through ongoing new employee orientations, supervisory training programs, and existing house publications. Also, most group health insurance policies cover from half to all of the costs for most problems dealt with by an EAP. Experience shows that EAPs, in the long run, decrease insurance premiums as health, disability, sick leave, and workers compensation claims decline.

Program Evaluation

Valid and objective methods for assessing the effectiveness of an EAP should be a part of the program. Criteria for evaluating the program should be tied into initial program objectives. Have an impartial evaluation team rather than the EAP staff or the original planning group conduct the follow-up assessment. It is important that confidentiality be maintained in this phase also. Typical criteria used to evaluate EAPs include these questions:

- How does the actual number of referrals compare to the expected number of referrals (based on statistical estimates of impaired employees per company size)?
- What is the recovery rate of those served?
- Have there been measurable improvements in job performance of those served?

- Have health insurance claims and costs declined with EAP implementation?

Consortium Approach

A consortium is a cooperative agreement among companies and agencies that do not have enough employees to warrant their own EAP. Typically, they pool resources to obtain a single assessment-and-referral source. This person should be located at a neutral site rather than in one of the consortium companies. Companies and the agencies involved should have a steering committee consisting of representatives from each company to develop the consortium (if one does not already exist in the community), to coordinate its operation, and to evaluate the cooperative venture. Experience shows that consortiums work best for companies with fewer than 2,000 employees.

The company representative to the consortium should work with key people internally to develop a company policy statement, make employees aware of the EAP, and train supervisors and managers for their roles. While it is cost-effective for small companies to use a single assessment-and-referral counselor, many support functions should be separate and tailored to meet the needs of individual companies. In many cases confidentiality is easier to maintain and employees use the EAP more readily when all EAP services (assessment-and-referral counselor as well as community treatment resources) are located outside of the company.

[*See also* Family-Friendly Management; Substance Abuse; Management; Violence in the Workplace]

For Additional Information

Cunningham, Gloria. *Effective Employee Assistance Programs: A Guide for EAP Counselors and Managers.* Thousand Oaks, Calif.: Sage, 1994.
Scanlon, Walter. *Alcoholism and Drug Abuse in the Workplace: Man-*

aging Care and Costs Through Employee Assistance Programs. Westport, Conn.: Praeger, 1991.

Sonnenstuhl, William J., and Harrison M. Trice. *Strategies for Employee Assistance Programs: The Crucial Balance.* Ithaca, N.Y.: ILR Press, 1990.

Ethics in the Workplace

There are many reasons why organizations increasingly are concerned with matters of ethics. The pressure of competition is one factor. When the very survival of an organization seems at stake because of market competition, a company and its people may engage in behaviors once considered unacceptable but now deemed necessary. As companies merge, acquire other companies, downsize, or decentralize, organizational cultures often change, with questions of ethics and values bound to arise.

Also, a more heterogeneous workplace reflects differences in people's values, norms, and beliefs. A company with employees from different cultural, ethnic, racial, and gender groups may need to state explicitly its preferred ethical positions.

Finally, some would say that today's society presents more ethical challenges than earlier ones, and the workplace, as a microcosm of society, must deal with those challenges. Whatever the reasons, many organizations are making ethics a topic of discussion, policy, and practice. Contemporary organizations realize that good ethics makes good business sense. This chapter examines the role of ethics in the workplace, indicates the prevalence of ethics codes in organizations, and presents strategies for developing an ethics program.

The Role of Ethics

Whether managers realize it or not, their organizations already have a system of ethics that influences the behavior of all employees, from bottom to top. That ethical system may not have been developed consciously and may not have been communicated explicitly. Nevertheless, the company's ethical assumptions are revealed in its incentive system, promotion policy, management behavior, decision-making styles, and communication practices. And on a more explicit level, organizational ethics manifest themselves in top management speeches, board actions, concrete decisions, policies, and orientation and training programs.

Some organizations communicate their ethical positions in a written code of ethics.

But whether ethical assumptions are implicit and must be inferred or are communicated explicitly to all employees, the messages are there and influence day-to-day functioning.

Prevalence of Ethics Codes

Various studies show that more organizations have explicit codes of ethics now than did in the past. A 1987 Conference Board survey of over 2,000 organizations showed that 76 percent of companies in the United States have corporate codes of ethics. A similar 1992 Conference Board survey reported ethics codes in 83 percent of all U.S. firms. A 1992 study by the Center for Business Ethics surveyed the Fortune 1000 companies and found 93 percent of respondents have corporate ethics codes. Taken collectively these data suggest that ethics codes are increasingly prevalent in today's organizations.

Developing an Ethics Program

In developing an explicit ethics program, management must determine its goals or objectives for such a program. Why is the organization embarking on the project? Of course, there may be multiple objectives for establishing ethical values for the company, communicating ethical expectations to employees, and establishing an ethical reputation, internally and externally. Once the goals are clear, there is a three-stage process for developing an ethics program.

1. *Perform an ethics audit.* The organization should assess its existing state of affairs regarding ethics and values. The ethics audit, which can easily be done by an outside consultant, can help identify company values, both stated and implied. It can determine employee beliefs about company values as well as what employees value at work. Discrepancies between stated and enacted values may emerge. The audit can also identify issues on which employees need or want ethical guidance. It is important to develop such a picture of the status quo, so as to serve as the foundation for a formal ethics program.

2. *Determine the role of top management.* There should be discussion of the role of top management in setting the ethics culture of any organization. It is generally agreed that top management sets the tone for actions in a company. To what extent does top management model and support the ethical principles of the organization? How can top management be involved in the development and implementation of a formal ethics program?

3. *Prepare a specific ethics code.* Management must create, disseminate, and enforce its organizational code of ethics. Of course, the content of that code will depend on the objectives for the program and the nature of ethical challenges facing the organization. Some general questions can help guide the creation of an ethics code:

- What ethical problems have we encountered in the past?
- Are there ethical issues that may create problems in the future?
- What actions justify reprimanding or discharging an employee on ethical grounds?
- Do our competitors engage in practices we consider unethical?
- What is most important in this organization?

Organizations can look to the ethical standards developed within the industry or by professional groups as models. Another approach is to examine common elements in organizational codes of ethics and determine which issues apply to the organization. For example, studies show that the following issues appear in many corporate codes of ethics:

- Use of company equipment and supplies
- Use of company information
- Conflict of interest
- Policies on gifts, kickbacks, entertainment, and travel
- Harassment and discrimination
- Employee rights
- Political activity on company property
- Safety and security
- Moonlighting
- Whistleblowing

As part of the ethics policy, there should be procedures for monitoring compliance and consequences established for non-compliance. Ignoring ethics violations, no matter how small, will immediately serve to undermine an organization's ethics policy.

Implementing Ethics Policies

Typically, it is not enough to merely create a company code of ethics. That code must be discussed and questions concerning its application in the workplace be answered. Employees must learn the implications of the ethical code, and this is best done through orientation procedures, staff meetings, and training sessions. Training can help sensitize employees to the ethical decision-making processes.

At such ethics training sessions, the written code should be presented and discussed. Employees could complete surveys of individual values, with results related to organizational values. They need to see a fit between their personal values and organizational ethics. Cases that relate directly to a particular industry or profession should be analyzed. The employees could participate in role-plays of ethical situations applicable to their jobs. Ultimately, these sessions will motivate employees to behave ethically and to internalize the ethical values of the organization. Effective ethics training allows employees to realize that good ethics make good business sense.

Establishing an ombuds office is another way by which an organization can operationalize its code of ethics. An ombudsperson can serve as a resource to interpret the organization's ethics code as applied to real situations. Further, the ombudsperson can evaluate questionable actions or decisions, counsel individuals on particular ethical dilemmas, and resolve ethical complaints. Having an individual in such a role helps the organization live its ethical code, rather than having that code be a lifeless document.

As part of any ethics program, there should be an ongoing system to evaluate the company's ethical climate, make necessary adjustments, and reward ethical behavior by employees. The ethics audit described earlier could be used periodically to assess the program. Additional evaluative input could come from training sessions or via the ombuds office. It is not enough to merely develop an ethics program and assume that ethical issues are resolved as a result. That ethics program must be dynamic and flexible as management, employees, and ethical questions change and evolve.

To be truly effective, an ethics program must provide recognition and rewards for decisions and actions commensurate with organizational ethical standards. Supervisors at all levels must be held accountable for ethical behavior within their units. Once it becomes clear that unethical behavior will no longer be tolerated, and ethical behavior will be recognized and rewarded, ethical practices will be embraced by all organizational members.

[*See also* Family-Friendly Management; Meetings; Organizational Culture; Orienting New Employees; Training]

For Additional Information

Berenbeim, R. *Corporate Ethics Practices.* New York: The Conference Board, 1992.

Hodgson, K. *Rock and a Hard Place.* New York: AMACOM, 1992.

Manley, W. *Executive's Handbook of Model Business Conduct Codes.* Englewood Cliffs, N.J.: Prentice-Hall, 1991.

Navran, Frank J. "Develop an Ethics Policy Now." *Transportation and Distribution*, February 1992, pp. 27–30.

Family-Friendly Management

Increasingly, organizations are instituting policies and programs to help employees balance their work and family lives. Essentially, this means having an understanding attitude about the ways that family life impinges on work life, and giving employees some flexibility about where, when, and how their work gets done. While being family-friendly can be considered a humanitarian effort, there are compelling business reasons for such an approach. These days, being family-friendly is necessary for companies to recruit the best personnel from a diverse workforce. Women and men alike are increasingly unwilling to sacrifice their personal needs for the sake of a career. More employees are selecting places of employment based in part on the organization's tolerance and flexibility for balancing work and family concerns.

Additionally, family-friendly companies appear to have lower rates of absenteeism and turnover. By making sometimes small changes and minimal cost adjustments in workplace policies, organizations can retain good employees who might otherwise leave. The costs associated with absenteeism and turnover mitigate the costs of developing family-friendly management practices.

Trends Encouraging Family-Friendly Management

There are many societal and workplace trends encouraging family-friendly management practices. To begin, there is the increasing number of women in organizations of all types. While large numbers of women are not at the top levels of organizations, women have moved into middle-management positions in sufficient numbers to begin to affect organizational culture. In many organizations, the culture may be evolving into a more family-friendly one by virtue of women's management styles.

Correspondingly, men are taking a larger role with family responsibilities than did men in previous generations. Many men seek jobs that allow them to be full participants in the lives of their children. Thus, family-friendly management is not just a women's issue.

Another societal trend is our aging population. Increasingly, employees—be they male or female—are caring for elderly parents. These employees need flexible workplace climates that enable them to fulfill these caretaking roles. Government regulation is also a factor leading to family-friendly companies. The Family and Medical Leave Act (FMLA) of 1993 is one such government mandate to provide a work environment that accommodates employees' family demands. Thus, increased competition for top-quality employees is making family-friendly management a necessity for recruiting and retaining a quality workforce.

The Impact of Family Concerns on the Workplace

When employees are unable to balance the demands of the job with demands at home, their productivity suffers. Such role conflict leads to stress, tardiness, increased telephone usage for personnel business, absenteeism, sick leave, and perhaps turnover. Estimates place the cost to business of employees' dependent-care responsibilities at $3 billion per year. Workplace surveys of employees show the majority of employees have either child-care or elder-care responsibilities—indeed, about 40 percent of the U.S. workforce is providing both child care and elder care simultaneously. The stresses felt by this "sandwich generation" inevitably impinge on workplace productivity. Thus, the conflict between family and work responsibilities is no longer an issue that organizations can avoid.

The Family and Medical Leave Act

Provisions of the Family and Medical Leave Act became effective for nonunion employees in August of 1993 and for union employees in February of 1994. The act requires organizations with fifty or more employees to provide eligible employees with unpaid leaves for certain family or medical situations. Eligible employees include those who have worked at least 1,250 hours for the employer in a twelve-month period preceding the leave. Such employees may take a maximum of twelve weeks' leave per year to provide care for a newborn or adopted child, foster care, care for a spouse, child or parent with a serious health condition, or for the employee's own serious medical condition.

The FMLA requires that the employee's medical benefits will be continued during the leave and that the employee will be returned, at the conclusion of the leave, to the same or equivalent job with comparable pay, benefits, and terms of employment.

The twelve weeks of leave may be taken consecutively or intermittently. Intermittent leave means the employee may take separate periods of time owing to a single medical circumstance. For example, an employee may request one day off per week or one hour of leave per day for doctors' visits or elder care until the twelve weeks of leave is exhausted. Intermittent leave may not be taken to care for a healthy child.

Family-Friendly Options in Organizations

There are a number of ways that organizations can provide a family-friendly workplace. The organization need not provide all of these, but may select those that best fit the needs of its employees and the type and size of the organization.

1. *Family Care.* Family care includes a variety of needs, such as day care for infants and toddlers, before- and after-school care, summer care, sick child care, and elder care. Organizations can assist employees in obtaining and paying for child and elder care in a number of ways. For example, some employers pay a portion of employees' care-provider costs through dependent-care ac-

counts. Here, employees can designate pre-tax dollars from their own salary to use for dependent-care expenses; the only cost to employers is the record keeping. Organizations can also provide referral services to assist employees in finding quality dependent care. This entails providing lists of dependent-care options available in the community. Companies can contract with such referral services at nominal costs. Referral assistance is useful for organizations in which there are frequent transfers of personnel.

Some organizations have established on-site day-care facilities. This is a very attractive benefit for many employees, but a costly one to employers. Another way to assist with employee child care is for the organization to help pay the costs of an off-site child-care facility in exchange for preferential treatment for the organization's employees. Organizations can join dependent-care consortiums in some communities. By collaborating with other organizations in arranging for dependent care, an organization can lower its costs in providing such a benefit. Some states offer tax credits to businesses for providing child-care assistance.

2. *Flexible work arrangements.* Flexible work arrangements take many forms, including flex-time, part-time work, work at home, job sharing, and a compressed work week. The family responsibilities of most employees are not so demanding that they need to use the provisions of the Family and Medical Leave Act. Rather, in many cases family emergencies come up sporadically, and some flexibility in the work schedule is all that is needed to enable a productive employee to handle a family responsibility. Flexible work arrangements may cost an organization very little, but they serve to greatly accommodate employees' needs.

Flex-time involves negotiating with the employee for varied start and end times to a workday. For example, an employee might start earlier in the morning so as to end the work day at the same time as a child's school day ends. The employee is still on-site the same number of hours, but may have a slightly different work schedule than other employees.

Since organizations increasingly are using *part-time* employees, part-time work is an option that might first be offered to existing employees before hiring new part-time staff. Some employees may need temporary part-time work during a family crisis, while others may elect part-time work on a permanent basis. And advances in technology have expanded the options for work at home. For certain job categories, an employee working at home with a personal computer, fax, and telephone can be more productive than working on-site. Of course, not all jobs lend themselves to off-site work.

In *job sharing*, two employees perform the functions of one job. With dedicated employees, the organization may actually get more work done at less cost in a job-sharing arrangement. While each person presumably does 50 percent of the work at 50 percent of the salary, many professionals in job-sharing arrangements actually do more than 50 percent of the work for that half-time salary. The company also realizes the costs savings for both employees, while having two qualified employees on which to rely.

Many organizations are moving to a *compressed work week*, whereby employee work four 10-hour days in lieu of five 8-hour days. Such an arrangement can lower employees' child-care and commuting costs while maintaining the productivity for the organization.

3. *Work-life programs.* While not as common as family-care or flexible-work arrangements, work-life programs can be a viable strategy for assisting employees with work and family conflicts. Work-life programs provide training to employees on whole-life planning, stress and time management, conflict-resolution skills, communication strategies, and exercise and nutrition programs. Such programs not only help employees better manage their family and work demands but also provide competencies that can transfer to workplace behavior. By participating in work-life programs, employees may improve their communication and efficiency on the job.

4. *Employee assistance programs.* Complete and effective employee-assistance programs (EAP) can serve to create a family-friendly organizational climate. While not designed for that purpose, EAPs involve counseling services and referrals to enable employees to better manage their dependent-care and health-care needs. Companies may want to examine the range of services provided by their EAP to determine if more family-friendly services can be added.

Organizations can no longer expect employees to leave their personal problems at the door. They must offer work arrangements and benefits that enable productive employees to remain productive in light of family responsibilities. They must train managers to have compassion for employees' family crises while continuing to expect high levels of quality performance. To be family-friendly is not to sacrifice productivity or profits. Rather, family-friendly management enables a workforce to handle family demands in a way that allows for maximum productivity. Family-friendly management makes good business sense.

[*See also* Disabled Employees; Employee Assistance Programs; Motivation]

For Additional Information

Durity, Art. "The Sandwich Generation Feels the Squeeze." *Management Review* 80, No. 12 (December 1991), pp. 38–41.

Geber, Beverly. "The Bendable, Flexible, Open-Minded Manager." *Training* 30, No. 2 (February 1993), pp. 46–52.

Hand, Shirley, and Robert A. Zawacki. "Family-friendly Benefits: More Than A Frill." *HR Magazine* 39, No. 10 (October 1994), pp. 79–84.

Olmsted, Barney, and Suzanne Smith. *Creating a Flexible Workplace: How to Select and Manage Alternative Work Options.* New York: AMACOM, 1994.

Wilkof, Marcia V., and Joy Schneer. "Is Your Company and Its Culture Women-Friendly?" *Journal for Quality and Participation* 18, No. 3 (June 1995), pp. 66–69.

Feedback

Almost all aspects of a manager's job involve feedback, or giving and getting information about work-related performance. You must give feedback to your employees and receive information from your supervisors about your own managerial performance. Customers give feedback to organizations about products and service. Employees give feedback through various means to their bosses. Smart managers solicit feedback about their own behavior, new ideas, and organizational procedures and programs. In essence, feedback or information about workplace performance permeates the communication system of an organization. Feedforward and feedback are the first steps in the cycle of continuous improvement.

This chapter examines the prevalence of feedback in organizational life, the need for communicating clear expectations (feedforward) prior to evaluating performance, the advantages to managers of enhancing feedback skills, and guidelines for giving and receiving work-related feedforward and feedback.

Why Consider Feedback?

Though you may not use the term *feedback* to describe sharing information about work performance, hardly a day goes by when you do not evaluate others' work and communicate your reactions to it. Anytime managers give reactions to other people's work, they are engaged in the process of giving feedback. Raising your eyebrow or critically scowling constitutes feedback. It can be subtle and fleeting or explicit and thorough.

Because feedback is inextricably tied to the managerial role, you should be acutely conscious of the feedback process. Become aware of unintentional displays of feedback and realize the advantages of developing feedback skills. By being direct and clear with feedback to others, managers, employees, and the entire organization will benefit. Here are some of the advantages of developing feedback skills:

1. *Feedback reduces uncertainty.* Most people need to know what is expected of them, and they crave reactions to their work. We look for subtle signs from others and then try to guess what they think of our performance. Not knowing how supervisors, in particular, perceive our work can be quite stressful. All employees need to know where they stand on the job.

2. *Feedback solves problems.* If a subordinate has a performance problem, then early feedback about that problem can solve it before it magnifies or becomes ingrained. A manager who has a problem relationship with another manager can use feedback to attempt to resolve their differences. Withholding information or reactions will not make the problem disappear. Only through direct, clear feedback about the problem and discussion of alternative courses of action will problems be solved.

3. *Feedback can build trust.* Trust means being comfortable in your predictions of others' behavior. You are in a much better position to predict others' behavior if they have been upfront with you in the past. By directly communicating with others, you can help reduce suspicions and fears among work colleagues. Managers who regularly communicate feedforward and give feedback to subordinates are predictable managers. Subordinates know what to expect, appreciate that predictability, and show less defensiveness.

4. *Feedback can strengthen relationships.* People who can be honest in their reactions to each other tend to have stronger relationships. While the feedback process can be painful, the ability to communicate openly leads ultimately to stronger relationships. Managers who care about their subordinates' success will give them lots of performance feedback and will coach them to greater achievements.

5. *Feedback improves work quality.* Employees cannot be expected to improve their work quality unless they have a clear understanding of what quality is and how their work compares

to quality standards. Likewise, praise for performance excellence creates incentives for even more quality. You can build quality and productivity by continually giving your employees feedback about their performance and working with them to meet higher performance goals.

Communicating Expectations or Giving Feedforward

Before one's performance can be fairly and objectively measured, that person must have a clear understanding of the expectations the manager has for the job. Such feedforward should include time frames, measures of quality and quantity, financial parameters, factors for formally measuring performance on performance evaluations, and customers' expectations. The manager should describe even subtle and less obvious expectations for the employee. These subtle expectations may cover such things as where to go for help, limits or expectations for employee authority to get the job done, and training progressions.

The best time to communicate feedforward is all the time. Certainly, it makes sense to discuss expectations with new or newly transferred employees. Managers also must give detailed discussions of their expectations when starting projects and before communicating employee evaluations. Yet wise managers realize that routinely reviewing their expectations, daily or weekly, increases the possibility that employees will meet or exceed those expectations. Indeed, feedforward motivates both employees and managers alike.

Giving Feedback to Others

There are some managerial guidelines for giving both solicited and unsolicited feedback about the work performance of others.

1. *Feedback should be specific.* Give examples of the behavior or performance at hand. The more specific you can be with examples and complete descriptions of behavior, the more the other person

will understand your feedback. Telling someone to take more initiative, use more common sense, or change a negative attitude are meaningless generalities. To be more specific with the feedback, you must provide examples of when the person should have but did not take initiative. Explain what is meant by common sense. Show how the so-called negative attitude manifested itself in a specific, problematic job-related behavior.

2. *Feedback should be descriptive, not evaluative.* This means describing behavior in observable terms rather than using judgmental words. Notice the difference between feedback that calls an employee irresponsible with deadlines and feedback that describes the three times in the last month when the person missed work deadlines. Referring to observable behavior deals in the realm of fact—either the employee missed the deadlines or did not. Using evaluative labels and character attacks moves the feedback into the emotional arena and deals with opinions.

3. *Feedback uses appropriate timing.* Feedback is most effective if given right after the work performance occurs or immediately after it is solicited. Delayed feedback is not as effective as immediate feedback. Timing also means giving feedback privately and when there is enough time for a discussion.

4. *Feedback should be ongoing.* Giving feedback should not be a sporadic event in a work relationship, but an ongoing, natural part of the manager-employee relationship. Feedback offered only once a year at the formal performance review is insufficient and will have little impact on performance. If feedback becomes a regular part of the work relationship and you comment at least weekly on the positive and negative features of employees' performances, the feedback process will be less traumatic and more effective.

Soliciting Feedback From Others

Feedback should be a reciprocal process. Not only do you give feedback to others, but you should solicit it from others as well. Employee feedback on company programs, for example, can serve as a barometer of the effectiveness of those programs.

Participants in orientation sessions, training programs, assessment centers, employee-assistance programs, quality efforts, teleconferences, or career-development, outplacement, or retirement counseling sessions always should have opportunities to evaluate the programs. These are but a few of the places where employees can give feedback to management.

Additionally, employees can provide their reactions to your behavior in such routine areas as performance review, delegated projects, disciplinary procedures, meetings, and decisions. Certain features of the workplace, such as employee-involvement programs, exit interviews, and suggestion boxes, exist for the very purpose of soliciting employee feedback. Indeed, there are few areas of organizational life in which employees cannot provide feedback, and many managers are surprised at the insight and professionalism of employee feedback to them.

When soliciting feedback, follow these guidelines in obtaining and reacting to others' evaluations of your performance or programs:

1. *Try to get as much specific information as possible.* The more specific the feedback, the more useful it is. Whether you informally ask for a colleague's reaction or structure a questionnaire to solicit program participants' reviews, make sure your questions are specific. Ask follow-up questions to get more detail. It is up to the recipient of feedback to probe for enough detail to make the information useful. If you intend to use the feedback to make changes in your performance or program, it must be sufficiently detailed so you know what to change.

2. *Do not become defensive when receiving negative feedback.* The automatic tendency when receiving critical evaluations is to become defensive. We want to deny the evaluation and to provide refutation. Sometimes we resent the person who provides the negative feedback. Managers who receive negative reactions from employees regarding a new program or procedure may consider the employees ungrateful or uninformed. In some cases, you discount others' feedback by calling it wrong or incorrect. Such defensive responses defeat the purpose of obtaining others' feedback.

3. *Use feedback.* It is worse to solicit others' feedback and not use it than to ask for no feedback at all. Employees feel manipulated, for example, when they are asked to provide input to management and their reactions are not taken seriously or used in any way. Ignoring employee suggestions has been the downfall of many employee-input programs.

The feedback we receive from others is often very valid. We should welcome feedback, study it, and use it to make improvements in managerial performance, procedures, and programs. Successful managers seriously entertain the feedback they receive, no matter whom it comes from. They appreciate others' evaluations, use feedback to make improvements, and offer explanations to others when they cannot implement their suggestions.

4. *Conduct employee-opinion surveys.* Employee-opinion surveys are a great way of receiving candid, anonymous reactions from employees. They can monitor discontent or pinpoint problems among employees. By structuring a series of questions on any number of issues and having an outsider administer the survey and summarize results, you can receive substantial feedback from employees. If done regularly with findings disclosed and deficiencies corrected, the opinion survey can be a valuable feedback tool. The method can be applied to customers, the public, or other groups whose feedback is important to the organization.

[*See also* Coaching Employees; Delegation and Empowerment; Motivation; Performance Appraisal, Time Management]

For Additional Information

Baumgartner, Jerry. "Give It To Me Straight." *Training and Development* 48, No. 5 (June 1994), pp. 48–51.

Kilbourn, Brent. *Constructive Feedback: Learning the Art.* Cambridge, Mass.: Brookline Books, 1990.

Kushel, Gerald. *Reaching the Peak Performance Zone: How to Motivate Yourself and Others to Excel.* New York: AMACOM, 1994.

Romano, Catherine. "Conquering the Fear of Feedback." *HR Focus* 71, No. 3 (March 1994), pp. 5–10.

Stone, Florence, and Randi Sachs. *The High Value Manager: Developing the Core Competencies Your Organization Demands.* New York: AMACOM, 1996.

Innovation and Creativity

Once considered the domain of artists, musicians, and writers, creativity is now regarded as a necessary characteristic for leaders, managers, and administrators as well. There is a growing literature on managing innovation, aimed at business and nonprofit organizations. Creativity workshops and materials are designed for managers and executives in various types of organizations. And today's managers must refine their own creativity while also fostering creativity in their subordinates.

Such a focus on innovation can prove to be a good counterbalance to the typical managerial emphasis on logic, fact, data, and objective analyses. Successfully cultivating the innovative side of management is considered by many to be a key to survival and growth in the increasingly competitive marketplace. Innovative thinking and creative problem solving certainly are necessary for such management activities as planning, product development, customer service orientation, and production improvements.

What Is Innovation Management?

Managing innovation means fostering the kind of environment in which people can think outside of established parameters. It means helping employees figure out new ways to do a job better. It requires taking truly novel approaches to tasks and decisions.

The concept of organizational innovation is somewhat contradictory to the very ways that organizations are typically managed. In large part, managing in an organization means establishing standard policies and practices, and then ensuring that behavior follows established norms. Conformity is necessary to prevent chaos. Yet innovation and creativity mean breaking out of established ways of doing things.

Conformity does not promote creativity and innovation is inherently nonconformist. So while the concept of creativity may seem antithetical to the management role, there is room within the managerial function to develop and enhance creativity in self and others. This chapter describes the characteristics of highly creative individuals, examines the stages in the creative process, describes two processes for engaging in creative thinking and decision making, and provides suggestions for enhancing and managing innovation in organizations.

Characteristics of Creative Individuals

While it is difficult to create a profile of the creative individual, in part because creativity defies categorization, highly creative people do seem to have a number of traits and behaviors in common. Managers wanting to foster innovative thinking would be well advised to seek out employees with such characteristics. Likewise, such behaviors can be rewarded in the workplace. Some of these behaviors can also be the target of creativity training sessions.

1. *Curiosity.* Creative individuals tend to have a highly developed sense of curiosity. They are attentive to their surroundings and see the world with a sense of awe and wonder. Like children, they are interested in everything, are not inhibited by established ways of doing things, and often wonder "why" or "what if." Creative people are imaginative. They like to daydream, fantasize, and wonder. They can visualize, in their vivid imaginations, new ways of doing things.

2. *Self-confidence.* Creative people have sufficient self-esteem to be independent thinkers and nonconformists. Creative individuals rarely take no for an answer. In other words, they are persistent. They can find ways around rules and procedures. Often, they are driven to create despite obstacles.

3. *Take risks.* Risk taking is another element associated with creativity. Creative people are adventurous and enjoy the exhilaration of challenges, risks, and the unknown. Oftentimes, highly creative people are very sensitive. The artistic personality frequently is associated with heightened sensitivity and a quickness of temper.

Stages in the Creative Process

Despite the fact that creativity is freewheeling and not bound by rules, in business there seem to be some recurring stages in the process by which people create.

1. *Saturation.* The initial part of the creative process involves saturation, or total immersion in the topic or task at hand. In business, one must be well read or experienced in a subject before being able to have insight about that subject. To become saturated in an area of business is to become familiar with all the available information in that area.

2. *Deliberation.* Deliberation refers to the careful thought, study, or discussion of the task at hand. By giving a great deal of unhurried thought to an issue on which one is knowledgeable, creative insight can occur.

3. *Incubation.* The waiting period when one does not focus on the task at hand, but allows a relaxed period for the mulling of ideas, is referred to as incubation. During the incubation period, the results of saturation and deliberation can work in the subconscious. Setting a project aside temporarily or "sleeping" on a problem gives a person distance from the task so that ideas may incubate.

4. *Illumination.* Often there is a sudden insight during the creative process. Indeed, the symbol of a lightbulb is often used as a graphic representation of insight. Such flashes of brilliance are a natural outgrowth of immersing oneself in a topic, giving slow and deliberate thought to the topic, and then resting the mind so that insight can occur.

5. *Accommodation.* This refers to the activity of revising and refining the insight into a workable solution to the task. The insight is altered, elaborated, and refined into a clear or precise answer or direction.

Tools of Creativity

A familiar procedure that can assist with innovative thinking is *brainstorming.* This is a structured technique by which a group generates a large number of innovative ideas. The assumption behind brainstorming is that the larger the quantity of ideas, the greater the chance of a truly innovative idea. To be truly effective, brainstorming should follow some established procedures.

- There should be a "try anything" attitude.
- As people generate wild and imaginative ideas to a question, freewheeling is encouraged.
- Participants should think of as many ideas as possible, without commenting on or judging any.
- Ideas may be original or they may combine or revise previously suggested ideas.
- While the group quickly lists all possible ideas, someone records all the ideas in full view of the group.

Only after the group has exhausted all possible ideas do the participants evaluate the ideas. Because of the tendency of managers to approach decision making with a critical eye, brainstorming is an effective tool for withholding criticism so that imagination can run rampant.

Another technique for enhancing creativity is *storyboarding.* This is a process by which ideas are placed on movable cards so that they can be shifted and reorganized. The ability to visually move ideas around lets people perceive things in new sequences or combine ideas in unusual fashions.

Storyboarding can be used in combination with brainstorming. The brainstorming process generates a long list of ideas on a given topic. Then the ideas are recorded on cards that are organized in a variety of ways. For example, the cards could be grouped by similarities or by differences. They could be rank-ordered by preference. They could be arranged by most to least costly, or least to most disruptive to the organization. There is no limit on the ways the cards can be arranged. Indeed, the point of storyboarding is to find as many different ways to order and combine ideas as possible.

Suggestions for Managing Innovation

There are several ways a manager can encourage creativity and innovation on the job.

1. *Cultivate a sense of enjoyment at work.* Innovation rarely occurs when tasks involve drudgery. Managers can create a work culture that is fun and enjoyable. Indeed, employees who enjoy their work will be more productive than those who dislike their jobs. Managers should develop strategies to enhance the enjoyment of work.

2. *Encourage silliness and risk taking.* Some of the most innovative organizations have toys in the workplace. By encouraging a childlike sense of play and rewarding employees for unusual ideas, managers can foster innovative thinking.

3. *Allow a balance of thinking and resting.* A relaxed mind is more likely to generate innovative ideas than will a stressed mind. Managers who burden their subordinates with inordinate amounts of work and unreasonable deadlines hinder innovative thinking and creativity among their staff.

4. *Change organizational routines.* Organizations thrive on established procedures and regular routines. Since a routine calls for repetitive behavior, it precludes original or innovative approaches. One way of enhancing innovation is to eliminate routines and to have employees function in ways they think best.

5. *Rely on instincts, intuition, and hunches.* Often, we fail to realize that for knowledgeable and experienced managers and employees, instincts are not random but informed. Intuitions are based on recall of past experiences, keen observation, the

combining of ideas, and analogous reasoning. Such gut-level reasoning is a most valid form of decision making.

6. *Seek naïve views.* The nonexpert on a task may bring a very different perspective to a problem than will experts. The layperson may have an innovative approach to a task that experts cannot see because they are blinded by past practice. Outsiders to a problem—be they consultants, clients, customers, or employees from a different function—should be valued for their unique perspectives and creative insights.

7. *Think in terms of opposites.* Consider doing the very opposite of what you would normally do on a task, problem, or decision. This strategy breaks with established patterns of thinking and keeps managers from getting conditioned to respond in predictable ways.

8. *Use trial and error.* Many new discoveries occurred because of an accident or an error. When attempting to solve a problem, try various approaches until discovering the one that works best. Remember, creativity involves a willingness to take risks, even risks that prove to be wrong.

9. *Ask hypothetical questions.* Questioning assumptions allows for speculation and theorizing. It leads to the imagining of alternatives. Like a child, ask "what would happen if . . ." when dealing with a task.

10. *Practice envisioning.* Most managers get so caught up in the immediate, day-to-day activities that there is little time to envision new things. To have vision is to imagine the future, to think, to contemplate, to speculate. In other words, envisioning is part of managing innovation.

[*See also* Change Management; Delegation and Empowerment]

For Additional Information

DeCock, Christian. "Imagination: The Art of Creative Management." *Journal of Management Studies* 31, Issue 1 (Mar. 1994), pp. 283–85.
Mattimore, Bryan W. *99% Inspiration: Tips, Tales, and Techniques for*

Liberating Your Business Creativity. New York: AMACOM, 1993.

Van Gundy, Arthur B. *Idea Power: Techniques and Resources to Unleash the Creativity in Your Organization*. New York: AMACOM, 1992.

Vyas, Niren M. "Promoting and Managing Creativity." *Business and Economic Review* 40, Issue 3 (Apr.-June 1994), pp. 7–10.

Intercultural
Communication

Managers operate in a global business economy. Many large corporations are international, with branches or offices in other countries. American-owned companies frequently use foreign labor or materials. Clearly, the market for products and services spans the world. And the number of foreign-owned companies operating in the United States is growing. Indeed, the concept of jointly managed firms, with Japanese and American partnerships, for example, is increasing in popularity. Nor is international exchange limited to the corporate environment. The scientific, medical, educational, and artistic communities are global in scope and cooperation also.

The global workplace requires managers to travel internationally. Some relocate to work in other countries. You may be asked to entertain foreign visitors. Marketing managers may be called on to develop plans for doing business in other countries. Supervisors or managers in the United States may work with a largely immigrant labor force.

Thus, to enhance international success, managers must understand intercultural communication—the customs, etiquette, and methods of communicating with people in or from other countries. Organizations with the best international agreements and relationships are those that understand the nuances of international behavior and can avoid offending business leaders in a host country because of ignorance of that country's culture. A rudimentary knowledge of cultural variations in values and work attitudes helps in the supervision of a culturally diverse workforce. Knowing the rules for intercultural communication enhances the image of individual managers, as well as that of their organizations and the nation as a whole.

Intercultural communication is a very broad concept. Books are available on the culture of most every country. Obviously, you will want to familiarize yourself with the intricacies of the particular culture with which you will be involved. Competent managers are aware of the various categories of typical cultural differences and have basic competence for communicating in another culture.

Areas of Cultural Difference

Almost any aspect of behavior may have cultural variations. However, some categories of behavior related to international business may have wide variations across cultures. It is important to learn the target culture's norms in each of the areas described below.

Greeting and Terms of Address

First impressions will be formed about the appropriateness of your behavior when you are introduced to a colleague from another country. What greeting behavior is considered polite? By what term or title should you address the other person? What degree of formality is expected?

You may have to learn the pronunciations of certain names and practice saying them. Some Spanish-speaking cultures use double surnames; the first name is the surname in China. In some cultures, the nonverbal greeting gesture is a handshake; in others, it is a bow or a kiss on the cheek. There can be variation within such greeting gestures as well. How one shakes hands or how low one bows may convey meaning. Of course, the rules become even more complicated for a woman manager in another culture. In certain cultures, appropriate behaviors for women differ from the norms for men. In regard to greetings and terms of address, it is always better to use the more formal style until invited to become more familiar or informal.

Dining Etiquette

Host colleagues will surely present the international traveler with food and drink as a sign of hospitality. Knowing how to behave while dining is crucial to intercultural success. You may be expected to eat unusual foods. To decline a food offering may offend the host. You may be expected to engage in such rituals as offering toasts or making elaborate welcome speeches. Who is expected to sample the food first, host or visitor? Food may be presented on individual plates, served by the host, or eaten from a common serving dish. There may be norms about whether food should be passed or received with the left or the right hand. Lunch may consist of a five-course meal spanning two hours. There may be obligatory drinking and dancing until the early morning hours.

Knowing how to entertain foreign visitors in your country is equally as important. Among other considerations, it is imperative that you not serve guests foods that are prohibited in their cultures.

Gift Giving

The protocol of giving and receiving gifts is another important area of intercultural awareness. International business often begins with the exchange of gifts. Visiting the host's home means bringing an appropriate gift. Consider the nature of appropriate gifts, how to present them, when to present them, how to receive a gift, and how to communicate appreciation for a gift.

An appropriate gift for an international host can be an item that represents your own culture of something appropriate for doing business, like a pen or an office decoration. Flowers, candy, or toys for the host's children may be appropriate when you visit the home of your host. Sometimes, gifts with the organizational logo are presented. However, personal or intimate items should never be given.

Learn the items that are considered offensive gifts in certain cultures. For example, leather is inappropriate in India, liquor is taboo in Islamic regions, and even the color of presents may have negative connotations!

There may be cultural expectations about whether a gift is presented initially in the relationship, before doing business, after deals are negotiated, or at the time of departure. Cultural norms govern whether to present it publicly or privately. The appropriate value or expense of the present varies across cultures. Always send prompt written thank-you notes for gifts received.

Since gift exchange is a symbol of relationship development and appreciation for hospitality, make yourself aware of cultural norms so that you do not inadvertently destroy the goodwill associated with this behavior.

Dress and Appearance

Styles of clothing differ worldwide. Clothing is an obvious sign of a foreign visitor, although managers worldwide are increasingly adopting Western styles of business attire. It is advisable to wear conservative business dress, appropriate to the weather of the host country, when you travel internationally. Local attire you are expected to wear should be provided for you, since it may be offensive to mimic local appearance customs without first being invited to do so. Certain cultures may have rigid dress codes for businesswomen. You may be expected to remove your shoes in buildings in Eastern cultures. In casual dress when touring a country, certain colors may be considered offensive. For example, white (not black) is associated with death in many Asian countries; green may symbolize freshness in the United States but disease in jungle areas.

Time Consciousness

People regard and use time differently in various cultures. Americans tend to be very schedule-conscious and may be perceived as rushing. When doing business in another culture, you should know the meaning of time in that culture and adjust to the host country's time values.

Will a meeting start at the scheduled time? Will there even be a scheduled meeting time? In some cultures, you may be kept waiting for hours or for days until the host is ready to see you. Arriving early for a meeting may be evaluated negatively. You may be expected to arrive promptly even though the host is not subject to the same rule.

In some cultures, procrastination is a virtue and punctuality is not. Deadlines and agendas may be regarded as a sign of efficiency or of impatience. Each culture emphasizes one time orientation (past, present, or future) or another. Knowing this can affect your approach to business. Appealing to tradition in some cultures may be a more appropriate negotiation tactic than a reference to future progress.

Communication and Language

Language obviously is a distinctive feature of nations and regions within nations. Other aspects of oral communication vary culturally. You would be wise to learn some aspects of the host country's language and to consider becoming conversationally fluent in that language. Americans may be perceived as arrogant when they expect the rest of the business world to speak English. Surely there are business advantages to knowing the language of the area in which you are conducting business.

Even if the business transaction occurs in English, there are other communication features to consider. Avoid using jargon and slang expressions, as well as certain topics of conversation. Politics, religion, and personal issues are topics that probably should be avoided in all foreign countries.

People have different styles of communicating in various cultures. These are often subtle differences that can make the uninformed businessperson seem impolite. For example, Americans communicate directly and assertively. In some other cultures, people may hint at what they mean or soften the impact of messages. Americans may come across as rude or pushy in such cultures. American business leaders may develop impatience with foreign colleagues who will not give a direct answer to a question. In some cultures, people will not communicate rejection or bad news. They may tell you what they think you want to hear rather than what they actually believe. Emotion and conflict in conversations may be appropriate in some cultures, but not in others.

Nonverbal Behavior

The meaning attached to gestures, eye contact, and the use of space is not universal. Nonverbal behavior is very culture specific. So the manager doing business in another country must be aware of the norms for nonverbal behavior as well as those for oral communication. This way you will not offend your host nor take offense at the nonverbal styles of others.

People from Latin cultures use many gestures while speaking; the British are more subdued. You may want to adjust your own level of gesturing to approximate that of people in the host country so that you do not come across as listless or flamboyant. Certain standard gestures have very different meanings internationally. For example, in some countries, the thumbs-up gesture or "A-OK" sign is considered obscene.

Making eye contact shows respect in the United States, while in many Asian cultures it is considered disrespectful. Staring or pointing may also be considered either appropriate or offensive.

Space is another nonverbal cultural variable. Japanese work environments are open while Americans prefer separate offices or cubicles. Arab and South American people stand close and touch while talking, which is considered crowding by people from cultures with larger space zones. An Arab colleague may perceive an American manager who feels an invasion of personal space and who backs away as rude.

Work Attitudes

There are cultural differences in people's attitudes toward work. What motivates a person from one cultural background may not motivate someone from a different culture. The priority given to work, family, or leisure time is culturally determined. Competition is valued in some cultures, whereas others prefer collaboration. Some cultures are individualistic, and others value group loyalty. Dignity and face-saving is paramount in some cultures; harsh criticism has little effect in others.

Such essential features of cultural identity, values, and habits affect all aspects of international business. Cultural work attitudes affect hiring, supervising, motivating, disciplining, selling, and marketing strategies, among other things. Cultural identity runs deep. An employer will have little success when encouraging workers to behave in ways that contradict cultural conditioning. Likewise, when doing business outside of your own country, you must adjust your work attitudes and behavior appropriately.

Developing Intercultural Communication Competence

Getting along well with people of other cultures is largely a matter of opening your eyes to other ways of seeing the world. Here are some tips for doing that.

1. *Become aware of variations in cultural traditions.* Examine your own assumptions about greetings, hospitality, appearance, work attitudes, communication, and nonverbal behavior in order to recognize your own habits and how they might be perceived by others. Self-awareness will make you more attuned to the customs of others.

2. *Learn as much as possible about the target country.* Become familiar with the country's politics, economic system, religions, history, social structure, educational system, business customs, food, sports, music, art, and daily life. Such information can be obtained through libraries, by taking courses at local colleges or universities, by watching travel videotapes, or by contacting consultants, embassies, cultural organizations, or experienced travelers.

3. *Learn the language.* Take a language course, hire an individual tutor, or use self-study foreign-language tapes. With an understanding of some of the basics of the language, you will be surprised at how rapidly you develop your proficiency once you are in the target country.

4. *Use a cultural go-between.* This could be someone in your organization or country who can coach you or call ahead to make introductions and arrangements for you—an American expatriate living in the foreign country or an interpreter who can travel with you.

5. *Try cultural-awareness training.* If your company or industry frequently does business in other countries, you might request cultural-awareness training sponsored by your company or professional association. Such an investment in training could have far-reaching business benefits.

To develop intercultural communication competence, you must be willing to learn, adapt, and adjust. You cannot expect the culture to adapt to you, nor should you label another culture's traditions as alien or inferior. Remember, you are the foreigner. With open-mindedness, flexibility, some knowledge about the culture, and support people, you will find that international business travel or relocation is a valuable and exciting experience.

For Additional Information

Brislin, Richard W., and Tomoko Yoshida. *Intercultural Communication Training: An Introduction.* Thousand Oaks, Calif.: Sage Publications, 1994.

Hoecklin, Lisa Adent. *Managing Cultural Differences: Strategies for Competitive Advantage.* Reading, Mass.: Addison-Wesley, 1995.

Munter, Mary. "Cross Cultural Communication for Managers." *Business Horizons,* May/June 1993, pp. 69–78.

Thiederman, Sondra B. *Bridging Cultural Barriers for Corporate Success: How to Manage the Multicultural Workforce.* Lexington, Mass.: Lexington Books, 1991.

Interviewing

Interviewing skills are essential to the managerial role. Managers interview job candidates in order to make selection decisions, conduct performance-appraisal interviews with employees to give feedback about job performance, and conduct counseling interviews with troubled employees to seek behavioral change. Whenever an employee is discharged or resigns, managers should conduct an exit interview to get the employee's reactions to various aspects of the workplace and to discuss severance issues. Managers may interview consultants before using their services or may interview staff members before giving them delegated assignments, leadership roles, or promotions. Then there are the situations in which managers are interviewed by others—the media, the public, regulatory agencies, or students. This chapter discusses selection, performance-appraisal, counseling, and exit interviews and examines interviewing as an information-exchange process.

Selection Interviews

The goal in a selection interview is to obtain relevant and detailed information about job candidates in order to make the best match between an individual and an organization. The interviewer of job applicants functions like a detective uncovering clues about performance and personality in order to make a prediction of how well each candidate will perform the job. The interviewer must dig out information because candidates naturally will distort and hide information to put themselves in a good light. While doing the detective work, the interviewer must develop rapport, facilitate a smooth conversation, and present an accurate picture of the job and the organization.

The interviewer should develop a set of questions around certain categories relevant to the job. Equal Employment Opportunity Commission (EEOC) guidelines prohibit questions about marital status, children, age, national origin, birthplace, religion, sex, race, ownership of a house or car, credit rating, or type of military discharge. Interviewers should become familiar with EEOC requirements for wording questions in permissible areas of inquiry.

The interviewer should plan the question sequence, balance question categories with time limitations, know how to probe for more information, become familiar with the candidate's written materials, and plan a note-taking method. The goal is not to amass a great deal of facts from an interview, but to get at intangible information such as how a candidate performed in past jobs, reasons for work-related decisions, priorities and values, maturity, temperament, shortcomings, and aspirations.

The interviewer must carefully structure the interview, direct it, focus on relevant areas, probe beneath the surface, and keep track of time. Yet the interview should not resemble an interrogation. Questions should flow easily. Probes should not be threatening. The format should resemble a spontaneous and lively conversation rather than a question-and-answer session.

Probing below the surface is key to effective selection interviewing. First responses to a question typically are well-thought-out answers that put the candidate in the best light. It is important to seek the "why" or the "how" behind the responses. Ask candidates to elaborate, go into more detail, or explain their reasoning. Patient listening, nonverbal signs of encouragement, silent pauses, paraphrasing, and requests for elaboration will get the candidate talking. The less talking the interviewer does, the more the candidate will talk.

Novice interviewers waste time asking questions about facts that have already been obtained through resumes and applications. Becoming familiar with factual information on written materials lets the interviewer move immediately to substantive, new information.

Good note taking will record the wealth of information disclosed in an interview. It is impossible to recall information after the interview, and details become muddled if more than one candidate is being interviewed.

Performance Appraisal Interviews

The purpose of performance appraisal interviews is to give employees feedback on how well their performance measures up to job standards and to set future performance goals. Just as in selection interviews, you must review written materials, plan the interview, know how to probe, use time wisely, answer questions and provide information, and record responses. Prior to conducting a performance appraisal, review the person's job description, reread the last performance evaluation, and consult documentation accumulated on the employee's job performance. Interview time should not be wasted in becoming familiar with written materials.

You should also plan the series of questions and statements so as to structure the interview. Communicate ratings on the various criteria, discuss the employee perceptions of performance in various areas, uncover reasons for performance problems, and coordinate with the employee the objectives for the next work period.

Probing is an important ingredient of performance appraisal interviews. Probe to see if employees understand job standards and are capable of and motivated to meet job performance expectations. Try to learn what motivates employees so you can use appropriate incentive when coaching them. Discover what resources would help them perform the job better.

Finally, you must record information during and after the performance appraisal interview. During the discussion, employees typically provide information that helps you understand their work performance, motivation, constraints, and goals. Record agreements you reach during the interview. After the interview, elaborate on the notes you took during the performance appraisal and record the tone of the discussion. Comprehensive documentation of performance is necessary to support discharge, demotion, or promotion decisions.

Counseling Interviews

In some cases, poor employee performance is due to personal problems, such as alcohol and drug dependency, emotional or psychological difficulties, or marital or family concerns. When personal problems impair work performance, conduct a counseling interview. This does not mean that you conduct psychological counseling. In a counseling interview, you attempt to get the employee to recognize inappropriate behaviors and to commit to change. You need not diagnose the personal problem that allegedly affects work performance.

The best approach in a counseling interview is to indicate the exact nature of the poor work performance and ask the individual for explanations of that poor performance. If the employee discloses a personal problem, then you can recommend professional assistance, preferably through an employer-paid benefit such as medical insurance or an employee assistance program. If the employee does not disclose a personal problem, you can suggest professional referral options in case the employee has personal problems that may be impairing work productivity.

As with other types of interviews, the counseling interview presents similar challenges of reviewing written materials, planning, probing, using time wisely, providing information, and taking notes. This type of interview also calls for assertiveness and empathy skills. You must be assertive in confronting the performance problem and suggesting professional help while simultaneously showing a caring and supportive attitude toward the troubled employee.

Exit Interviews

Whenever an employee leaves the organization, either willingly or through termination, the manager should conduct an exit interview. This allows managers and employees to discuss the reasons for separation and make separation agreements. You can learn a great deal from terminated employees about how to restructure the job for the next person hired. In the case of a termination, you must explain to the employee the reasons for dismissal and discuss both the cover story that others will be told and severance benefits.

Whether the separation be through resignation or termination, you should try to create a conversation to give and get information. Plan initial questions and become skilled at using follow-up probes. You must provide information about the details of separation from the organization—paperwork to be completed, benefits to be continued for a certain length of time, and the organizational policy regarding references. Notes should be taken about the content and tone of the exit interview, as well any separation agreements.

The Interviewing Process

There are certain elements of the interview process that cross all types of workplace interviews. Whether you conduct selection, performance appraisal, counseling, or exit interviews, you must know how to set the appropriate climate, ask and answer questions, control the interview, and take notes and maintain documentation.

Setting the Climate

Interviews present a certain degree of tension for both the interviewer and the interviewee. In order to reduce tension and to enhance the quality of information shared, you must be skilled in creating rapport. Create an appropriate climate by selecting a comfortable, private place for the interview. There should be no interruptions or distractions. You can develop rapport through some initial small talk and then state the purpose of the interview. By making smooth transitions between answers and subsequent questions, and by listening more than talking, you reduce threat and build a comfortable climate.

Certain interviews, such as counseling discussions with highly emotional people or exit interview with very defensive individuals, never develop a pleasant climate. But it is the manager's responsibility to develop and maintain a professional climate, however the person behaves.

Asking and Answering Questions

Questioning is the heart of the interviewing process and the most important feature of all interviews. In order to obtain substantive, candid information, you must know what questions to ask, how to ask them, and how to use follow-up probes. Ask questions in such a way that they are hardly apparent.

The best type of interview questions are open-ended, neutral questions. Open-ended question call for broad, lengthy responses. They cannot be answered with one-word or short replies. Neutral questions do not cue the respondent to the correct answer to lead to an obvious response. You can create open-ended questions by beginning the question with the words "What," "Why," "How did you," "To what extent," and "What would you do if."

Prepared questions are just one type to use in interviews, however. A more important type of question is the follow-up probe—that is, the spontaneous question that follows after the interviewee has provided a response. You should probe all answers to get more detailed, more accurate, and less rehearsed responses.

To be effective, probes must be smooth, relevant, and conversational. Interrogating probes will create defensiveness and hinder spontaneity. This means that interviewers must be skilled listeners so they can ask logical follow-up questions. Obviously, the person's answers determine the nature of the follow-up probes.

Vary the types of follow-up probes you use. An occasional "why" will not threaten people, but following every answer with a "why" question will sound interrogating. An excellent device for getting an interviewee to elaborate is to ask no question at all. Instead, a comment on the previous answer, a paraphrase of the answer, or a silent pause likely will produce elaboration.

Your job is not only to ask questions but to answer them as well. Thus, you must know how to encourage interviewees' questions, be skilled at understanding questions, and be able to provide information. Managers in all types of interviews must encourage the other person to ask questions.

A pleasant climate, sufficient time for the interview, and the manager's encouraging style will help interviewees feel comfortable about asking questions. Periodically throughout the discussion, indicate a willingness to answer questions. Imply that questions from the interviewee are natural and expected, and that all questions are acceptable.

When presented with a question, you should paraphrase it to check understanding. After paraphrasing the question, provide an answer, and then check back with the questioner to see if the response was satisfactory. It is important to provide information at a level that the questioner can understand. By considering the interviewee's perspective, you can provide a sufficient depth of information.

Controlling the Interview to Achieve Objectives

Managers must be skilled in controlling the interview without appearing directive or overbearing. There are several techniques for controlling an interview. First, plan categories of questions with a tentative schedule. In addition to planning an interview schedule, you must watch the time closely and keep the pace moving. Effective interviewers learn to tactfully and unobtrusively interrupt statements to steer the direction of the conversation. You can interrupt at logical points, such as during pauses or during transitions.

Taking Notes and Documenting Information

Another feature crossing all types of interviews is the need to take notes during the discussion and to maintain documentation following the interview. Note taking during the interview must be unobtrusive, a background activity that does not hinder the communication or call attention to itself. Some interviewers develop checklists or forms to facilitate their recording of pertinent information.

After the interview is completed, spend some time elaborating on your sketchy notes, writing down additional information and impressions, and summarizing the interview. Do this immediately after the interview, while impressions are fresh. The more detail you record during and after the interview, the more informed and more justifiable your position or decision will be.

[*See also* Performance Appraisal; Recruiting and Selecting New Employees; Terminating Employee and Downsizing]

For Additional Information

Arthur, Diane. *Recruiting, Interviewing, Selecting & Orienting New Employees*. New York: AMACOM, 1991.

Goodale, James G. *One to One: Interviewing, Selecting, Appraising, and Counseling Employees*. Englewood Cliffs, N.J.: Prentice-Hall, 1992.

Mercer, Michael W. *Hire the Best . . . and Avoid the Rest*. New York: AMACOM, 1993.

Risser, Rita. "Interviewing Pitfalls for the Unwary." *Manage* 48, No. 1 (July 1994), pp. 25–29.

Listening

Listening is a communication activity required of all managers at any function or level. According to some estimates, about half the total time a person spends communicating is devoted to listening. While listening is a process that many of us take for granted, poor listening can be costly and can result in production errors, disgruntled employees, conflicts, rumors, workplace accidents, and lost sales. Listening mistakes waste time, anger others, affect productivity, and hurt a company's reputation. Many organizations realize the importance of effective listening on the job and, consequently, train employees to be better listeners. The following information can help you identify poor listening habits in yourself and in others and can provide the basis for improvement.

The Listening Process

Listening involves more than just hearing a message. When we listen, we receive a stimulus, convert it to words, attach meaning to the words, relate the message to our past experiences in order to comprehend it, and choose a response. Because we do all this in a matter of seconds, there is room for error. Let us examine each element in the process of listening to understand where mistakes are likely to occur.

Listening can be divided into four major steps:

1. Sensing
2. Interpreting
3. Evaluating
4. Responding

We must receive a signal through the *sense of hearing*. That means that we must be paying attention and must have good hearing skills. If we have hearing problems or are not paying attention, then listening efficiently will be hindered in this first step.

After sensing the stimulus, we *interpret* it in a way that makes sense to us. We take sounds that we hear, translate those sounds into words, and attach meaning to the total message. What meaning we attach to the message is a matter of individual interpretation. Our backgrounds, experiences, attitudes, self-concepts, and moods will affect how we interpret another person's words. Because we differ, our interpretations of each other's messages differ. Correctly interpreting another person's words entails some negotiating and checking until our understanding matches the other person's original meaning.

Once we feel that we understand the other person, we usually have an *evaluative* reaction to the message. We decide if the information is good, accurate, useful, important, and so on. While listening, we tend to judge the message: what is evidence and what is opinion? Is the speaker believable or not? Do we agree or disagree with the message? Do we need the information or not? Sometimes our judgments are premature or erroneous. There is the tendency to evaluate before completely comprehending.

Finally, in the listening process, we *respond*. The response is based on what we have heard, how we have interpreted it, and the judgments we have made about the message. Any errors along the way will lead to an inappropriate response. The response is the only external element of the listening process. Sensing, interpretation, and evaluation occur in our heads. How we respond, then, becomes the measure of our listening success. Until we make a concrete response, the speaker does not know if the point was made and understood.

Common Listening Problems

Managers who want to improve their own listening efficiency or develop their employees' listening skills should try to eliminate these poor listening habits:

- *Tolerating or creating distractions.* Noise interferes with hearing. External noise in the physical environment as well as internal distractions (lack of concentration) will impede listening.
- *Faking listening.* Poor listeners pretend to be paying attention when they are not. They fake facial expressions, eye contact, and head nods to signal interest while they actually daydream or go off on a mental tangent.
- *Tuning out dry subjects.* Poor listeners quickly declare a message boring, develop a "who cares" attitude, and refuse to put forth listening effort. If the message is not captivating or entertaining, poor listeners become lazy and give up.
- *Mentally disagreeing.* Some listeners cannot remain objective enough to understand a message before evaluating it. They let their emotions take charge and internally refute or argue all the points they hear.
- *Focusing on the speaker's delivery.* Poor listeners pay more attention to the speaker's voice and appearance than they do to the message. They have trouble paying attention to content and instead focus on the speaker's mannerisms.
- *Daydreaming.* Many of us fall into the trap of daydreaming because we can think faster than anyone can talk. The average person speaks about 175 words per minute but can think at a rate of over 400 words per minute. Poor listeners do not use this extra thought speed productively. They think about unrelated topics and tune into the speaker only occasionally.

Ways to Improve Listening

You can improve your own or your employees' listening efficiency by developing these good listening habits:

1. *Develop powers of concentration.* Good listeners can ignore distractions in the environment and seem to will themselves into listening. Also, they actively reduce controllable noise by closing doors, holding calls, and clearing their minds. The more we

work at concentrating while listening, the more our powers of concentration develop and the easier listening becomes.

2. *Generate interest in information.* Good listeners can find areas of interest in most any message. They are receptive to information and try to find ways to apply or use the information, which builds tolerance and patience into listening. Rather than declaring a subject boring and tuning out, good listeners develop an inquiring mind.

3. *Overlook speaker's mannerisms.* If we focus on the content of a message, the style in which the message is delivered becomes secondary. Good listeners do not prejudge the value of a message on the basis of a speaker's delivery or appearance. Important information can be obtained from an unimpressive messenger. The content of the message is much more important than the way it is packaged.

4. *Focus on central ideas.* Learning to identify the major points of a message improves listening efficiency. Central ideas and subpoints anchor the facts and details of a message. It is difficult to grasp detailed information without organizing it into a few major points. Good listeners are concept listeners rather than fact listeners.

5. *Hold your fire.* Good listeners separate the tasks of interpreting and evaluating messages. They make sure comprehension is complete before judging the message and resist the temptation to mentally debate instead of listening. It is wise to slow down the listening process. Ask questions to check your understanding before agreeing or disagreeing with the information. Holding your fire also means paying total attention to the speaker without mentally framing a response.

6. *Work at listening.* Listening is not a passive activity. Active listening is hard work. It involves an expenditure of energy characterized by a rise in body temperature, increased heart beat, and higher levels of adrenaline. Good listeners realize that listening entails work, not relaxation.

7. *Pay attention to body language.* Visual cues can help us more accurately interpret the meaning of a person's words. When communicating face-to-face, we can look to the speaker's facial

expressions, posture, and gestures to give added meaning to the message. A good listener observes as well as hears.

8. *Capitalize on thought speed.* Our capacity to think faster than we can speak should not be a drawback to communication. Rather than daydreaming, we can use our thought speed to mentally summarize information, anticipate the next point, and listen between the lines to the tone of voice.

9. *Paraphrase remarks.* Good listeners practice the skill of paraphrasing what they hear. This entails summarizing a speaker's point back to the speaker to check understanding and seeking feedback. This way misunderstandings or faulty assumptions can be discovered early and corrected.

Eliminating any bad habit takes motivation, determination, and support. Replacing bad listening habits with effective listening techniques takes time and commitment. Managers who want to improve their listening skills should work one at a time on each suggestion provided until mastering it. Trying to accomplish all of the suggestions at once would be overwhelming. Through self-discipline and practice, you can realize the benefits of listening efficiency. Good listening is good business.

For Additional Information

Nichols, Michael P. *The Lost Art of Listening.* New York: Guilford Press, 1994.

Robertson, Arthur K. *Listen for Success: A Guide to Effective Listening.* Burr Ridge, Ill.: Irwin Professional Publications, 1994.

Meetings

Supervisors, managers, executives, and administrators alike spend an inordinate amount of time in meetings. In addition to the usual staff, department, sales, or team meetings, we have special committees, task forces, or projects that require us to work together in groups. The increased emphasis on teamwork, employee involvement, quality, and participatory management create the need for more meetings. Business meetings can be useful tools for communicating ideas, disseminating information, solving problems, and making decisions. Unfortunately, few meetings are as effective as they could be. By realizing common problems, understanding the purpose of meetings, and following guidelines for leading and participating in meetings, we can eliminate all the wasted time and make meetings useful and enjoyable.

Common Problems With Meetings

The following are some common pitfalls of business meetings:

1. *We are not informed of the purpose of the meeting.* Little work can be accomplished if members do not know why the meeting was called or what the outcome of the meeting should be. In this situation, the group spends the entire time trying to figure out its task.

2. *We are not given a detailed agenda ahead of time.* Participants should know exactly what issues will be discussed, what items will be covered, or what reports will be given. Without a specific agenda in advance, we come to meetings unprepared. We do not have the necessary information with us; nor have we given thought to the issues under discussion.

3. *The leader does not control the meeting.* Even with clear objectives and specific agendas, meetings can go astray. Some leaders do not follow the prepared agenda or fail to keep the group on target. Once they go off on tangents or other agenda items are introduced, the session becomes disorganized and chaotic.

4. *The meeting is long and tedious.* Some meetings start out organized but deteriorate into long, boring ordeals. The meeting is scheduled for too long of a period of time, or the leader does not keep the pace moving. Participants lose concentration and energy in meetings that last longer than one hour. Effective meetings are fast-placed. If the group is not pushed through the agenda, it will become bogged down on each issue.

5. *Individuals are allowed to dominate.* Many a productive meeting has been ruined by one person who rambles, takes the discussion in a different direction, or blocks the group's productive work.

There may be other reasons why meetings fail. These are merely the most common problems. If you and your colleagues find yourselves dreading or resenting business meetings, try to identify the pitfalls that plague meetings in your organization. That is the first step in creating more effective meetings in the workplace.

Reasons for Holding Meetings

Managers who lead meetings will want to give specific thought to the particular reason they schedule a meeting. Such reasons include:

▪ *Obtaining information.* We often present information via reports (oral or written) in a meeting. If many people need the information, then a series of succinct reports in a group meeting can be an effective way to exchange information. Report givers must be skilled at presentation for this type of meeting to be effective. Listeners can ask questions or engage in discussion about the material presented. If there is no opportunity or need for follow-up discussion, then the meeting was unnecessary. If there is no need to hear or discuss the reports, then distributing the information in writing to individuals would be a better approach.

• *Solving a problem or making a decision.* Some decisions are best made by a group. We give more support to a decision that affects us if we have input into the decision. Many complex decisions need the deliberation of several individuals who hold different perspectives. A problem-solving team working together through meetings can thoroughly analyze a problem and creatively discover solutions.

• *Motivating people.* Bringing individuals together for a meeting can be motivational. This is the basis of sales meetings and major conventions. A group energy develops when many people with the same goals assemble. The excitement and interaction provides a momentum that can be harnessed by the organization.

• *Developing new ideas.* Creative ideas can occur when a group of individuals bounce thoughts off of one another in a meeting. Members use their imaginations to discover innovative concepts or approaches. They replace evaluation and analysis with speculation and curiosity. While one creative person can develop new ideas working alone, a group meeting has the potential of producing many more ideas. Members build on each others' ideas.

• *Making announcements.* You can use meetings to announce and explain new policies, programs, systems, or products. A meeting can be an effective alternative to memos, electronic mail, and reports. By getting everyone together, you can go into more detail, use visual demonstrations, answer questions, and clear up misunderstandings.

Characteristics of a Good Group Meeting

Effective group meetings look and feel different from ineffective meetings. A good meeting could be characterized by the following six attributes:

1. *Participants have a strong sense of belonging or unity.* There is a sense of mission and cooperation. Members want to be part of

the group and see a common purpose. In essence, there is a strong commitment and loyalty to the group, which translates into good attendance at each session, prepared and informed members, and a willingness to work hard for the group or the company.

2. *Everybody participates.* In good meetings, everyone feels comfortable contributing. There is a shared interaction among members. Regardless of actual status or position, each person feels that all remarks will be considered by the rest of the group.

3. *Discussion follows a clear plan.* Effective meetings have clear purposes, published agendas, and prepared members who stick to the purpose and stay on course. Everyone knows why the meeting was called, what the group is trying to accomplish, and where it stands in relation to the task.

4. *Conflicts are managed.* Whenever we meet in groups to give or get information, to make decisions, to generate ideas, or to solve problems, differences of opinion occur. When meetings are operating properly, we feel free to disagree. Organizations that stifle conflict restrict the good ideas collegial bickering or friction can produce. On the other hand, meetings must not deteriorate into aggressive free-for-alls. In effective meetings, people can disagree while maintaining respect for one another.

5. *Task and people issues are considered.* In effective meetings, the group does its work while maintaining good relationships among the people involved. Both the task and the morale of the group are important considerations.

6. *The group is aware of its process.* Effective groups have ways to examine themselves and their progress. At times, they step back from their job and look at their procedures, membership, and internal communication. Members can suggest alternative meeting times, propose new ways of operating, and comment on group problems.

The Leader's Role

The leader of a meeting has several tasks before, during, and after the meeting. In preparation, you must decide if a meeting is the best way to achieve a particular objective. If you decide that a meeting is the best strategy, then plans are necessary. You must decide who should attend, what the agenda will be, when and where the meeting should occur, and what information, materials, or equipment will be needed.

Strategically selecting meeting participants is an important consideration for effective meetings. Some meetings automatically dictate the participants. Rather than having a standard composition of members for all meetings, however, consider the issue carefully. Selecting the right mix of people for a meeting is a crucial factor in its success or failure.

You should carefully prepare and circulate an agenda ahead of time. It is important to be realistic about what can be accomplished in the allotted time period. Some leaders provide suggested time limits for each agenda item. Sometimes it is necessary to circulate a tentative agenda and ask participants to suggest additional agenda items. You then circulate a revised agenda to members before the meeting. If members are expected to bring information to the meeting or to present reports, they should receive advance notice.

The time and place of a meeting are other important considerations. Choose a time that accommodates members' schedules and energy levels. Monday mornings, Friday afternoons, and time slots immediately after lunch should be avoided. Likewise, people will not be at their peak concentration level the day before holidays or vacations. The location of a meeting can also affect its outcome. Rooms that are too crowded, too hot, or have poor acoustics lead to lifeless sessions. Chairs should be arranged to best serve the purpose of the meeting. Motivational meetings should be held in exciting, off-site locations. This adds a note of importance and visibility to the meeting and can make participants feel special.

You should also arrange for necessary materials and technological equipment to be used at a meeting. Such fine points of preparation give the meeting an atmosphere of efficiency and enhance your credibility.

You must take an active role in running a meeting. The following are some suggestions for conducting an effective meeting:

1. *Create a member-centered meeting.* A dominant leader will stifle a meeting. Members resent meetings where the leader does all the talking and they cannot have input or ask questions. Some authorities suggest that the leader talk less than 20 percent of the time in a meeting. You should not give opinions or evaluations until everyone has had a chance to be heard. Good ideas are lost when subordinates are reluctant to contradict or disagree with a manager who has already stated a position.

2. *Stimulate discussion by asking questions.* An effective meeting is more than a series of monologs. It should be an exchange of information and ideas. To accomplish real interaction, you should be skilled at questioning. A good way to stimulate discussion is to ask open-ended questions, which cannot be answered by yes/no responses or short reactions. Examples of open-ended question are "What do you think?" "How should we proceed?" "Why?" "What should we do?"

3. *Avoid idea killers.* Make sure that everyone has a chance to be heard and that everyone's comments are taken seriously. Comments and behaviors that kill enthusiasm must be prohibited. Treating a participant as inferior, uninformed, inexperienced, or naïve will suppress discussion. Sometimes the best comments come from organizational newcomers whose ideals are not dimmed by skepticism.

4. *Keep the group on the subject.* It is your role to move through the agenda and keep the group from going off on tangents. Frequent summaries are a good device for keeping the group organized and for keeping the pace moving. If several members are interested in discussing another subject, make that a topic for a subsequent meeting. Make sure that no one dominates or sabotages the meeting. You must be skilled at maintaining control of the meeting without being dominant.

5. *Summarize the meeting and give assignments.* A good leader does not let meeting time run out. You should draw the session to a close by summarizing information, suggesting unresolved issues for future meetings and giving participants tasks to work on before the next meeting. Thus, people leave the meeting with a sense of accomplishment and future direction.

There are still some tasks after the meeting has concluded. Prepare and distribute minutes, notes, or publicity of the meeting as soon as possible. You may want to begin planning the agenda of a subsequent meeting while ideas about this meeting are still fresh in mind. Finally, good leaders review and analyze the meeting process. Assess the meeting effectiveness and your own leadership style, then use that information to make the next meeting better.

Special Techniques

Some techniques are especially useful for achieving certain meeting purposes or facilitating the meeting process. Three techniques applicable to business meetings are the problem-solving method, brainstorming, and videoconferencing.

The Problem-Solving Method

The problem-solving method is a logical format for working through a problem to a solution. Groups engaged in problem-solving meetings should follow these five steps:

1. *Describe the problem.* What exactly is the problem at hand? Are there several interrelated problems? Are there problems underlying the obvious one?

2. *Discuss history, causes, and effects of the problem.* How long has the problem existed? Has anything been done to solve it before? What are its obvious and subtle causes? Who is affected by this problem? How serious are the effects?

3. *Suggest many possible solutions.* What are all the possible actions that could be taken to solve this problem? What are some immediate solutions, long-term solutions, and creative solutions?

4. *Identify the best solution.* Which solution is most practical, easiest to implement, most cost-effective, most acceptable, or most permanent? The best solution is one that fits whatever criteria the group thinks is important.

5. *Make recommendations for implementation.* Who will implement the solution? How? By what timetable? What resources will be required? Whose support is essential? By what means will the effectiveness of the solution be evaluated?

Brainstorming

Brainstorming is a method for stimulating the creative thinking of meeting participants. It encourages the free flow of ideas. It is especially useful to generate many ideas. The rules of brainstorming follow:

1. Members present ideas rapidly as they come to mind. Do not self-censor thoughts. Free-associate without worrying about the logic or quality of ideas.
2. Members should briefly suggest ideas. Speak just long enough to present an idea. Do not explain it or justify it.
3. Members should not analyze or evaluate others' ideas. The goal is a quantity of ideas. The quality of the ideas will be considered later. Members are not allowed to comment on, criticize, praise, or debate ideas that have already been presented.
4. Members are encouraged to build on the ideas of others. The advantage of group brainstorming is that one person's idea can trigger another person's thoughts. Piggybacking on previous comments is part of the creativity of this activity.
5. Someone records each idea where everyone in the group can see it. By putting ideas on newsprint or on a board visible to the entire group, members can see and build on previous comments.

Videoconferencing

Videoconferencing is the use of telecommunication systems by groups of people at two or more locations for the purpose of meeting with each other. Participants can be geographically dispersed and meet via technology rather than through face-to-face contact. Videoconferences can range in size from three to thousands of participants at two or two hundred different locations.

Using videoconferencing for meetings has its advantages and drawbacks. Perhaps its greatest attraction is that it saves time because it reduces the need for travel. Additionally, it allows more people to have easy access to communication, provides a greater sense of participation in the organization as a whole, and creates an improved organizational image because of state-of-the-art technology.

The limitations of videoconferencing include the cost of the technology to provide full-motion, interactive video; the resistance of some participants to this technology; the impersonal nature of videoconferencing meetings; and technical or security concerns.

The following are suggestions for conducting effective meetings via videoconferencing technology:

- The individual scheduling a videoconference should determine its purpose, set an agenda with time estimates for each item, determine the list of participants, invite the participants in advance, disseminate the participant list and agenda ahead of time, gather all support material, and moderate the meeting by keeping the group on the agenda and time line.

- Those speaking in a videoconference other than for the purpose of a lecture should keep their remarks short and solicit frequent responses. Always give your name and location before making a remark, and solicit responses from specific individuals. Address other persons by name. Wait for a break in the discussion before contributing. Try to avoid off-microphone discussions in the background and extraneous movement. Never call on an individual or site without some warning.

- The videoconference room should look more like a meeting room and less like a radio or television studio. If the equipment and the technical production become the focus, people will become formal, rigid, and uncommunicative. It is important to preserve the spontaneity and informal exchange of a face-to-face meeting.

- Use some techniques to enhance individuals' visual images. Do not wear white or close-knit plaids. Look at the camera.

Do not read from notes. Avoid nervous mannerisms. If image is very important, practice speaking before a camera or with a teleprompter before the actual videoconference.

• When using graphics, make sure all material can be seen or read. Opt for less rather than more information per graphic. Determine your worst-case viewing situation when judging the readability of material.

[*See also* Team Building; Project Management]

For Additional Information

Daniels, William R. *Group Power: A Manager's Guide to Conducting Regular Meetings*. San Diego: University Associates, 1990.

Drew, Jeannine. *Mastering Meetings: Discovering the Hidden Potential of Effective Business Meetings*. New York: McGraw-Hill, 1994.

Silva, Karen. *Meetings That Work*. Homewood, Ill.: Business One Irwin, 1994.

Weissinger, Suzanne Stewart. *A Guide to Successful Meeting Planning*. New York: Wiley, 1992.

Mentoring

Mentoring involves the formation of relationships between senior and junior employees for the purpose of career development. The mentor (or sponsor) holds a higher position in the hierarchy and has demonstrated some degree of organizational success. Thus, the protégé can benefit from the mentor's information and advice. The mentor is interested in the career growth of capable junior colleagues and is willing to devote time and emotional energy to helping them. The mentor receives satisfaction and recognition from assisting the protégé. In some organizations, mentors receive tangible rewards for their involvement in mentoring relationships.

Benefits of Mentoring

Junior employees receive the most obvious benefits from mentoring. But mentors themselves and the organization as a whole reap advantages as well. Some advantages mentoring relationships provide to protégés are:

- *Assimilation into the organization.* Mentors can help newcomers learn about organizational norms, understand the unique culture of a particular organization, and deal with corporate politics. There is no way, other than through observation over time, to learn about the subtle, yet important aspects of a workplace without the help of a seasoned veteran of the organization.

- *Sharing information.* A mentor can provide "inside" information that a protégé cannot obtain as easily or as quickly through other means. The mentor can be a direct conduit to supervisors' thoughts and reactions. The wise protégé listens carefully, honors the trust in the relationship, and is discreet with confidential information provided by the mentor.

▪ *Opportunities for career growth.* The many valuable functions performed by a mentor combine to offer career growth opportunities to a protégé. Mentors can help less experienced colleagues set goals, plan careers, and develop skills necessary for career advancement. They can nominate protégés for key projects, bring them visibility, speak favorably about them to others, and introduce them to key people in the organization.

▪ *Support and understanding.* Mentors are workplace friends. They can listen to problems, calm fears, and boost the confidence of protégés. Because mentors are more experienced and trusted colleagues, they can be an excellent sounding board for concerns and offer empathy and advice.

▪ *Provision of a role model.* Individuals who have achieved success in an organization can serve as valuable role models to newcomers. Astute protégés learn by observing the subtle behaviors and reactions of the mentor and incorporating such observation into their own repertoire of behavior.

Mentors can also realize benefits from their relationship with protégés. The fresh insights of new talent can challenge and motivate long-term employees. Protégés can help senior employees stay abreast of new developments in a field or refine their outdated skills. Mentors can obtain information about employees from protégés that they could not obtain from other employees, who are often reluctant to share negative information with supervisors. Competent protégés make a mentor look good. A senior employee who has helped develop a young "star" shares in the visibility and prestige of the protégé's success. The protégé speaks favorably of the mentor and offers admiration and respect to the mentor, who in turn realizes great satisfaction by passing on information, insights, and wisdom and seeing these ideas continue through others. Some organizations formalize the mentoring process and offer rewards such as recognition dinners, travel perks, or funding for pet projects to those willing to serve as organizational mentors.

Organizations benefit whenever talent is nurtured. Mentored

individuals learn faster, become socialized into the organization more easily, and enhance their chances for success. Through mentoring, the talents of younger employees are tapped and the motivation and skills of older employees are maintained. Thus, organizations can reduce turnover and realize a greater human resources potential.

Issues of Cross-Gender Mentoring

Many organizations use mentoring relationships to assist women and minority employees, who may face unique career challenges in traditional organizations. There are some dynamics of cross-gender mentor relationships that must be dealt with if such mentoring is to succeed in an organization.

For example, some women report difficulty in using male mentors as role models. What is considered appropriate behavior for a male in the workplace may not be considered appropriate for a female employee. At the very least, a female protégé must adapt behaviors modeled from a male mentor to fit her own style. The relationship of a male mentor to a female protégé may reinforce stereotypical roles of male power and female dependence. Issues of intimacy and sexuality may surface in cross-gender mentoring relationships. Frequently, cross-gender mentor relationships receive more attention and resentment from co-workers than same-gender mentor relationships do. Workers may become suspicious of and impugn the motive of a male senior manager who takes special interest in a new female employee.

It is difficult to provide remedies to problems of sex-role stereotypes and sexual tensions that can affect cross-gender mentoring. At the very least, mentors, protégés, and organizations should be aware of such possible complications and should ensure that mentoring facilitates rather than impedes career growth.

Fostering Mentoring in Organizations

Mentoring is an aspect of human resources development. To encourage it, organizations must relate mentoring to its overall human resources development effort. If a company pays lip service to the importance of employees, then mentoring will not work. An organizational culture to support mentoring must exist. A teamwork environment is more conducive to mentoring relationships than an environment of individual competitiveness.

Managers should be made aware of the mentoring process, functions, and advantages. Educational programs can highlight the topic of mentoring and teach support skills such as listening, coaching, counseling, motivating, and giving feedback.

The mentoring function can be built into goal setting and performance appraisal criteria for managers. If you are aware of the need to mentor junior employees and possess mentoring skills, you can allocate part of your time for this activity. Likewise, if mentoring becomes a management function in an organization, the performance appraisal system can review and reward your success at mentoring others.

Organizations committed to mentoring can establish a formal mentoring program by disseminating a policy and setting up procedures for paring senior- with junior-level employees. In such programs, however, participation should be voluntary. Once employees have expressed interest, a formal system can encourage the development of mentor relationships. There should be a mechanism for reassigning mismatched pairs and for evaluating the effectiveness of a formal mentoring program.

[*See also* Career Development]

For Additional Information

Hensler, D. Jack. "Mentoring at the Management Level." *Industrial Management* 36, No. 6 (Nov./Dec. 1994), pp. 20–21.

Murray, Margo, and Marna A. Owen. *Beyond the Myths and Magic of Mentoring: How to Facilitate an Effective Mentoring Program.* San Francisco: Jossey-Bass Publishers, 1991.

Shea, Gordon F. *Mentoring: Partnerships for Exceptional Employee Development.* New York: AMA Membership Publications Division, 1994.

Motivation

Because productivity is a goal in all workplace organizations, managers must be skilled at motivating others. You must understand the concept of motivation and the complex array of factors that affect it in order to influence others toward greater productivity.

The Concept of Motivation

The term motivation relates to the energy that initiates and directs behavior and concerns the choices that we make about our goal-directed behavior. Presumably, we have a wide range of choices about behavior. Motives prompt us to act in certain ways as opposed to other ways. Motives are the "why" of behavior. An understanding of the following five characteristics of motives will help you motivate your employees more effectively:

1. *Motives are hierarchical.* The motives for our behavior vary in strength and importance. Some are more powerful than others. They exist in a type of rank order. When contradictory motives exist, the more powerful motive will guide our behavior.

2. *Motives may be unconscious.* Frequently, we are unaware of the motives for our behavior. When asked why we are behaving a certain way, we may state a variety of reasons unrelated to our actual behavior. We may think these are our motives or wish they were our motives. Rarely are we fully aware of the inner needs and drives affecting our behavior.

3. *Motives must be inferred.* We can observe behavior, but we can only infer the motives underlying that behavior. Trying to understand our own and others' motivations is guesswork. At

best, we can try to extrapolate motives from observed behavior coupled with stated beliefs and intentions.

4. *Motives are individualistic.* The motives of each of us differ. We each have a different motivational hierarchy composed of different desires and different priorities. Because motives are based on needs, rewards, and values, they obviously vary from person to person.

5. *Motives change.* Motives are not stable. Because our motives fit together as a set, different ingredients of that set may change or vary in importance over time. What motivates us today may not motivate us tomorrow. Even if we could ascertain all of the elements in a person's motivational system, the dynamic nature of motives would complicate our understanding.

Job and Organizational Factors Affecting Motivation

You must take many factors into account when trying to understand the process of motivation. In addition to understanding inner needs and goals, you must identify factors of the job and the organization that influence behavior if you are to understand the motivational process.

Many characteristics of a job affect an employee's motivational level and either encourage or discourage the desire to perform well. Some types of jobs are more intrinsically satisfying than others—that is, in certain types of jobs an employee is motivated by the work itself. Studies of motivation based on job content show that employees want to feel challenged in a job, they want feedback about their performance, they want to feel that the job is valued or important, and they want some degree of control or autonomy over setting work goals and determining the paths to reaching those goals. Keep in mind that because motives are individualistic, the extent to which employees are motivated by these job requirements will vary. But in general, employees find them intrinsically rewarding.

Many features of the organizational environment also affect motivation. Employee motivation can be affected by the company's personnel selection and placement procedures, training and development systems, performance appraisal methods, supervisory styles and practices, and reward and compensation system. Indeed, just about everything in an organization can affect an employee's motivation to perform.

If the wrong people are hired for jobs, then motivation will suffer. An underqualified person will be discouraged by the inability to perform well and may be motivated to avoid work-related behavior because of a fear or failure. An overqualified person will be discouraged by the lack of a challenge.

Employee training and development can be a valuable tool for developing motivation. Through training, employees can gain the skills necessary for success, can develop positive attitudes toward performance, and can develop challenging career goals.

Performance feedback is an essential ingredient of intrinsically motivating jobs and a prerequisite to performance-based rewards. It is difficult to encourage employees to improve if you have no reliable way of assessing their current performance. Likewise, you cannot reward excellent performance without a means of judging excellence. A good performance appraisal system should support your methods of motivating employees.

Effective supervision is closely tied to employee motivation. Employees will be motivated to perform well if they have a good relationship with their supervisor and feel that supervisory practices are fair. Indeed, supervisors are the key motivators of their staff. Effective supervisors motivate by giving regular and specific performance feedback, by coaching employees to improve their performance, by encouraging employee growth and development, and by rewarding good performance.

Motivation increases when employees receive desired rewards as a result of their performance. Rewards can take the form of raises, bonuses, promotions, recognition, prizes, or time off. The key points are that the employee must value the reward and the reward must be based on performance. Obviously, the importance of compensation and rewards as motivators will vary from person to person. But an organization with a fair compensation and reward system is likely to have an easier time motivating its members.

Types of Motivators

There are a variety of strategies you can use to motivate employees. Four types of workplace motivators are needs satisfiers, rewards, job design, and employee participation.

Needs and Motivation

Some outcomes are desired by employees and others are not. One reason for this involves the concept of human needs. If certain needs are important to individuals, then they will act in ways to satisfy those needs. By understanding what pressing, unfulfilled needs people have, we can motivate them. Psychologists have theorized that any of the following sets of needs may govern human behavior:

1. *Need for achievement.* Employees motivated by a need for achievement want the satisfaction of accomplishing something challenging. They want to exercise their talents, to surpass others, to attain success. Such people are self-motivated, given a sufficiently challenging job to do. They set realistic goals and achieve them. To allow these employees opportunities for meeting their needs for achievement, you must provide new and challenging assignments.

2. *Need for power.* Employees with a high need for power derive satisfaction from influencing and controlling others. They like to lead, to persuade, and have an impact on situations. Such people are motivated by positions of power, leadership, and authority. They become informal group leaders, hold leadership positions in community or civic groups, and strive for supervisory or management positions. These people should be given opportunities to influence others, to make decisions, and to direct projects.

3. *Need for affiliation.* Employees motivated by an affiliation need derive satisfaction from interacting with others. They like to be with people, develop friendly relationships, and find the social aspects of the workplace rewarding. You can motivate such people by providing them with opportunities for interaction in

the workplace: teamwork projects, group meetings, company athletic teams, or jobs involving communication with others.

4. *Need for autonomy.* Employees with the need for autonomy want freedom and independence. They want to direct their own efforts and will resist close supervision. You can motivate them by allowing them to make their own choices, set their own schedules, and work independently of others.

5. *Need for esteem.* Employees with high esteem needs like to be recognized and praised. They want others to acknowledge and appreciate their work. Attention and respect from others motivates their work. Give them ample feedback, public recognition, or tokens of appreciation for good work.

6. *Need for safety or security.* Employees motivated by this need derive satisfaction from job security, a steady income, health and life insurance, and a hazard-free work environment. They will seek jobs with tenure or protection. They may also want predictable work with little risk or uncertainty. Salary and fringe benefits are very important to them.

7. *Need for equity.* People driven by a need for equity want to be treated fairly. They have a strong sense of conscience or ethics. They may compare their work hours, job duties, salary, and privileges to those of other employees and become discouraged if they perceive inequities. They want to see that standards are being applied consistently and that dishonesty and favoritism are not being tolerated in the organization.

8. *Need for self-actualization.* This refers to the satisfaction gained from growth and self-development. It may mean creative expression on a job or learning just for the sake of learning. People motivated by this need may take on challenging work not for the sense of accomplishment or to gain recognition but only for the sheer enjoyment of a new experience and self-discovery. Such people need jobs that help them reach their potential.

Rewards and Motivation

Extrinsic rewards are another type of motivator. Managers typically give tangible rewards based on performance, such as raises, bonuses, status symbols, fringe benefits, prizes, and incentives.

Employees who value such rewards put forth considerable effort to obtain one. But extrinsic awards can be quite costly to an organization. If you want to use extrinsic rewards to motivate employees, make sure that the following conditions are met, without which any reward system can actually hinder motivation and negatively affect performance.

1. *Employees must perceive the rewards as valuable.* Some companies offer trinkets as rewards and wonder why employees are not motivated to earn them. You should determine what rewards employees desire.

2. *The rewards must be tied clearly to performance.* Both the recipients of rewards and their colleagues who observe the process must see that the reward was earned through superior performance. If employees perceive that rewards are given on a capricious or arbitrary basis, then motivation will suffer.

3. *There must be objective criteria for evaluating performance.* People must know exactly what they have to do to obtain the reward. There should be no surprises. When employees disagree on who deserves the rewards because assessment methods are vague or invalid, then morale and motivation will decrease. But rewards linked to clear and attainable standards of performance are effective motivators.

4. *Information about the allocation of rewards should be shared openly.* There should be no secrecy about who got what rewards and why. A performance-based reward system will serve as a motivator only in an atmosphere of trust and open communication.

Job Design and Motivation

Because certain job features are intrinsically satisfying, redesigning jobs can be a way to motivate employees. It is, after all, easier to change jobs in an organization than it is to change the people in an organization. Basically, there are three ways to redesign jobs:

1. *Job rotation.* Move employees through a variety of jobs, departments, or functions. This is especially useful for someone

who has been on job for a long time, who is no longer challenged by a job, or who has a strong need for activity or change. By giving an employee the opportunity to change jobs, you can prevent boredom and develop a more versatile worker.

2. *Job enlargement.* Expand an employee's duties. Once an employee has demonstrated the capacity to handle the current workload and has indicated a desire to expand into new areas, adding new responsibilities may be necessary to keep the employee motivated. Talented employees become especially frustrated and de-motivated if a job is too simple or too limited.

3. *Job enrichment.* Make jobs more desirable or satisfying. Give employees more autonomy, input into decision making, more interesting projects, whole rather than fragmented tasks, or more information about company goals.

Participation and Motivation

Many organizations use systems of employee involvement to increase motivation, company loyalty, and quality performance. Organizing employees into teams can serve to enhance both motivation and quality. Employees who feel that they are an integral part of an organization will be motivated to do good work. Those who merely put in their time to earn a paycheck will care little about the quality of their work. Through a teamwork approach, employees can fulfill many of their job-related motivational needs, team members can provide rewards to each other, and the organization can benefit from a more engaged workforce.

[*See also* Coaching Employees; Feedback; Team Building]

For Additional Information

Jaffe, Dennis T., Cynthia D. Scott, and Glenn R. Tobe. *Rekindling Commitment: How to Revitalize Yourself, Your Work, and Your Organization.* San Francisco: Jossey-Bass Publishers, 1994.

McCoy, Thomas J. *Compensation and Motivation.* New York: AMA-COM, 1992.

Smigel, Lloyd. *Management Plus: Leadership, Motivation, and Power in the Changing Workplace.* Chicago: Contemporary Books, 1994.

Spitzer, Dean R. *Supermotivation: A Blueprint for Energizing Your Organization from Top to Bottom.* New York: AMACOM, 1995.

Whetten, David A., and Kim S. Cameron. *Developing Management Skills: Motivating Others.* New York: HarperCollins, 1993.

Negotiation

Whenever we exchange information with the aim of influencing or persuading others in order to meet our own needs, we are involved in the process of negotiation. Sellers and buyers negotiate the price and terms of large-scale purchases such as real estate. Husbands and wives negotiate to settle arguments. Teenagers negotiate with parents for privileges and freedoms. Unions and management negotiate labor contracts. And managers negotiate with countless numbers of people in the course of a week to make decisions, promote projects, or settle problems. The managerial role fits the very definition of negotiation. We share information for the purpose of reaching an agreement that achieves our needs and the needs of our departments and organizations.

The essential characteristics of negotiation, which distinguish it from other types of communication, are the notion of give-and-take, mutual fulfillment of needs, the use of strategies to influence the other party, and some amount of conflict that must be resolved. People usually enter negotiations with predetermined objectives that they expect to adjust along the way. Through the mutual exchange of information and concessions, they expect to be able to reach agreements. Needs fulfillment is the very purpose of negotiation. Each party is dependent on the other for something. Both parties want their needs to be met. Conflict occurs because the needs of each party are often different or mutually exclusive. The achievement of one person's needs may automatically frustrate the fulfillment of the other's needs. Finally, strategies come into play whenever negotiators plan methods or tactics to influence each other. Strategies of negotiation need not be devious schemes to manipulate or deceive. More often than not, they are merely well-conceived plans and preparations developed prior to the face-to-face interaction of a negotiation.

Types of Negotiations

There are three primary types or styles of negotiations: controlling or "lose-lose" negotiation, competitive or "win-lose" negotiation, and collaborative or "win-win" negotiation. It is important for all negotiators to be aware of the three types of negotiations so that you can identify the style of the other party and make necessary adjustments to your plans and strategy accordingly.

Controlling, or Lose-Lose, Negotiation

Some labor negotiations and political negotiations can be categorized as controlling negotiations. Failing to agree to a disadvantageous labor contract, thus causing a strike, may be seen as winning control for your side. Lose-lose negotiations are characterized by the following:

- The negotiator claims there is a central control such that the negotiator has little control.
- Controlling negotiations drag on painfully slow, with every minute detail seen as contestable. The controller typically does not give an inch on any point.
- The negotiations start with tough, nearly impossible demands and end in a similar state.
- Adversary concessions are viewed as weakness.
- The negotiators and their organizations are feared by the other party.
- Usually there is a prolonged history of animosity and high levels of distrust between the parties.
- The style of making demands is more important than the demands themselves. Appearing to be tough and nonconciliatory are of paramount importance to the lose-lose negotiators and their organizations.

There are several tactics you can use with lose-lose negotiators.

1. Discuss the issue of control at prenegotiations planning sessions and with the other party prior to the negotiations.

2. Insist that all negotiations be private and away from media or public attention. Limelight is fertile soil for the lose-lose negotiators.
3. Spend much time debating and negotiating the rules and format for the negotiations. Rules surrounding impasse or breakoff points are important.
4. Insist on stalemates as being acceptable only if they can be resolved by subcommittee later during the negotiation process.
5. Try to control the time, place, and environment of the negotiations. Hostile turf or a neutral site for the negotiations can be a deterrent to lose-lose negotiators.

Competitive, or Win-Lose, Negotiations

Competitive, or win-lose, negotiations are similar to lose-lose negotiations in that they start with tough demands. Adversary concessions are viewed as weakness, and the negotiator claims there is a central control such that the negotiator has little control. There are many differences, though, as the following characteristics of win-lose negotiation style indicate:

- Negotiators use premediated emotional appeals.
- Win-lose negotiators make concessions infrequently and grudgingly.
- Negotiators ignore and manipulate deadlines.
- Parties have a take-it-or-leave-it attitude.
- Competitive negotiators make one-time, exclusive offers.
- Almost without fail, competitive negotiators have a hidden agenda behind the smoke and mirrors of minor issues. They use these items as positioning tools so that when the true agenda surfaces, they are in position to claim victory.

Such negotiations have drawbacks. Unless there is historical precedence for such a type of negotiation, competitive negotiations are good for only one deal. This type of negotiation alienates opponents and friends of opponents. The competitive negotiator also risks losing past gains.

Your best strategy with this type of negotiator is to strongly remind the person of the aforementioned drawbacks. Personalize the risks to the negotiator and his or her organization. Offer the alternative of the win-win style, sometimes referred to as collaborative, or mutual gains, negotiations.

Win-Win, Collaborative, or Mutual-Gains Negotiation

A simple and highly successful strategy for negotiation is based on mutual gain; there is no fixed sum or set amount of the pie from which one party wins and the other loses. Instead, the pie itself is expandable and through joint creative problem solving, can be enlarged so that both parties stand to gain. This requires fresh ideas, an understanding of the needs of both parties, and collaboration to satisfy both parties. Rather than proposing a single option for a tightly held position, the win-win negotiators from both sides uncover numerous options so that everyone wins.

Negotiators using a mutual-gains approach negotiate over principles, not positions. In the previous styles, negotiators usually articulate positions that must be defended. Egos become inextricably linked to each position. Any movement from a position is seen as a concession, a loss, or a weakness.

Mutual gains offer a better approach. Identify your principles or needs. State your objectives or needs rather than a position. There can be many options for satisfying an objective or need, but there is only one position. When each party has directly communicated its needs, some clear overlap will be revealed. By revealing principles or needs, you are discussing a mutual problem. By stating positions, you are imposing predetermined solutions. It is wise to find creative solutions once you both understand each other's needs.

This increasingly popular and effective negotiation style has eight essential elements:

1. The outcome must call for either both parties to win or a stalemate to occur so that neither party loses.

2. The negotiating environment must promote trust and an open exchange of ideas, without any hidden agenda. Trust involves an accurate prediction of the other person, means for

knowing what behavior to expect, having faith in the accuracy of information, and seeing integrity in the other person's motives. Negotiators can develop trust by acknowledging common ground, by presenting accurate information, by listening to each other, and by aiming for an agreement that is fair to both parties.

3. Negotiators must be empowered to decide and must be fully aware of one another's parameters.

4. Both parties must be willing to work hard as partners to search for new options to satisfy the needs of both parties. A key difference in the philosophies of collaborative versus competitive or controlling negotiation is the perception of each party as a partner rather than an opponent. To view the other as an opponent automatically creates an atmosphere of hostility and a style of negotiation consistent with win-lose or lose-lose. Viewing the other as a partner acknowledges that you depend on each other for the fulfillment of needs and that you want to be able to reach an agreement.

5. Negotiators must openly disclose their human needs. Often, personal needs such as the need to win, to look good to others, to have ideas accepted, or to save face drive negotiators far more than do specific issues or amounts. You must know the other negotiator and determine his or her personal needs. Then you may satisfy the negotiator's needs while resolving issues favorably.

6. There must exist a mutual desire to positively continue the relationship.

7. Creative problem solving is a separate process from decision making in win-win mutual-gains negotiations. Creative problem solving relies heavily on brainstorming techniques. Once the partners understand each other's needs, they generate as many options for meeting those needs as they possibly can. Many of the options will be unfeasible or will be rejected by the negotiators after careful consideration. But in that long list there may be one or two unconventional or unusual options that have merit and are acceptable to both negotiators. Other suggestions for promoting creative thinking involve being open-minded, having a questioning attitude, drawing examples from seemingly unrelated situations, and persevering in problem solving.

8. Both parties must be satisfied with the outcome.

There are but a few drawbacks to this style: (1) both sides must sacrifice on issues; (2) compromise now may lead to future negotiations on these same matters; and (3) both parties must be forthcoming with their needs and other disclosures, unlike negotiators in either win-lose or lose-lose negotiations.

Preparing to Negotiate

In many instances, effective negotiators spend more time preparing for a negotiation than they do in a negotiation session. The exact nature of the preparation depends on the type and importance of the negotiation, though all negotiations require that you set objectives, collect information, analyze the other party's objectives, identify needs of both sides, determine limits to concessions you are willing to make, set parameters or boundaries for such issues as time, money, personnel, etc; and give considerable thought to the process of negotiating.

Setting Your Own Objectives

What do you want to accomplish by negotiation? You may have several objectives or goals that may relate to long-term or short-term needs. It is wise to establish some priorities to your set of objectives: Which goals are least important and most important? Clearly, some points are major and others are minor. Make these distinctions ahead of time. Also, whenever possible, think of objectives not as fixed goals but as flexible ranges.

Collecting Information

The more informed you are as a negotiator, the more effective you will be. It is imperative that you collect all the facts related to a particular negotiation. What led up to this negotiation? What agreements were made between the parties in the past? What is the history of the situation? What solutions have other groups used in similar situations? What risks you are willing to take? You must begin to think of barriers to reaching your goals that may arise and plan for contingencies to overcome them.

Analyzing the Other Party's Objectives

Besides knowing your own goals, knowing barriers to these goals, preparing contingencies for these barriers, and being well informed about the negotiation issues, try to identify the objectives of the other party. With some knowledge of whom you are negotiating with and why you are negotiating, you should be able to estimate some of your partner's goals and priorities. Imagine yourself in your partner's position. If you were on the other wise of the negotiation, what would you be attempting to obtain? How would you go about obtaining your major goals?

Obviously, your negotiating partner can have many objectives. The more accurately you assess your partner's priorities, the more prepared you will be for the negotiating session. Similarly, the more you know about the other negotiator and the negotiation methods he or she employed in the past, the more likely you will attain your goals.

Analyzing Both Parties' Needs

All negotiators are trying to meet human needs, which underlie all negotiation objectives. In fact, successful influence or persuasion usually appeals to basic human needs. By understanding how human needs relate to motivation and action, we can be more skilled negotiators.

In addition to identifying the needs that underlie your own negotiating goals, try to analyze the needs of your negotiation partner. By matching your strategies to the other person's needs, you will enhance your negotiating success. Remember, in the mutual-gains approach of win-win negotiations, both parties disclose their goals. Successful negotiators also discuss their human needs.

Thinking About the Negotiation Process

The final step in preparing to negotiate involves learning about the negotiation process. It helps to be aware of specific skills involved in negotiating. Think of all the situations in which you practice negotiation. Analyze behaviors that help and hinder the achievement of desired outcomes. Give thought to the particular negotiating situation you are about to face. What is the time frame for negotiating? Will there be several interactions over a period of time before agreement is reached, or is there only one shot for agreement? Will you continue to have a relationship with this person after the negotiation? Or is it unlikely that the negotiating parties will ever interact again? Are you negotiating as individuals or do you each represent constituencies? What is the distribution of power between you and the other negotiating party? While there are no automatic strategies based on the answers to these questions, it is wise to consider such aspects of an upcoming negotiation.

Developing the Right Attitude and Atmosphere

Somehow, the process of negotiating has earned a negative reputation. Negotiation conjures up images of stalwart opponents in poker-faced deliberations who fight for their positions by using misinformation and manipulation. In reality, negotiators can be more effective if they discuss principles rather than positions, promote trust, allow each other to save face, use a collaborative style of communication, and try creative problem solving. It helps to create an atmosphere of collaboration and a goal of win-war or mutual problem solving.

Conducting a Negotiation

A negotiation is a type of communication and should follow principles that promote clarity and understanding. If negotiators look at each other as partners trying to solve a problem together, rather than as adversaries, they will be clear and direct in their communication. They will realize the value of stating specific needs, sharing information, listening, questioning, and building a good working relationship. What follows are not negotiating tricks but principles of effective communication in negotiations:

1. *State your principles directly.* Early on, both parties should clearly indicate their needs, principles, or objectives. Remember, this is not a position, but a statement of problem parameters. Do not hold back in indicating your objectives. Do not exaggerate or distort your needs.

2. *Listen to each other.* Pay attention to what is being said. Paraphrase to show your understanding. Check out assumptions. The sooner you understand the other's needs, the sooner you will find points of commonalty and divergence. Once you clearly understand where the points of divergence are, you can begin to develop options to satisfy differing needs.

3. *Take your time.* It takes time to find equitable solutions to problems. Creative options do not come easily; they require much deliberation and contemplation. Partners must avoid defensiveness and be patient with the negotiation process.

4. *Use questions.* Questions enable you to clarify your partner's point of view, separate facts from assumptions, and check out your perceptions. Straightforward questions allow negotiators to deals in specifics. Imagine the progress that a negotiation could take if each person honestly answer the question "What would you like to accomplish from this negotiation?" Effective questions in a negotiation are sincere attempts to elicit information or clarify understanding. They should not be devices to steer the conversation or lead to a particular answer. They should not come across as hostile or interrogating.

5. *Allow emotions.* It is appropriate to have an explicit discussion of feelings in a negotiation. Feelings cannot help but underlie issues and contribute to the atmosphere in a negotiation. To deny emotions is to fuel an eruption. When negotiators can release their feelings, they talk more rationally. The best way to deal with feelings in a negotiation is to state them and to discuss them rather than to make a dramatic display of them.

6. *Summarize agreements.* Negotiators frequently focus more on points of disagreement than on points of agreement. It is important during a negotiation, and especially at the closing of a

negotiation, to summarize each element of an agreement. That way, each party knows exactly what has transpired and each defines outcomes similarly. A summary prevents people from selectively perceiving agreements in ways that favor them. If you hear an inaccurate statement during a negotiation, say "No, that's not how I understood our decision. I thought. . . ." Then you can eliminate misunderstandings.

Special Forms of Negotiation

Not all negotiations involve just two parties in a face-to-face deliberation. There may be negotiating teams, mediators, or arbitrators involved in the process.

Some negotiations are so complex that they require the involvement of two groups of people. A labor contract negotiation may involve various divisional heads and personnel specialists from management as well as elected union representatives. Team negotiations provide the advantage of broader perspectives, informational expertise, and specialized roles. With more people present, more issues can be represented and more information provided. Each person brings a particular skill to the process, such as listening, questioning, creative thinking, summarizing, or trust building. The disadvantages of team negotiations include scheduling difficulties, human resources costs, and role coordination. If each negotiating team has four or five members, it may be difficult to find time for discussions amenable to everyone's schedule. It is also more expensive to use several people rather than one person. Finally, team members may contradict each other, may disagree about desired outcomes, or may have difficulty working together as a team.

Alternative Dispute Resolution

Alternative dispute resolution (ADR) is a low-cost, attractive alternative to resolving disputes typically heard in expensive and time-consuming courtrooms. Arbitration and mediation are long-standing forms of ADR. Until recently, arbitration and mediation have been available only to employers facing labor disputes, and have been limited to cases involving labor contracts or legal action. Now, some nonunion employers are looking to ADR as a remedy for employment and disciplinary conflicts. Federal, state, and local governments also increasingly seek ADR for regulatory disputes with employers, such as EEOC hearings involving sexual harassment or the Americans with Disabilities Act. Also, some employers are creating ADR systems internally for such areas as employee appeals to disciplinary decisions, potential employee lawsuits, and employee-employee disputes.

Besides the cost and time savings of ADR, this alternative gives both parties many benefits. They determine the process rules and jointly determine a facilitator. Since no juries are involved, decisions are more predictable and consistent. When employees join in appellate panels on disciplinary hearings, the decisions receive greater acceptance from the parties involved and from other employees. For most cases involving federal regulatory agencies, employers using ADR have input in the selection of the arbitrator or mediator. When outside arbitrators are used, their decisions, though less costly, are final and binding.

The role of arbitrators, mediators, or hearing panels is not to determine right and wrong, but to find a durable outcome that restores, perseveres, or enhances the relationship between the parties. Since these hearings are private, there is no public record, and both parties may agree to keep the matter confidential.

Critics of ADR complain of the lack of regulatory control over the process, the limited scope for review or appeal, and that arbitrators, mediators, and panelists may lack legal experience. Some who dislike ADR criticize the secrecy or closed-door nature of these hearings.

Mediators can be used when a negotiation reaches an impasse. If negotiators have taken sides and are rigidly defending their positions, progress is impossible without the help of a third party. The mediator intervenes to promote understanding and agreement; the mediator does not make decisions or impose solutions, but helps establish cooperation. Mediation looks for areas for mutual gain, with balanced decisions that promote a healthy relationship for the long term. Also, mediation allows parties to walk away from decisions. Mediators help negotiators clarify objectives, understand needs, and identify areas of agreement and disagreement.

Arbitration is used when the negotiation process breaks down and is beyond repair. While associated with negotiation, arbitration actually discourages negotiation. Arbitrators hear the issues of both sides and make a binding decision. Once a problem is in the hands of an arbitrator, the negotiators lose all power to make decisions. In effect, because they cannot agree, they seek a solution from someone else. Because not all traditional face-to-face negotiations can produce settlements, arbitration is a necessary and valuable option.

[*See also* Conflict Management]

For Additional Information

Hall, Lavinia, ed. *Negotiation: Strategies for Mutual Gain: The Basic Seminar of the Harvard Program on Negotiation*. Newbury Park, Calif.: Sage, 1993.

Hawkins, Michael W. "Alternative Dispute Resolution: An Alternative for Resolving Employment Litigation and Disputes." *Northern Kentucky Law Review* 20, No. 2 (1993), pp. 493–504.

Fisher, Roger, and William Ury. *Getting to Yes: Negotiating Agreement Without Giving In*. New York: Penguin Books, 1983.

Networking

Successful managers usually develop methods for staying abreast of developments in their fields; for meeting important people in their organizations, professions, or industries; for getting informal information useful for performing their jobs; and for cultivating a circle of allies or helpful colleagues. This process of establishing connections within and across organizations is called networking. Many women in the workplace have embraced the concept of networking as a way to penetrate the "old boys network." Successful managers, be they male or female, understand the networking phenomenon and engage in it for career advancement.

Networking is the process of developing and using contacts for career support or advancement. Networking means building a system of interrelationships of people who can help each other's careers. By expanding the number of people you know and linking together the people you know with the people they know, a network of organizational contacts can be created. The number of connecting points in the network can grow exponentially. An examination of the types of possible networks, their purposes, and methods of developing networks helps define and illustrate the concept.

Types of Networks

Some examples of career networks include the following categories:

- *Occupational.* Anyone in a particular occupation can affiliate with others in the same occupation. The affiliation can be through informal contact or through formal organizations. Accountants meet with other accountants; journalists, architects, machinists, plumbers, or nurses meet with others in their occupation to learn from each other.

- *Horizontal.* People at similar job levels, whatever the field, meet together. Presidents of various organizations in a city, for example, can have contact with each other. Groups form for professionals or executives from a variety of fields, with the assumption that people from similar career levels have common concerns.

- *Special interests.* Individuals seek contact with others who are demographically or philosophically similar. Groups based on gender, race, age, ethnicity, or other demographic factors related to career progress are common network types. Likewise, employees can seek contact with others, internal or external to their organizations, who share views about their treatment, benefits, or company policies. Professional groups of women, blacks, Latinos, environmentalists, older citizens, gay people, political activists, or handicapped people are a few examples of special-interest networking.

- *Occupation/horizontal.* This type of network involves people at the same level in the same occupation. Examples include high school principals, hospital administrators, construction company owners, general managers of automobile dealerships, or personnel administrators in the transportation industry.

Purposes of Networks

There are many reasons why people develop career networks. Most important, you can learn from organizational contacts. Talking to someone in the same profession or someone with the same job title can give you insights into how to better perform your own job. You can share stories, examples, ideas, or advice. You can borrow techniques from each other. By interacting with someone else in your occupation, you may learn about new developments in your field. Clearly, more heads are better than one. Managers who do their jobs in isolation, without seeking out professional colleagues, will tend to become parochial and outdated in their ideas and methods.

Another reason to develop career connections is to acquire sounding boards. If it is risky to test new ideas within workplace organizations, an associate in a different organization who understands your job can provide valuable feedback about your new ideas, methods, or projects. Likewise, when your job is frustrating or a relationship with a supervisor is troublesome, complaining to an associate across town or across the country can be helpful.

A well-developed network of business associates can provide referrals for a variety of needs. By meeting with or interacting online with acquaintances in the world of work, networkers have found clients, customers, new jobs, consultants, partners, and friends, to name a few. Anytime you need to reach a large number of people or to expand the number of people you know, networking is an effective strategy.

Networking is especially useful for people who feel isolated in their work. The self-employed, employees of small organizations, people in remote geographic areas, salespeople in one-person branch offices, or the sole woman in an organization all must develop a network of people if they are to have work colleagues at all. Going to a meeting or having lunch with others who can understand your job is imperative to work motivation and career growth.

Overall, people engage in networking to promote their careers. Knowing someone in a particular company can improve your chances of getting a job in that organization. Attending meetings or conferences with colleagues in your field keeps you current and enhances your promotability. Having lunch regularly with other women executives provides business contacts that may develop your organization's revenues. Knowing influential leaders in your city increases your visibility and prestige on the job.

Finally, networking can be fun. It gives you a chance to meet new people, socialize with business associates, and expand your horizons. For most managers, talking shop with people in similar or even in different occupations is an enjoyable way to spend time. Discussing common business interests, empathizing with each other's workplace experiences, or discovering people you know in common is an exciting part of the organizational environment. Work would be boring without networking.

Networking Methods

There are as many ways to cultivate career networks as there are unique compositions of networks. Managers who are skilled at networking use all the available resources. You never know what the source of contacts, information, or opportunities will be.

Meeting lots of people and discovering the ways in which you can help each other's careers are the key points of networking. Possible sources for meeting people who could help your career include professional associations, volunteer organizations, classes and lectures, network directories, computer bulletin boards, community groups, alumni associations, social events, and the people you already know.

Every job has some type of affiliated professional or trade association to which you can belong. Joining the groups related to your occupation or industry is an excellent way to make career contacts. But this method of networking is effective only if you are an active, outgoing member of the group. Merely paying membership dues or attending an occasional meeting is not enough. Joining committees and working on behalf of the organization will have greater career payoffs than will passive membership.

The business and professional leaders of a community often volunteer their time and talents to nonprofit organizations in the community. Your willingness to participate in volunteer organizations could have long-term career benefits. By helping with artistic, educational, or civic endeavors, ambitious managers contribute to their own career contacts as well as to their communities.

Taking classes related to your line of work or attending business lectures in the community is another method of networking. Such educational activities attract a motivated group of individuals who have a common interest in the topic of the class or lecture.

There are countless formal groups that exist to unite individuals with occupational, demographic, philosophical, or lifestyle similarities. Checking directories of network groups would be a wise way to locate sources of organizational contacts.

Many people with common interests interact electronically through computer networks and bulletin boards. This is an easy way to reach large numbers of people, to tap into a wealth of business information, and to interact spontaneously without ever leaving your office.

Having attended the same school often creates a psychological bond between people. Strangers who are graduates of the same school have been known to help each other. Typically, the alumni of any school will include many individuals with prestigious positions. Being active in alumni associations and contacting fellow graduates who may be valuable business associates is another networking strategy.

Many astute managers have stumbled on valuable business contacts at social events. Merely mingling with others and introducing yourself to people in social situations can expand a career network. Follow up on the casual meeting with a lunch invitation or with some business correspondence to develop the business relationship.

Finally, using your existing network of familiar people is an easy and effective way to make career contacts. Think of everyone with whom you have a relationship—relatives, friends, coworkers, neighbors. Talk to them about the people they know. Ask for an introduction or for permission to use their name when contacting other people. Make contact with potential business associates. Discuss ways in which developing an association may be mutually beneficial.

Do's and Don'ts of Networking

Networking can have a negative connotation because of a seemingly callous purpose or because of inappropriate methods. Some people are overzealous in making career connections. Others try to use networking as a substitute for professional competence. By following some guidelines for networking, you can retain it as a valuable tool for professional growth and career advancement.

1. *Make sure networking benefits both parties.* Just like mentoring, networking should benefit both people in the relationship. Some managers make the mistake of developing contacts only as a way to benefit their own careers. They forget that networking is a two-way street. Successful networking means that you give as much as you get from the relationship. It is presumptuous to expect people to help you in your career if you cannot help them in return.

2. *Always practice businesslike conduct.* Treat a networking relationship as you would treat any important business relationship. It is important that you not impose yourself on the contact person. You must make appointments and adhere to schedules. Realize that people are busy and workplace demands must always take precedence over networking activities. Networking relationships should be characterized by respect and professional integrity rather than pushiness and self-interest.

3. *Don't expect miracles.* Effectively developing career contacts should be an ongoing process of your working life. It is not something that you do intensively for a short period of time and then reap startling rewards. The positive outcomes of networking are not immediately apparent. The benefits often are subtle. A network contact may affect your career without your even knowing it. Networking is a slow, steady process of building workplace alliances. It may be years before you realize the benefits of a networking connection.

4. *Make time for networking.* Because the results of networking are intangible and work deadlines must be met, some managers claim that networking is not worth the time. Attending meetings, actively participating in professional associations, and cultivating business relationships can be time-consuming activities. But if done effectively, networking is time well spent. It is important to schedule a certain amount of time into your work routine just for networking purposes. Make sure you touch base with business acquaintances often enough to maintain the relationship.

5. *Networking presumes competence.* Competent individuals make successful networkers. Nobody wants to invest in relationships with incompetent associates. Successful, capable managers want to surround themselves with competent associates.

Networking is a tool to advance your career, but the foundation of the career rests on competence in your profession.

[*See also* Career Development]

For Additional Information

Baker, Wayne E. *Networking Smart: How to Build Relationships for Personal and Organizational Success.* New York: McGraw-Hill, 1994.

Olson, A. Andrew. "Long-Term Networking: A Strategy for Career Success." *Management Review* 63, No. 4 (April 1994), pp. 33–35.

Organizational Culture

The concept of organizational culture refers to a set of assumptions or beliefs that are shared by members of an organization. A system of shared values in the workplace can be considered a culture. Culture encompasses the assumptions, habits, customs, stories, practices, and traditions of a group. Corporate cultures specify how employees communicate, dress, think, behave, work, and make decisions. While the idea has been intuitively understood for some time, the explicit discussion of corporate culture is a relatively new phenomenon in management literature.

Why Care About Organizational Culture?

Culture has a powerful influence throughout an organization. It guides behavior, affects morale, and creates an organization's identity. There are many reasons why managers should understand their organization's culture:

1. *Fitting in.* Being in a new culture creates uncertainty and tension. You do not know what is expected of you in a new organization, function, company site, or department. Assessing the culture helps you to respond appropriately. You can get cues about how to act and what to value. As a newcomer, the only way to understand subtle organizational norms is to observe them through behavioral manifestations of the culture.

2. *Understanding others' behavior.* Effective managers have insights into people and their behavior. Since an organization's culture shapes its people's assumptions, values, and behavior,

you must work to understand cultural forces in the workplace. Perhaps a culture of competition is preventing people from working effectively as a team. Or maybe employee input is stifled because supervisors ask to be alerted to problems but reward workers who keep quiet. An awareness of culture helps you to understand people's motivations, standards of performance, and seemingly contradictory behavior.

3. *Managing intraorganizational conflicts.* Sometimes subgroups in an organization do not get along because they represent two very different cultures. Research and development specialists may be accustomed to a data-gathering, deliberate, slow, analytical type of environment and may not be able to work effectively with the action-oriented, fast-paced, flamboyant marketing people in the same company. An understanding of these different subcultures in your organization will lead to more realistic expectations of cross-functional teams and prepare you to handle intergroup conflicts.

4. *Coping with marketplace diversity and international business.* In a heterogeneous society, organizations employ and serve people who differ according to racial, gender, ethnic, religious, age, geographic, and lifestyle factors. Organizations that understand how culture affects people can provide more enlightened and nondiscriminatory places to work. You can use cultural information to market products and services more effectively and to meet the needs of a diverse clientele or customer base. For multinational corporations or executives who travel to different parts of the world to do business, an understanding of culture as it affects the workplace is essential.

5. *Shaping or redirecting organizational cultures.* If you want to take a proactive stance in shaping your company's image, values, and standards of behavior for employees, you must understand cultural forces in the workplace. Indeed, you shape organizational culture by most everything you do: the behaviors you show as a role model; your hiring, promotion, and termination decisions; what you pay attention to and reward; organizational creeds you create and stories you tell; organizational structures and policies you develop; and the physical space you occupy and allocate. Strategic planning or organizational development goals must be developed in light of the organizational culture.

Elements of Organizational Culture

Because an organization's culture derives from all its structural, procedural, and personnel aspects, the concept of culture is broad and elusive. There are identifiable elements, however. Managers interested in examining the culture of their organization should focus on these elements:

Values

Strong business leaders clearly indicate what they consider to be important. By communicating values—the underlying assumptions upon which organizations are based—you establish common goals and standards of behavior and help shape your organization's identity. By identifying the values of your corporate culture, you discover preferences for how the organization should be run and guidelines for individual behavior in the organization.

Values as clues to organizational culture can be discovered in a number of ways. Sometimes they are explicitly stated in company philosophies, creeds, or policy statements. A company's slogans and mottoes usually reveal the essence of its mission. In addition, you can analyze the physical environment created by an organization.

Communication

Every workplace culture will include assumptions about the correct ways for people to relate to each other. Indeed, the styles of interaction and rules governing relationships in an organization reveal much about its culture. Some cultures promote informal interaction, reward dissent, and encourage social relationships between employees. Other organizations allow communication only through a strict chain of command or even discourage disagreement.

To discover communication aspects of an organization's culture, pay attention to who communicates about what to whom. Culture dictates the topics worthy of communication in the workplace. An organization's culture can be characterized by the content, amount, and direction of its communication as well as by the nature of workplace relationships.

History

Corporate founders are frequently colorful characters whose visions shape the organizations they develop. Founding figures and leaders throughout an organization's history have a powerful influence on its culture. Major developments or crises chart its course and image. An organization's culture is the sum of the major leaders and events of its past.

Thus, to understand your organization's culture, you must learn its history. Just as a nation of people can appreciate its culture by learning its history, so organizational members can understand workplace culture through learning about significant people, events, and crises that affected the organization. Reading corporate histories, talking to veterans of the company, and listening to stories and legends can provide insights into present-day culture.

Symbols and Ceremonies

Organizations create objects and emblems to represent themselves. These contribute to an organizational identity. Employees can look to them as a source of pride, loyalty, and personal identity. Outsiders recognize companies by their symbols. Likewise, organizations stage many events for both insiders and outsiders that reveal their cultures. Company literature, advertisements, press releases, meetings, recognition ceremonies, and social events say something about the organizational culture.

To discover workplace culture through symbols, you can analyze company logos, mottos, and slogans. What image do they portray and what values do they embody? Decorations, artwork, or interior design in company facilities may be symbolic of organizational philosophies or attitudes. Documents such as annual reports, recruiting brochures, and employee handbooks serve symbolic as well as informative functions. Routine events such as departmental meetings or extravagant occurrences such as trade shows or stockholders meetings shed light on organizational culture.

Managing Organizational Culture

Astute managers are aware of the concept of culture and understand their roles in shaping or redirecting the cultures of their organizations. In essence, effectively managing a corporate culture means understanding it, consciously shaping it, and changing it, if necessary.

Understanding culture means recognizing the values, communication rules, history, symbols, and ceremonies of a particular organization and how they both affect and reflect everyday decisions and actions of people on the job. Paying attention to the more subtle aspects of the workplace, including both human and structural factors, provides a larger perspective on the organization. Enlightened managers do not underestimate the role of culture. They can articulate their organization's culture, point to its elements, and understand how culture influences their own and others' behavior.

Effective leaders of organizations realize that they can actively *shape the culture* of their companies. In many ways, business leadership is synonymous with the creation of organizational culture. Strong leaders have a vision of the type of organization they want to develop and they take steps to bring that vision to action. Through your own behavior, you provide role models of the values and practices you want others to embody. You reinforce your cultural vision every time you make decisions, delegate projects, reward performance, or preside over organizational events.

Rather than haphazardly affecting workplace culture through random actions and messages, wise managers build and shape the culture of their organizations through clear and consistent actions. The ability to shape organizational culture rather than be constrained by it can distinguish legendary from average leaders.

When organizational leaders set out to *change aspects of their organization's culture,* their motivation may stem from changing marketplace dynamics, organizational restructuring, or the need for more effective management styles. They can affect cultural change through such intervention strategies as organizational development, team building, or training. Leaders who seek to change the culture of an organization must realize the enormous commitment their goal requires and must follow certain basic tactics to succeed.

Because culture is so pervasive and deep-rooted, it is not easy to change. Change projects may take years to accomplish, cost considerable money, and try the patience of leaders and employees alike. External consultants are often necessary to help organizations embark on change and to cope with the resulting upheaval, confusion, and anxiety. Upper-level management must demonstrate visible commitment to change and must help others through the painful transition of organizational assumptions and values. A strong, visible person to spearhead a change project is necessary as a symbol and consensus builder. To accomplish change in an organization's culture, committed leaders must embrace the change process, equip the organization with skills for managing change, and have patience to let cultural change evolve over time.

New Organizational Cultures

Contemporary scholars of corporate culture point to evidence of a transformation in the American workplace. Some predict that traditional, hierarchical organizations with power centralized in the hands of a few will give way to decentralized, smaller, entrepreneurial organizations. Visions of this emerging work culture include information-oriented business with increased levels of productivity through the utilization of new technologies; more participation and involvement of employees especially through the use of telecommunication; smaller, highly motivated work units; egalitarian and flexible workplace structures; work environments that emphasize creativity, reward risk, and enhance the quality of life; and increased employee autonomy and control.

[*See also* Team Building, Change Management]

For Additional Information

Denison, Daniel. *Corporate Culture and Organizational Effectiveness.* New York: Wiley, 1990.

Kotter, John P., and James L. Heskett. *Corporate Culture and Performance.* New York: Free Press, 1992.

Lahiry, Sugato. "Building Commitment Through Organizational Culture." *Training and Development* 48, No. 4 (April 1994), pp. 50–52.

McAuley, John. "Exploring Issues in Culture and Competence." *Human Relations* 47, No. 4 (April 1994), pp. 417–30.

Orienting New Employees

Some companies go to great lengths to recruit and select the right employees for jobs and then fail to provide adequate job orientation. For many new employees, orientation consists of nothing more than a few introductions, a brief tour of the facility, and the suggestion that fellow employees can answer further questions later. Consequently, the first few days on the job are filled with tension, uncertainty, embarrassment, self-doubt, resentments, and pessimism about future success in the position. This bad start may spill over to affect long-term perceptions about the job and the company.

Instead, an effective orientation program should ease the employee into the organization, celebrate the new employer-employee relationship, and provide information vital to functioning productively in the organization. Orientation sessions may seem like a waste of time because the employee is not working, but the commitment to new employee orientation will pay for itself in less turnover and in more motivated, productive, and loyal employees.

New employees should receive two kinds of orientation training: orientation to the organization and orientation to the work unit and job. Each complements the other and contributes to a comprehensive new-employee orientation program. A discussion of the purposes and components of each follows.

Orientation to the Organization

The purpose of this information is to acquaint new hires with the nature of the organization—its structure, mission, philosophy, and goals. Also, new employees should learn their responsibilities to the organization and the organization's responsibilities to them. This aspect of orientation gives them a sense of organizational identity. The specific topics of an organizational orientation should include:

1. *Company history.* Explain the founding of your company, its progress, accomplishments, key figures, and the path it took to its present status. This helps new employees see the larger picture and feel proud to be affiliated with the company.

2. *Nature of the industry or profession.* Explain how the organization fits into the overall picture of the industry or profession. This acquaints employees with the forces and constraints affecting the organization and can provide background information about why the company functions as it does.

3. *Organizational philosophy, mission, and structure.* The new employee should learn about the guiding principles of the organization. A sense of the organizational structure should be provided. Understanding the organizational chart will help new hires see how they fit into its structure. An introduction to the organization's philosophy, mission, and structure provides a sense of identity, helps shape work values, and creates pride in and loyalty to the organization.

4. *Employment benefits.* New employees should be made aware of the various benefits provided by the organization, such as medical insurance, life insurance, sick leave, vacations, holidays, retirement plans, education and training, and child care. New hires should be aware of their benefits options, and should schedule an individual appointment with a benefits counselor to make decisions and to process paperwork.

5. *Organizational policies and procedures.* These are general rules about how the company functions. For example, statements should be made about affirmative action and equal employment opportunity (EEO) policies, performance standards and evaluation processes, safety and security practices, and any standards regarding salary increases and promotions. New hires should acquire a sense of what is considered acceptable behavior in the workplace.

6. *Facility tour and introduction to key people.* It is essential for new employees to see how the organization operates, learn their way around the physical facility, and be able to associate names with faces of key people. They should be escorted to all departments, and receive a brief statement about the function of each department and the interrelationships of departments. The tour should point out the location of employee lounges, lunch rooms, vending machines, and other pertinent areas, such as exercise rooms, lockers, or medical or child-care facilities.

During the orientation program, new hires should receive an employee handbook that typically includes information about company history, philosophy, mission, structure, policies, procedures, and benefits. The personnel department should provide brochures about various benefits and distribute policy manuals, facility maps, and organizational directories. New employees may be overwhelmed with the amount of information provided in orientation sessions. Written materials to read at home or to consult later can ease the feeling of information overload. All aspects of organizational information are not pertinent to new employees on the first day of work. They are more concerned with their daily jobs duties. However, general information about the organization provides a framework for doing a job and will interest the new employee more after a few days in the organization. Thus, it is important that the employee have written materials to consult and avenues for asking questions both during and after the formal orientation program.

Orientation to the Department and the Job

Once the new employee has been introduced to the organization, it is time to provide an orientation to the particular work unit and job duties. This session should take place in the work unit and be conducted by a member of that department. The topics to be covered in the departmental orientation typically include:

1. *Department mission and relationship to the organization.* What are the responsibilities of the department? What is its role and

how does that role relate to the overall organizational mission? The new employee should learn what the work unit does in the short and long term, and how work flows into and out of this work unit. It is important to explain how the work in this unit affects and is affected by work done in other units.

2. *Departmental structure.* Who is in charge of what in the department? Who supervises whom? New employees should be aware of their reporting relationship and, in the case of supervisory positions, should know what employees they supervise.

3. *Work supplies.* The person doing the departmental orientation must show new employees their work station or office and explain where to get necessary supplies, tools, or equipment; the phone system; and policies regarding the use of office equipment or clerical staff.

4. *Job description and standards of performance.* Employees should know exactly what they are responsible and accountable for. What tasks are they expected to perform in the new job? How are they to complete their job duties? What are acceptable standards of performance? By what criteria will their job performance be measured? During the departmental orientation, they should be guided through the actual work performance. Perhaps they can watch others perform the job and then do it themselves with follow-up coaching. Information about work priorities should be provided. Trainees should be encouraged to ask questions and be given ample feedback by supervisors.

One method of orienting new employees to the job is to provide a work buddy or coach, who provides on-the-job training for a limited period of time. This role must be taken seriously and far surpasses the question-answering role that colleagues often perform for new hires. Of course, the buddy must show excellent work performance and be skilled as a teacher or coach

5. *Work schedule.* Departmental orientation sessions should acquaint new employees with expectations about work hours: starting and stopping time, lunch and coffee breaks, overtime, and scheduling sick days and vacations.

6. *Departmental policies.* New employees will need to know work unit rules about dress codes, smoking, personal calls,

visitors, and disciplinary and grievance procedures. They should be apprised about norms of acceptable and unacceptable behavior in the work unit.

Interspersed with all the orientation information, there should be attempts at hospitality and rapport building. Small talk about non-work-related topics can ease the stress of those first few days on the job. New employees should be invited to lunch during the orientation period. In short, they should feel special and welcome during the first few days on the job. The more coworkers take new employees under their wing, the more successful and formal orientation program will be.

Do's and Don'ts of New-Employee Orientation

1. *Don't neglect new-employee orientation.* Take the time to provide a comprehensive introduction to the company and to the job, which will reduce misinformation and job errors and create a more satisfied and productive worker.

2. *Provide follow-up to orientation training.* Don't think that a new employee is acclimated after a few days or weeks. Provide detailed information, at a later time, about policies and procedures and company benefits. Schedule several feedback sessions about job performance. Give new employees plenty of opportunity to ask questions, even months into the job tenure.

3. *Make orientation exciting.* Since this is the introduction to the firm and to the job, the first impression should be positive. Orientation should not entail an endless stream of factual information. Group orientation sessions for all new hires in the company can lend an air of excitement to the process. Social events mixed with various formats for presenting information can have a memorable and beneficial impact. Make sure speakers are dynamic, discussions are lively, tours are productive, and orientation leaders are helpful and friendly. Orientation should make new hires happy about their decision to join the organization and make them look forward to beginning their actual work.

4. *Don't sour new employees.* All organizations have problems, drawbacks, and troublesome people. Orientation is no the time

to alert new hires to problems or to make disparaging remarks about the company or any of its people.

5. *Hold separate orientation sessions for exempt and nonexempt employees.* While information about company history, philosophy, and mission will be applicable to all levels of employees, much of the information and tone of orientation sessions will vary according to employee status. Supervisors and managers may be more interested in organizational structure, training opportunities, and career advancement issues than nonexempt employees would be. Information on policies, rules, and disciplinary procedures may vary across employee groups. Benefits likely will differ. Rather than trying to orient diverse employees together, tailor separate sessions to meet specific needs.

6. *Solicit feedback about orientation effectiveness.* New hires should provide feedback to orientation leaders about the effectiveness of both organizational and departmental information sessions. Participants should indicate to what extent their needs were met and their questions answered during the orientation period. The input should be used to revise subsequent orientation training.

[*See also* Training]

For Additional Information

Arthur, Diane. *Recruiting, Interviewing, Selecting, and Orienting New Employees.* New York: AMACOM, 1991.

Part-Time, Temporary, and Contingent Workers

Part-time, temporary, and contingent workers are becoming a more prevalent and important part of the U.S. workforce. For this reason, organizations need to learn how to better manage these employees. We use the term *contingent worker* here to mean anyone who is not a permanent, full-time employee in the organization. Independent contractors who provide services to a variety of companies and who do not desire permanent work in one organization are a type of contingent worker.

Likewise, interim or seasonal workers brought into a company to handle projects or peak work loads are another example of contingent workers. Employees provided by temporary services agencies and part-time employees may also be considered part of the contingent workforce. Numerous terms, including *leased employees, contract employees, complementary workers, just-in-time employees, outsourced labor,* and *supplementary workers,* are used to refer to this category of personnel.

At one time, temporary or part-time employees were found only in clerical or low-level positions. This is no longer the case. Contingent workers today typically include professionals, such as doctors, nurses, lawyers, scientists, engineers, professors, financial analysts, and business executives, as well as secretaries, data processors, computer programmers, and retail sales people. In some cases, CEOs or CFOs may be brought into an organization on a temporary or contingent basis. There is hardly an occupation that has not developed its share of contingent workers.

Prevalence of Contingent Workers

The Bureau of Labor Statistics estimates that about 25 percent of the U.S. labor force consists of contingent workers. This is the fastest-growing segment of the labor market. Indeed, since 1980, the number of contingent workers has grown three times faster than the labor force as a whole. It is difficult to accurately determine the numbers of contingent workers, but estimates do exist. The National Association of Temporary Workers reports that there are about 1.5 million temporary workers; about 24 percent of those are interim professionals. There are about 21.5 million part-time workers, with the majority being voluntary part-timers, according to Bureau of Labor Statistics data. An approximate 10 million independent contractors can be added to this mix, according to General Accounting Office reports. By any estimate, contingent workers constitute a sizable portion of the U.S. workforce.

Why Organizations Use Contingent Workers

There are many factors accounting for the high use of contingent workers, related to issues of organizational size and structure, finances, and employment philosophy.

1. *Flexible staffing ability.* The size and structure of organizations continue to evolve, with organizational downsizing creating leaner companies. When business demands warrant adding personnel, companies are more likely to hire temporary workers, whom they can discharge easily during economic downturns rather than adding to their permanent ranks.

Also, because of corporate downsizing, there are more qualified people seeking work on an interim basis. Indeed, it is less risky to use contingent employees than to hire permanent employees when business climates are uncertain. Using contingent workers allows organizations to respond flexibly to the ever-changing marketplace.

2. *Lower costs.* There are many financial incentives for organizations to expand their number of contingent workers. With contingent workers, a company pays for labor only when it needs it. An organization can rapidly expand and contract the size of its workforce through contingent staffing and thereby contain its personnel costs while linking payroll costs directly to workload. Typically there are no benefits costs or reduced benefits costs associated with a contingent workforce. Because temporary and part-time workers receive few benefits, this can be an enormous savings. Hiring temporary employees through an agency also saves companies recruitment, selection, and training expenses. The agency typically bears the costs of advertising the positions, screening applicants, and training new hires.

3. *Greater freedom.* The increase in temporary and part-time employees is also related to new individual and societal philosophies of employment. The nature of the relationship between employers and employees has changed greatly in recent years. Whereas employees used to seek lifetime employment in one field or even with one company, many people today prefer to pursue various careers in a lifetime. They enjoy the freedom and the flexibility of working for multiple companies on a part-time or temporary basis.

Contingent work arrangements can appeal in particular to entrepreneurs, free spirits, college students, young mothers, and retirees. Of course, one can question whether these changing philosophies of employment result from increases in contingent work or have created the phenomenon of a contingent workforce. Whatever the impetus for change, it is clear that more individuals are willing to join the contingent workforce and, in some cases, prefer this type of employment.

Advantages and Disadvantages to Organizations

Obviously, companies see many advantages in using part-time and temporary workers. Studies that have analyzed the role of contingent workers reveal that there are both advantages and disadvantages to organizations in using these types of employees.

In addition to the flexibility and financial benefits, some companies make contingent employment *a path to regular employment*. Employers can observe the skills of a contract worker and assess the employee-organizational fit before offering that employee a permanent position. By using contract employees in such a probationary period, employers can reduce the costs and risks of employee selection.

The *risks of litigation* may be reduced when using contingent workers. If the individual is defined as an employee of the agency providing contingent workers, and not as an employee of the company, then the company's liability for discrimination or wrongful discharge claims is reduced.

Opinions differ on whether contingent employees are *more or less productive* than their regular-employee counterparts. In many cases, temporary employees are less experienced in the jobs they are performing, less familiar with the organization in which they are working, and less committed to the organization. These factors, coupled with a second-class status in many organizations, less job security, and fewer benefits, would seem to make them less productive than regular employees.

On the other hand, contingent workers may increase an organization's productivity because they are paid only when they are working. Unlike regular workers, they are off the payroll when the lack of work dictates. And contingent workers are less likely to be involved in office gossip and politics. A Bureau of Labor Statistics study shows that temporary workers produce about two more hours of work per day than do their counterparts holding regular positions.

There are some clear disadvantages in using contingent workers. Almost all analyses report *tension* between contingent and regular employees in an organization. Regular employees resent what they perceive to be an invasion of temporary workers who perform less, address more questions to permanent employees, and threaten their job security. Many employees today fear that they will be replaced with cheaper contingent workers. Some forecasters predict a resurgence in unionism as more regular employees watch full-time, permanent jobs erode and the numbers of poorly treated contingent workers rise.

Effectively Using Contingent Workers

There are four steps for using contingent workers for maximum results.

1. *Determine your needs.* The organization needs to develop a staffing plan related to the use of both regular employees and contingent employees. The company should define what tasks need to be performed by regular employees and what tasks could be performed by part-time or temporary personnel. Such planning helps determine the ideal ratio of regular to contingent workers and eliminates hiring on an emergency basis. Most organizations can anticipate the general volume of work, the typical time needed to complete work, and the cyclical nature of work, and they can plan accordingly, even for contingent workforce needs.

2. *Decide whether to use an agency.* After developing a staffing plan, organizations should carefully hire contingent workers or carefully select the employment agency that will provide the temporary employees. The question of whether to hire directly or to use the services of a temporary employment agency is a complex one, affected by financial, legal, and other human resources factors. With the proliferation of temporary services agencies to provide professional and entry-level employees of all types, many organizations find it more convenient and cost-effective to work with an agency. As stated previously, the costs of employee selection and training are absorbed by the agency.

The employer's liability regarding EEO requirements depends on how the employee's status is defined and how the relationships are structured among the employee, the agency, and the organization. Companies are advised to consult an attorney to carefully define such relationships and to screen agencies for past practices of discriminatory conduct.

In small human resources departments, or when hiring needs are very specialized, using an employment agency can be preferable to directly hiring contingent workers. Most agencies have greater resources than would be available in house for identifying and screening job candidates.

3. *Review possible benefits to be offered.* A consideration in hiring contingent workers is the extent and nature of any benefits to be provided by the organization. Some companies provide prorated benefits, especially for long-term part-timers or for contingent workers on specialized projects. It should be noted that some employment agencies provide some benefits as well.

4. *Make them feel at home.* After the contingent workers are in place, it is important that organizations avoid creating a two-tiered workforce, with regular employees getting choice assignments and contingent employees getting the worst projects. Contingent workers should be treated as an integral part of the workforce. This means they should be involved in the social network of the organization; they should be supervised to the same extent as regular employees are; they should have opportunities for input into decision making, training, and advancement. Such policies help lessen antagonism between regular and contingent employees.

Ideally, contingent and regular employees should not be readily identifiable in an organization. Only if contingent employees are treated as second-class citizens it will be apparent who falls into which category of employment. Distinguishing regular and contingent workers only by their payroll classification, and not by the nature of the work performed or the nature of treatment received, will help to create one cohesive, productive workforce.

Forecasts indicate that use of contingent employees will continue. It is in the best interests of all organizations, then, to effectively and humanely manage the contingent workforce so that these employees can be as satisfied and as productive as possible.

[*See also* Coaching Employees; Delegation and Empowerment; Motivation; Organizational Culture; Orienting New Employees; Terminating Employees and Downsizing; Training; Turnover]

For Additional Information

Caudron, Shari. "Contingent Workforce Spurs HR Planning." *Personnel Journal,* July 1994, pp. 52–60.

Ettorre, Barbara. "The Contingent Workforce Moves Mainstream." *Management Review*, February 1994, pp. 8–16.

Geber, Beverly. "The Flexible Workforce: Using Contingent Workers Wisely and Humanely." *Training* (December 1993), pp. 23–30.

Nollen, Stanley, and Helen Axel. *Managing Contingent Workers: How to Reap the Benefits and Reduce the Risks.* New York: AMACOM, 1995.

Olmsted, Barney, and Suzanne Smith. *Creating a Flexible Workplace: How to Select and Manage Alternative Work Options.* New York: AMACOM, 1994.

Performance Appraisal

Appraising performance is the act of observing and evaluating an employee's work behavior and accomplishments, with the purpose of measuring real performance against expected performance. Such analysis aids in making decisions about the employee concerning wages, salary, and benefits; promotion, demotion, transfer, or termination actions; and counseling, training, or career-development options. Systematic methods of identifying and measuring performance can assist human resources planning and improve an employee's future performance.

Many benefits result from an effective performance appraisal system. Organizations can control marginal performance, reduce losses from ineffective performance, and make more efficient use of personnel. Individuals can realize rewards for effective performance, and have a clear understanding of their career pathing.

Who Should Evaluate Performance?

There are various options for determining who will perform the assessment. Possibilities include immediate supervisors, self-appraisal, peer review, subordinate review, evaluation committees, personnel department staff, training department staff, and external sources. An organization can use one or any combination of these sources to conduct performance appraisals.

Probably the most common evaluator of performance is the employee's immediate supervisor. Employers regard supervisors as legitimate performance evaluators who are qualified to make career development-decisions.

Self-appraisals contribute to employee satisfaction with the evaluation process. When employees participate in setting performance goals, determining evaluation criteria, rating themselves, and discussing their performance with supervisors, they tend to be less defensive about appraisals and show greater improvement in performance.

Employee evaluations of supervisors and managers allow for multiple ratings and encourage employees to view workplace demands through the eyes of their supervisors. These workers are in an excellent position to comment on their supervisor's leadership ability, and the method promotes an environment of participation and provides valuable feedback to supervisors. On the other hand, some supervisors are threatened by employee evaluations and apply negative sanctions to the work group for poor reviews. On the other hand, employees may inflate ratings because they fear reprisals. Also, workers may not fully understand a supervisor's job requirements or may emphasize criteria relevant to their own relationship with the supervisor. Anonymity may remedy some of these conditions.

360 Degree Reviews

With greater frequency, employers are utilizing the 360 degree review. This is a process by which all internal people having contact with the person being reviewed give appraisal input. The method works well when reviewing all levels of management. In fact, it works quite well even when appraising the performance of senior managers. Contact people complete a questionnaire that includes specific open-ended questions linked to the manager's effectiveness and style. All input is based on observation through direct contact. Often consultants help administer the process and work with managers to develop an action plan for communicating results.

External evaluators, such as consultants or assessment-center raters, can also conduct performance appraisals. While they often employ standardized techniques that are statistically accurate and legally protected, external evaluators are costly and typically evaluate behavior in hypothetical rather than actual situations.

Peer Appraisals

Peers often have firsthand knowledge of one another's perform-ance. Research has shown peer appraisals to be reliable and valid predictors of job performance. The average of several peer ratings is probably more reliable than a single rating, however. Potential problems include the unwillingness of peers to evaluate one another, friendship biases, and competition within the work group. In spite of these potential problems, often employees will respond more earnestly to peer feedback than to management or supervisory feedback, since the power disadvantage is removed.

Additionally, some peer reviews remove the burden of deter-mining raises as the most important issue of the appraisal proc-ess. Experts believe that discussion of raises and promotions should be separate from performance appraisal discussions. They believe that focusing on raises muddies the waters of performance review talks. In other words, appraisal discussions must focus on past performance in view of expectations and needed behavioral modifications to meet future expectations. Simply put, talks on raises do not impact either phase of appraisal discussions. Such talk may demotivate an employee if he or she does not get a raise or the level of raise expected. Instead, feedback should target work performance relative to work demands and expectations. The peer review, or any review which does not deal with raises, reduces the likelihood that the employee will respond with, "So what! Did I get my raise?"—a remark so often heard in traditional appraisal discussions.

Performance Appraisal Techniques

Just as there are many options for deciding who should rate performance, there are numerous techniques for structuring and guiding a performance appraisal. Explanations, advantages, and disadvantages will be presented for the following common performance appraisal methods, such as trait-based measures, narrative essays, the critical-incident technique, checklists, graphic rating scales, behaviorally anchored rating scales, cost-related outcomes, and management by objectives.

Trait-Based Measures

In some organizations, performance appraisals are based on personal qualities or traits. Common traits included in performance evaluation forms are dependability, honesty, creativity, resourcefulness, integrity, decisiveness, judgment, tact, initiative, leadership, cooperation, enthusiasm, personality, and loyalty. The assumption underlying this approach is that such traits manifest themselves on the job and affect work performance. Raters indicate their perceptions of the employee regarding these factors via a checklist, yes/no scale, or graphic rating scale indicating a relative quantity of the trait.

As might be expected, there is ample room for error when you use trait-based measures. Raters may vary considerably in their perceptions or understandings of these traits, be forced into the role of judge, and have difficulty defending their decisions. By what criteria does a person award a numerical value of 3 versus 4 for creativity on a five-point scale, for example? Judgments based on trait-based measures are subjective and prone to litigation. Research shows that high ratings on trait-based measures do not necessarily correlate with good job performance. Organizations would be wise to use trait-based items sparingly, perhaps in conjunction with other techniques, or avoid them altogether in performance evaluations.

Narrative Essays

Essay appraisals involve a written description of an employee's qualities, attitudes, and behavior. The appraiser, who is familiar with the employee's performance, produces an unstructured, candid statement about the employee's strengths, weaknesses, and areas needing improvement. The method provides specific performance feedback to employees and can be a springboard for communication between a supervisor and an employee, as well as a catalyst for goal setting and individual development. Of course, the essay method is subjective, very questionable legally, and dependent on the appraiser's writing skills. Indeed, certain statements written by people unfamiliar with affirmative action laws may be difficult to defend in court or before federal, state, or local regulatory commissions.

Critical-Incident Technique

With this method, the supervisor makes periodic notations of important performance actions, both positive and negative, of employees. In essence, the supervisor develops files of effective and ineffective actions or performance by employees. The files can help jog the memory during a performance review, can give employees meaningful feedback about specific work-related behavior, can serve as the basis for completing other performance appraisal instruments, and can provide written documentation for personnel decisions in the event of appeals or litigation.

This is a time-consuming technique when performed conscientiously for all employees, however. Also, supervisors may be biased in what they choose to record, and for whom. They may record more negative incidents for a disliked employee or fail to document poor performance of a well-liked employee. Yet in a litigious environment, it is wise to have documentation to base any personnel decision, including performance appraisals.

Checklists

Checklists can range from lists of traits to descriptive statements of job-related behavior. The appraiser indicates with a check mark the traits employees manifest or job-related behaviors employees perform. Because a checklist ensures that all employees are assessed on the same items, comparisons to standard are easier. The more specific and descriptive the items are on the checklist, the more objective the method is likely to be. Checking a form to indicate whether an employee has "initiative," for example, requires much interpretation on the part of the evaluator. Checking an option on a continuum of "initiative" indicators, however, depends more on observation of an employee's behavior than on subjective judgment. Such categories on a checklist might include (1) "Needs substantial encouragement and direction in beginning projects," (2) "Starts some projects with minor prodding," and (3) "Launches new projects through individual motivation."

Graphic Rating Scales

Graphic rating scales contain a number of job-performance qualities and characteristics worded into statements. The appraiser typically responds in one of two ways: (1) how frequently the employee demonstrates the behavior or quality (always, often, sometimes, rarely, never), or (2) the extent of agreement with a descriptive statement about the employee (strongly agree, agree, undecided, disagree, strongly disagree). Examples of statements include "The manager takes corrective action to solve poor performance problems of subordinates," "The manager motivates subordinates to perform their jobs well," or "The manager meets reporting deadlines."

The items on graphic rating scales typically involve job behaviors rather than generalized traits. In that respect, they are more objective than some other evaluation techniques. Use specific statements, for example, of general "corrective actions," such as "Gives employees oral feedback about poor performance," "Sets goals with employees to improve performance," or "Coaches employees to improve work performance." Graphic rating scales constructed carefully, and used with reliability and validity data, can provide an efficient, standardized, and legally sound means of structuring performance evaluations. Graphic rating scales work well with peer reviews and 360 degree reviews.

Behaviorally Anchored Rating Scales

The behaviorally anchored rating scales (BARS) is a type of graphic rating system with specific behavioral descriptions for each point along the scale. The descriptions are anchors to aid the appraiser in defining outstanding, good, average, or poor performance.

Ideally, both evaluators and employees to be rated contribute to the development of the scale, which is a complex process essentially involving the collection of incidents describing competent, average, and poor performance of a particular job; categorization of those incidents into overall performance dimensions (technical ability, communication skills, leadership, and so on); and assignment of numerical values that translate into anchors along a continuum.

The following is an example of an item from a BARS for a training manager:

Dimension: Organizational skills

3 Excellent:	Follows a training outline; presents material in logical units; ties one idea into the next; summarizes information often.
2 Average:	Prepares a training outline but only follows it occasionally; presents material in no particular order; ties some ideas to others; summarizes information at times.
1 Poor:	Neither provides nor follows a training outline; presents material in random order; ideas seem unrelated to each other; rambles.

There are both advantages and disadvantages to the BARS method. The scales tend to be precise and objective because there are behavioral anchors for each decision option. There is little room for inference about what constitutes excellent, average, or poor behavior on a certain dimension of a particular job. The anchor descriptions, because they are created by people familiar with the job, tend to be accurate illustrations of the range of job performance. The descriptions use actual job terminology. However, BARS are time-consuming to develop for every job in an organization. Also, to be legally defensible, ratings must be backed by documentation for specific instances in which the employee performed or failed to perform a certain action.

Cost-Related Outcomes

This technique uses quantitative measures of performance outcomes or results. Criteria might include sales volume, claims processed, reports written, units produced, turnover rate, absences, and accidents, which can serve as absolute indicators of an individual's, a department's, or an organization's cost/revenue/profitability effectiveness. Measurement is very precise and objective.

The problem is that not all jobs or all aspects of jobs lend themselves to quantitative measures. How does one quantify problem solving or employee-development activities, for example? Nor do cost-related outcomes indicate how well something was done; they just tell how often something was done. A variety of factors beyond an employee's control can affect such quantitative criteria. But for jobs that lend themselves to cost-outcome criteria, such as sales, this method of performance appraisal may be effective when combined with other measures.

Management by Objectives

Management by objectives (MBO) is a technique whereby supervisors and subordinates mutually agree on measurable performance goals for a certain period. They develop plans of action and specify resources for achieving the goals. Then they monitor progress and evaluate goal achievement in a performance-review session.

Problems with MBO can occur if supervisors and employees disagree on performance goals for a given time period. Whose goals become the evaluation criteria? Also, MBO focuses on a number of small, specific accomplishments to the exclusion of broader, less measurable long-range objectives. Finally, resources must be provided for the attainment of goals. Otherwise, an employee's failure to meet objectives may be due to external forces, and the performance appraisals become unfair.

Problems With Performance Appraisals

Organizations must be conscientious about using an appraisal technique that is fair, objective, and related to the job requirements of the individual being evaluated. Nevertheless, because performance appraisals are based on human judgment, they are prone to subjectivity and error. In order to make the appraisal process as effective as possible, you will want to be aware of these common problems:

- Appraiser inflates ratings in a desire to be accepted, which interferes with objectivity.
- There may be friendship between appraiser and person being appraised.
- Some appraisers are reluctant to make negative evaluations of an employee's performance for fear of violent reactions, reprisal, or making their own departments look bad.
- Appraisers have fallible memories and fail to document behaviors.
- Appraisers often lack motivation to do a task they strongly dislike.
- Appraiser's often lack the skill or training to complete and communicate performance appraisals.
- There is little opportunity to observe employee behavior.
- Ranking employees is limiting and self-defeating to the organization while demotivating to many employees.*
- Errors occur because of unintentional bias or overt discrimination based on the sex, race, age, religion, political ideology, or any of a number of factors of the employee.
- Appraisers may increase a grade in order to appease an employee or because the employee needs a raise or favorable appraisal.
- A halo effect occurs when a strong perception of the employee's performance in one area distorts the appraiser's judgment in other areas. For instance, perceiving an employee as motivated may lead to erroneous judgment that the employee is competent.
- A spillover effect occurs when conclusions from a past

---

*Several experts on total quality, including the late Dr. W. Edwards Deming, believe that ranking people is grossly counterproductive. Rather than encouraging companywide excellence, ranking unnaturally limits high achievements to a few, thus disregarding the many. Therefore, an increasing number of companies are employing peer review and 360 degree reviews, without discussion of ranking or raises.

performance appraisal interfere with judgments on the current appraisal.

- A status effect is documentable when people in higher-status jobs automatically receive better ratings than people in lower-status jobs.
- A central-tendency effect refers to appraisers' judging all employees at the middle or average point on all performance dimensions on a rating scale.
- Sometimes appraisers are overly harsh or overly lenient in their evaluations.

Research shows that appraisers who receive training in how to conduct performance appraisals do a better job than do untrained appraisers. Organizations committed to the performance appraisal process should equip their appraisers with the knowledge and skills to be effective evaluators.

The Need for Documentation

There are many reasons why performance appraisals should be supported with thorough written documentation. Documentation, consisting of notes and files of specific actions during a review period, serves as a reminder at the time of a formal appraisal and guides the appraiser to an accurate judgment. Also, the appraiser can provide specific examples to clarify points and help employees understand the ratings. Thus, employees know not only how they were rated but why they received those ratings. Finally, and perhaps most important, proper documentation is imperative when you have to defend job evaluations and decisions legally.

The following guidelines should be followed to achieve proper and thorough documentation:

1. *Be fair.* Document all major job behaviors, not just positive or negative ones. Trying to build a case against an employee or showing favoritism toward an employee will be seen as prejudice. Logically, any employee file should include instances of good and bad behavior.

2. *State facts, not opinions.* The file should include examples of observable behavior, not inferences of attitudes or motives.
3. *Be timely.* Document actions when they occur.
4. *Keep documentation on all subordinates.* Keeping performance records just for poor performers could be viewed as unfair. It is important to keep thorough and balanced documentation on all employees.
5. *Be consistent.* Make documentation match your oral comments and actions.

Legal Considerations

Federal and state employee statutes, as well as court decisions, point to the following nine prescriptions for performance appraisal practices:

1. The appraisal process should be formalized, standardized, communicated more than once annually, and as objective as possible
2. The criteria in a performance appraisal method should be as job related as possible, based on a formal job analysis for all employment positions. Ratings should not be based on attributes of the employee.
3. Appraisal ratings should be uncontaminated (not affected by factors outside of the employee's control) and nondeficient (important aspects of job behavior are not omitted).
4. Employees must be aware of the performance standards to which they will be held accountable.
5. Evaluators should have substantial opportunities to observe job-related behaviors of the employees they appraise.
6. The validity of ratings should be determined. Organizations whose performance appraisal systems are questioned must show that ratings are valid reflections of past behavior and valid predictions of future behavior. It is wise to have specialists in psychometric testing document the adequacy of your performance appraisal system.

7. When possible, more than one appraiser should be used.
8. Documentation to support ratings should be kept.
9. Employees should have the recourse of a formal appeal process. Assure employees that using the appeals process will not result in punitive actions.

The Performance Interview: Feedback to Employees

The supervisor and employee should engage in an honest, two-way discussion about the latter's performance and set performance goals for the future. The interview process can be divided into three phases: preparation, communication, and follow-up.

Preparation

The appraiser should set a time, place, and agenda for the appraisal interview and notify the employee of those details. Both parties should have sufficient time to prepare for the appraisal interview. If self-review is part of the process, the employee will need time to complete a self-rating scale or set performance goals, in the case of an MBO approach. The appraiser must gather necessary data and complete appraisal forms.

The interview should be conducted in a private and comfortable location, preferably a neutral site, for the session. There should be enough time for both parties to discuss all points without feeling rushed. The appraiser should consider how to deliver feedback, how to handle employee reactions, and how to effectively coach for improved work performance.

Communication

The supervisor should try to put the employee at ease, discuss the purpose and agenda for the meeting, and then get to the information about job performance. Comments about job performance should be specific and illustrated with examples. Basically, the appraiser evaluates the employee's job performance against objectives and standards that have already been agreed to by the employee. If self-review has occurred, the supervisor and employee should examine and try to clarify areas of discrepancy in ratings. Together, in a problem-solving format, the two parties should discern causes for variations in ratings or causes for below-standard results.

The appraiser must be skilled in giving constructive criticism, showing empathy, listening, probing, managing conflict, and avoiding defensiveness. An appraiser skilled in interpersonal communication will be nonthreatening, sensitive, objective, firm, composed, and helpful in the interview.

After communicating ratings on the various dimensions, the supervisor moves on to plans for development. Areas needing improvement should be discussed, one at a time. Most important, the supervisor and employee should agree on work objectives for the next period and determine how each of them will contribute to meeting the goals. To conclude the interview, the supervisor summarizes what was discussed, what was agreed to, and what will happen next.

Follow-up

The appraiser should record all pertinent information as soon as possible after the interview. This includes an objective account of the information exchanged as well as personal reactions and impressions of the interview climate and tone. Both parties should keep written agreement of the understandings reached, actions planned, and commitments made.

Informal Appraisals

Although the formal performance appraisal process is a crucial aspect of all organizations, it should exist within a larger appraisal system. It is not enough to give performance feedback at periodic intervals, such as once or twice a year. Informal discussions of job goals and performance results, initiated by either the supervisor or the subordinate, should be a daily routine of the supervisor-employee relationship.

[*See also* Coaching Employees; Feedback; Interviewing]

For Additional Information

Allen, Peter. "Designing and Implementing an Effective Performance Appraisal System." *Review of Business* 16 No. 2 (Winter 1994), pp. 3–8.

Mohrman, Allan M. *Designing Performance Appraisal Systems: Aligning Appraisals and Organizational Realities.* San Francisco: Jossey-Bass, 1989.

Sachs, Randi T. *Productive Performance Appraisals.* New York: AMACOM, 1992.

Weiss, Donald H. *Fair, Square and Legal,* 2nd ed. New York: AMACOM, 1995.

Politics in Organizations

Everyone in an organization is aware of the concept of organizational politics. Intuitively, managers realize the need to have political savvy for surviving and thriving in an organization. But just what is organizational politics? And how does a politically astute manager behave? Being competent at organizational politics means understanding the concept of workplace politics, recognizing the ways that politics functions in organizations, and adopting appropriate behaviors to avoid political blunders in your organization.

The concept of being political in a workplace can have various meanings. Managers who are skilled in promoting themselves up the organizational ladder and in gaining power can be considered politically shrewd. Being political can mean getting your views, actions, or contributions recognized and accepted. Politically astute employees tend to be well-liked and possess much credibility. They see to it that their ideas are implemented and that they have many loyal followers. They have much influence on the organization, regardless of whether they hold key leadership positions.

Because of the ways in which organizational politics operates, the concept is somewhat amorphous. Politics is like a persistent but elusive undercurrent in the workplace. It operates with subtlety, below the surface. It is not explicit, and therefore not easy to describe or to grasp. Subtlety is one of the characteristics that makes political behavior successful. Someone who is blatantly trying to influence others or to gain power will meet with resistance. Attempting the same behavior inconspicuously will be more successful. For example, we are aware of the persuasive goal when a colleague is making a presentation in support of a pet project. We assume a critical posture and expect to question the validity of the proposal. The speaker, by being obvious in the influence attempt, will meet with resistance. But subtle attempts at influence, such as repeatedly portraying the project in a good light through brief comments exchanged in the hall or at lunch, may be powerful. Because you see these remarks as informational rather than persuasive, you will be less resistant and gradually become a proponent of the project.

Another characteristic of organizational politics is its pervasiveness. Political undercurrents exist in all organizations, though organizations vary in the extent to which political behavior is explicit and observable. But to deny the existence of politics in a workplace is to be naïve. If you think that a political atmosphere does not exist in your organization, then probably you have been overlooking or misinterpreting some signs. Because influence, power, and hierarchical structures characterize organizational life, political behavior is inevitable. Anytime you talk informally in the workplace, you have the opportunity to promote yourself and your projects. Such influence occurs naturally, casually, and almost imperceptibly during interpersonal conversations. If politics entails affecting others' perceptions of us and our work in order to gain credibility and power, then everything we do is political. Managers who understand the nature of politics in their organizations can see its pervasiveness.

In addition to being subtle and pervasive, organizational politics can be positive. Many of us think of workplace politics as devious and manipulative. Some managers leave certain organizations because they find the politics to be too stressful or destructive. But political behavior is not necessarily devious, back-biting actions, which are merely one form of organizational politics. For some reason, workplace politics has come to be equated with self-serving actions that necessarily hurt others or the organization. It is important to realize that organizational politics can be positive. Presenting accurate information behind the scenes to advance yourself or your project is both ethical and appropriate. Perhaps organizational politics becomes negative when false information is presented, when others are slandered, or when too much political activity interferes with work.

Many would argue that political savvy is necessary for managerial success. Technical competence alone does not ensure career advancement. Competent work, combined with the ability to influence others while not offending them, is the hallmark of successful managers. You must be able to sell yourself and your ideas both publicly and behind the scenes. Without an understanding of the political dynamics of your organization, you violate unwritten rules, undermine your own projects, and hinder your credibility and career opportunities.

By realizing the subtle, pervasive, necessary, and often positive nature of organizational politics, you will be well on your way to developing political awareness. Each organization has its own political rules of conduct. By being patient, cautious, and observant, you can learn to recognize and employ behavior that is appropriate to your particular workplace. In addition, there are some general guidelines for practicing organizational politics in most any workplace:

1. *Pay your dues.* You should not expect to receive any favors or support until you have contributed in significant ways to your department or organization. This is especially important advice for organizational newcomers. You earn credibility, support, and the right to influence others by working hard and demonstrating your trustworthiness. By accepting unpleasant tasks, assisting others, and working extra hours initially, you build up a reserve of credit for advancing yourself and your goals later on.

2. *Listen and observe.* Because the political atmosphere is implicit and subtle in most organizations, skills of listening and observing are important. By listening, you can notice who advances what ideas, who supports whom, what subtle suggestions are made, and what topics are awkward. Keen observation can reveal what projects receive high priority, where informal lines of communication occur, and what the nature is of alliances and animosities. The real power in organizations does not always lie with the visible power holders. By noticing the geographic placement of offices, seating arrangements in meetings, alternate meanings to statements, and the pattern of workplace friendships, you can begin to identify informal power, norms, and expectations.

3. *Understand the people in your organization.* In order to get along with and influence others, you must pay attention to the personality traits and organizational interests of the political players. Being a good judge of character is an ingredient of political savvy that helps you determine allies and methods of influence. Who are the fence sitters? Who are the opinion leaders? Which colleagues make decisions based on tradition, evidence, cost-effectiveness, or majority sentiment? Some people need to be coaxed, praised, or reassured. Others welcome directness and debate. Some people are risk takers and others are cautious. Still others block every attempt to change. Remember that employees in an organization want to protect their self-interests. By identifying those interests and styles of behavior, you will become skilled at dealing with people.

4. *Identify power sources.* Because organizational politics is so closely tied to power, it is important to appraise the relative power positions of individuals and organizational units. Who makes what decisions? Who controls what resources? Who has influence with supervisors? Learn to recognize both formal and informal power. For example, those in legitimate positions with the ability to reward or punish others are obviously powerful. But so are those who possess valuable information, indispensable skills, or charismatic personalities. Sometimes the least obvious person wields the most power.

5. *Build partnerships.* Most people operate according to the principle of reciprocal favors. If someone helps, supports, or acts kindly toward you, you are likely to feel obligated to return the favor. Maxims such as "One good turn deserves another" or "I owe you one" illustrate the reciprocity ethic. Politically wise managers build alliances base on this principle. By supporting each other, two colleagues have more strength as a team than they would individually.

Two points about the judicious use of this strategy are worth mentioning. First, it is rarely necessary to remind people that they owe you a favor. To make such an explicit statement is to bring the political process to an awkwardly obvious level. It also insults others to imply that they aren't holding up their end of the bargain. Indeed, the best alliances are implicitly understood rather than fully expressed in the first place. The second caution concerns the overuse of predictable alliances. If the work group realizes that two people always side with each other regardless of the issue, the group will discount the partnership.

6. *Never overuse power.* Being blatant with power is a sure way to lose it. Power can be regarded as your ability to influence others minus the others' ability to resist. It is a transaction between people, not an entity one person possesses. A manager who is tyrannical with power will create much resistance. A better approach is to avoid obvious displays of power. Managers, for example, who arbitrarily mandate new procedures for reports often get complaints, refusals, and sabotage from their staff members. By gradually and subtly influencing staff members to see the value of the new procedure instead, you will find compliance and support. Indeed, even in the absence of supervision, the staff will continue to do the reports in the new way because they have internalized your perspective on the issue.

7. *Learn to negotiate.* Politically savvy managers are good negotiators who know when to make concessions and when to hold out. By compromising several smaller points, they can often win on big issues. Effective negotiations involve careful listening, a sensitivity to nonverbal cues, the strategic use of questions, a knowledge of options, a sense of timing, and a confident style of communication. Negotiation is involved in many aspects of the managerial role. You may find yourself negotiating with supervisors, workers, colleagues, potential employees, unions, customers, or vendors. It is inherently a political process because it involves subtle attempts to influence others to gain power or achieve a goal.

8. *Never alienate supervisors.* It is political suicide to alienate supervisors. You do not have to agree completely with everything a supervisor does or says, because such obvious attempts to gain favor would hurt your credibility. But there are various aspects of maintaining a good relationship with supervisors. Never disagree publicly with them, nor create problems that make them look bad to their bosses. Get a supervisor's approval for unusual actions. Always follow the chain of command. Be a team player, not a pest or a constant complainer. Credit the contributions of your

boss to your own successes, and thank the supervisor for assisting, supporting, or developing you. Find ways to make your boss look good. Say yes to most requests your boss makes of you.

9. *Develop loyal and competent employees.* Being politically astute not only involves interactions with supervisors and colleagues but also relates to how you treat employees. Competent workers make you look good. Treating employees with respect and fairness will result in a group of loyal supporters. Managers who have good relationships with their employees can also receive essential information and perceptions from this level.

10. *Be patient.* Developing political awareness takes time. It can't be rushed. Asking someone to acquaint you with the political dynamics of your organization is self-defeating because the process cannot be articulated clearly; it must be sensed. Also, one person's perspective gives a limited and distorted picture of the political reality. Being patient also means taking time to build a reputation gradually, to influence slowly and subtly, and to acquire power incrementally. Being patient does not mean waiting idly for things to happen. Listen quietly, observe, and unobtrusively build good relationships and alliances, while cultivating competence, trust, and power.

[*See also* Conflict Management; Delegation and Empowerment; Negotiation]

For Additional Information

Buhler, Patricia. "Navigating the Waters of Organizational Politics." *Supervision* 55, No. 9 (Sept. 1994), pp. 24–26.

Presentations

Periodically, managers must make presentations to internal or external audiences. Internally, you may find yourself speaking to a group of supervisors, subordinates, or colleagues. External audiences include customers, stockholders, the community, or the press. Through presentations, you try to inform, educate, persuade, build consensus, affect decisions, or stimulate action. Whether it is an informal talk to a small group of colleagues or a speech to an audience of hundreds of unfamiliar faces, you need essentially the same skills to make successful presentations.

Overcoming Anxiety and Building Confidence

Most of us, even the most experienced and effective of speakers, feel some amount of anxiety before making a presentation. It is normal to feel some emotional tension when faced with a situation where performance is important and the outcome is uncertain. Minor stage fright can be advantageous. Such normal anxiety creates physiological reactions that you can convert into presentational advantages. For example, fear causes the heart to beat faster and causes more adrenaline to flow through the body. This mental and physical alertness can produce energy for a dynamic and enthusiastic delivery. The secret is not to let speaking anxiety run rampant but to control and channel it effectively.

The first step in building speaking confidence is to identify the specific causes of anxiety. Inadequate information, audience evaluation, hostile listeners, a weak delivery style, the attention of the spotlight, or question-and-answer sessions can all produce anxiety in a manager who must make a presentation. Some speakers fear that they will bore the audience, make themselves look foolish, appear overly nervous, or forget what they were going to say. By identifying the specific anxiety producers, you are in a better position to cope with anxiety.

Developing an appropriate attitude and relying on some anxiety-prevention strategies can help you build presentational confidence. The following are some general techniques. You can develop other devices for your own unique needs.

1. *Think positively.* Expecting failure will help to produce failure. By focusing on strengths and positive expectations, you will enhance your likelihood of success. Convince yourself that you will give the best presentation you can.

2. *Prepare thoroughly.* Once you have collected your information, organized your thoughts, and rehearsed your talk, anxiety about the presentation subsides. Never take a speaking situation for granted. Careful preparation builds confidence and success.

3. *Analyze the audience.* The more you know about the audience and can predict outcomes, the less nervous you will be. Analyzing the audience means knowing how many people will be present, who they are (gender, age, race, position), how much they know about the topic, why they are attending, and their attitude about you and your information.

4. *Learn to relax.* Techniques such as slow, rhythmic breathing, exercise, self-hypnosis, yoga, or meditation can help you relax. Some speakers take a few minutes before the presentation to think of something pleasant, go for a walk, talk to a friend, sit quietly alone, or engage in small talk with the audience. Discover whatever relaxation techniques work best for you.

5. *Acquire experience.* As in any hobby or sport, the more you do it, the better you become. Actual speaking experience is the best way to control anxiety and develop skills. Taking communication courses or volunteering to speak in professional or civic organizations can provide nonthreatening opportunities to practice presentational skills. Analyze your performance and seek improvement after each presentation you make.

Organizing the Message

An organized message is crucial if an audience is to pay attention to, understand, accept, or remember your information. It also enhances your image and credibility. No matter how dynamic your style, the presentation falls short if the substance of your message is not easy to understand and follow.

The first step in organizing a presentation is to determine the objective of the message. Every presentation needs a single purpose or central idea. Managers who cannot translate their purpose into a central idea of the presentation tend to ramble and confuse listeners. A central idea is a way to narrow the focus of the presentation topic. For example, a branch bank manager plans a presentation to inform customers about individual retirement accounts. At this point, the topic is determined, but the purpose or central idea is vague. A more specific purpose would be "To convince customers to purchase an individual retirement account by explaining its value and showing them how to open an account."

Once you have determined the purpose, select a few main points to cover in order to achieve it. In the preceding example, the manager may want to include three points regarding the value of individual retirement accounts: current tax savings, favorable interest rates, and the building of retirement income. After determining main points, select facts, examples, statistics, quotes, or stories to explain each point. This is the substantive information of the speech.

Next, outline the main points and supporting information to see that it flows logically. Points may have to be rearranged, or material added or deleted as appropriate. Some people use this outline as notes from which to deliver the presentation. By seeing the arrangement of points, you can plan smooth transitions between ideas. Finally, the presentation needs an introduction and conclusion—important elements that capture attention and provide lasting impressions of you.

By preparing a purpose, main points, supporting information, transitions, outline, introduction, and conclusion, you will present an organized, coherent message. Of all the skills of making presentations, organizing information is probably most crucial to speaking effectiveness.

Delivering the Presentation

Delivery is the packaging of a message. While it is essential to organize a message, the skillful presentation of information is another important ingredient of presentation success. Dynamic delivery keeps an audience's attention and makes listeners more receptive to your ideas. Excessive delivery problems can undermine your credibility and information.

One way to improve presentation style is to realize common pitfalls that managers encounter when making presentations. Examine this list of presentation errors to identify your own potential problems.

- Monotone voice
- Filled pauses
- Speaking too softly
- Speaking too quickly
- Distracting gestures
- Stiff, tense posture
- Lack of eye contact with listeners
- Mispronounced words
- Dependence on notes
- Nervous habits
- Ignoring audience cues
- Losing train of thought
- Pacing

With practice, speakers tend to get better at delivering messages. There are a few strategies for achieving the dynamic delivery of ideas.

1. *Be dynamic.* A lively, energetic speaker is much easier to listen to than a slow, deliberate one. As a speaker, you should try to be outgoing and enthusiastic. This means speaking loudly, using vocal variety, and keeping the pace moving. A confident,

prepared speaker can be more dynamic than a nervous, tentative one. Making presentations, at any level to any audience, involves a degree of showmanship. Listeners will pay attention to presentations that are interesting and enjoyable.

2. *Be conversational.* The best speaking style mimics ordinary conversation. Formal or pompous styles of talking strain listener concentration. Listeners will be captivated if they feel that the speaker is addressing them individually. To be conversational, voice tones should be informal, relaxed, and familiar. Avoid sounding as if you are lecturing or reciting information.

3. *Use appropriate physical movement.* Making an effective presentation involves nonverbal techniques as well as vocal ones. Natural gestures can illustrate or emphasize a point. Awkward or repetitive gestures can be distracting. Physical movement can parallel the movement through ideas in a presentation. Casually walking through the audience can capture attention and create an atmosphere of friendliness and informality. Remaining behind a podium or stiffly clinging to notes can undermine speaking effectiveness.

4. *Be fluent.* Speaking effortlessly and with grace captivates an audience and enhances your image. Successful presenters do not stumble over words, lose their train of thought, or clutter their talk with meaningless vocalizations. For many speakers, being fluent means eliminating words like "um," "ah," "OK," and "you know" from their delivery. By being aware of such pet, distracting words and by being comfortable with silent pauses, you can develop a fluent speaking style.

5. *Give eye contact throughout the audience.* Plan to have eye contact with every listener. Even in large audiences, you can scan all sections of the audience rather than looking just in the center. Eye contact during a presentation serves many purposes. It shows a speaker's confidence, credibility, and sincerity. It lets listeners feel that you are speaking directly to each and every one of them. It allows you to get feedback from the audience. By looking directly at all listeners, you can see signs of boredom, confusion, or disagreement. The effective speaker then adjusts to accommodate the audience mood.

6. *Use notes effectively.* Good speakers usually speak from limited, unobtrusive notes. Notes should serve only as a guide to the arrangement of ideas. Occasionally, they may include information, such as a statistic or quotation, that the presenter wants to deliver verbatim. Managers who use extensive notes or complete manuscripts often fall into the trap or reading from the notes. Reading information is not the same as presenting a message. Too much dependence on notes is a sure way of putting an audience to sleep.

7. *Do not call attention to your delivery.* The best presentation delivery is unnoticed. A speaking style that calls attention to itself defeats its purpose. Delivery is merely the mechanism for getting ideas across. The audience should be concentrating on the ideas, not the delivery style. If listeners are paying attention to the delivery, then you are probably using a distracting habit.

Choosing the Appropriate Language

To be effective, use words that are clear, specific, inoffensive, and vivid. In written communication, the reader can check the meaning of an unfamiliar word or reread a passage until it makes sense, but it is your responsibility to make sure that listeners understand the language in a presentation. That means avoiding specialized terms or jargon unless the audience understands it. If you must use jargon, take the time to define the technical or unfamiliar term. Simple concise ways to make points are needed in oral presentations. Avoid long, complex sentences and eloquent displays of vocabulary.

Other devices for achieving clarity include sequencing words, transition words, and frequent summaries. Words such as "first," "second," "next," and "finally" help the listener follow your movement through a sequence of ideas. Such sequencing words reveal the pattern of organization of ideas. Transition words who the relationship of ideas. Words such as "however," "on the other hand," and "similarly" help orient the listener to your points. Presentations need enough restatement to emphasize points and to assist listeners' recall. A few well-placed internal summaries as well as a final summary can help the audience grasp and remember your information.

In addition to using clear language, you should use specific language whenever possible in a presentation. Instead of saying, "We will know our budget allocations soon," say "We expect to know our budget allocation by July 1." Besides spelling out the meaning of ambiguous terms, being specific also means giving examples to illustrate a point. Instead of saying, "This company cares about employees," say "This company has established flexible benefits, a complaint procedure, and a new lunchroom because it cares about employees."

Choose you words carefully to avoid offending listeners. This means avoiding sexist language, racial slurs, ethnic aspersions, or remarks that would provoke defensiveness. Also, certain subtly offensive words hinder your purpose. For example, asking a group "Would anyone be willing to serve on a committee to plan the spring meeting?" discourages response. However, asking "Would anyone like the opportunity to help plan the spring meeting?" will invite more volunteers.

Vivid language is descriptive and captivating. It paints a picture for the listener. It uses active rather than passive words. Note the difference between these two sentences: "The report was done by us." "We did the report." Perhaps a more exciting verb, such as "prepared" or "completed," would make the sentence even more vivid. "Profits soared" is more exciting than "profits rose." "Diversified and increased attendance occurred this year" sounds boring and vague. "Hundreds of new people attended this year" is a more descriptive and vivid alternative.

Give careful thought to your word choice in presentations. Clear, specific, inoffensive, and vivid language will capture attention, emphasize points, and spur listeners to action

Using Visual Aids

Most business presentations call for the use of visual aids. Frequently, you place crucial information on flip charts, transparencies, computer multimedia, or slides to include in a presentation. Some information, especially numerical data, is difficult to grasp except in visual form. Talking about accident rates over a ten-year period will overwhelm listeners, but showing those rates in a graph presented on a transparency will allow you to highlight points and the audience to study the information. A chart to show redesigns in the organizational structure or sales growth will have more impact than words alone. Slides or a video showing a foreign manufacturing location go far beyond a mere verbal description.

As a speaker, you should determine whether visual aids will enhance a presentation, the best form of visual aid, and the effective use of visual material. Visuals will enhance a talk if they allow you to accomplish something you could not achieve through words alone. To visually present a few key words from a presentation will probably detract from rather than enhance a talk. Unless the words represent technical jargon, there is no reason to display them. When considering visuals, determine their purpose. If you cannot identify a specific purpose, then they are probably unnecessary. Another method for determining whether you should use visual aids is to assess their potential benefit in relation to the cost of preparation. For example, slides that are expensive and time-consuming to prepare are not worth the effort unless they make a significant impact on the presentation. Putting some figures on a flip chart may be worth the minimal effort involved, even if their impact is not great.

Once you decide that visuals will aid your presentation, it is important to select the appropriate form of visual material. The type you use will depend on your speaking purpose, the nature of the information you are presenting visually, the size of your audience, and your visual resources. An informative presentation to a few colleagues will not require elaborate use of visuals. A slide presentation in this situation is inappropriate. On the other hand, convincing potential investors to support a new project suggests the use of professionally prepared visual material as opposed to a few figures scrawled on a flip chart.

Certain information lends itself to particular forms of visual presentation. Illustrating a distribution system may require a manual; a film may be needed to show how a piece of equipment operates; computation of data or tables of information lend themselves to computer generated multimedia presentation, and a chart may be the best way to show operating costs. Give careful consideration to the most effective means of presenting information.

Finally, in terms of selecting visual aids, consider your available resources. Do you have the time, the money, or the professional assistance for producing slides? Is it possible to have a videotape produced professionally? Perhaps someone with excellent lettering skills could draw flip charts by hand. It is better to use less sophisticated methods such as flip charts or transparencies than to create sloppy or amateur slide or video presentations. Remember that visuals must not be distracting nor call attention to themselves in any way.

You must be skilled in the use of visual aids. While it is important that visuals be selected and prepared carefully, they must be presented effectively as well. Even professionally prepared visual material will fail if you do not know how to use the material. The following are some guidelines for the use of any type of visual aid in a presentation:

1. *Check legibility.* Visual material should be large, bold, and simple. Excessive amounts of information, small printing, or delicate drawings cannot be seen even from a short distance. Light-color markers on flip charts or transparencies do not show up well. After preparing a visual, test its legibility by positioning yourself at the back of the presentation room. If you cannot easily see the visual from there, then an audience member in that position will not be able to see it either.

2. *Have all materials with you at the time of presentation.* Many a presentation has been ruined by a missing chart, by the lack of an extension cord to run the slide projector, or by a marker that has run out of ink. Never search for materials during a presentation or leave the podium to retrieve anything. A practice session using the visual aids will alert you to any malfunctioning equipment or missing material. Some speakers have backup equipment or material just in case.

3. *Don't block the view of visual aids.* You must be able to refer to visual material without standing in front of it or looking at it rather than at the audience. Practice standing to the side of a flip

chart and using a pointer. Become proficient at using overlays or pointers with overhead transparencies.

4. *Plan time appropriately.* Visuals add time to a presentation. It is essential to determine how much time you will need for showing visual material. Give the group enough time to see, and in some cases to study, the visual material. You can quickly pace a slide presentation, where the impact comes from the total show rather than from any one slide. You need to display financial charts or graphs, on the other hand, for a long enough time for the audience to examine them.

5. *Make the visual aid secondary to the presentation.* Visuals assist, but do not replace, the speaker. Some speakers fall into the trap of becoming narrators. Their entire presentation is nothing more than a series of visuals, with their announcing or reading from one. Orient listeners to a visual presentation and summarize after showing the visual material.

Handling Questions

It is a rare business presentation where the speaker is not called on to answer questions. For most managerial presentations, the question-and-answer session is more important than the prepared talk.

Handling questions is the more difficult part of a presentation. You can never be as thoroughly prepared for this aspect of speaking as you can be for the planned remarks. If you can handle listeners' questions effectively, you have passed a major hurdle to the success of your presentation. Follow these guidelines for becoming skilled at fielding audience questions:

1. *Anticipate questions.* Most questions are typical and can be expected to emerge from a certain topic or from a particular audience. Put yourself in the place of your audience. What questions would you be likely to ask? By analyzing the common fears, assumptions, needs, or problems that listeners experience, you can identify likely questions.

2. *Always repeat the question.* This will allow the entire group to hear the question. It is annoying for the audience to listen to a

speaker give an answer to a question they did not hear. Repeating the question allows you to see if you understood the question correctly. Finally, it provides you some time to frame a response.

3. *Keep answers short and simple.* Remember that what is important to one person may be boring to the rest of the group. If the questioner wants detailed information and you can see signs of disinterest from the rest of the group, plan to discuss the question privately after the session or to send additional information to the questioner later. Providing short and simple answers keeps the pace moving.

4. *Discourage monopolizers.* Never allow one person to ask several questions if there are others who have not had a chance to ask a question. It may be necessary to interrupt the monopolizer diplomatically. Say something like "You're raising some interesting points, but in the interest of time, let's move on to some other questions."

5. *Realize that some questions cannot be answered.* You cannot be expected to have answers to all questions that could possibly be asked. It is appropriate to say that you do not have that particular information. You might suggest an alternative information source to the questioner or promise to provide information as soon as possible. Never fake an answer.

In some cases, you may not want to answer a question because it is sensitive or embarrassing. There are some techniques for gracefully sidestepping a question. You can talk generally about the topic of the question without directly addressing the specific question. You can answer a slightly different question. You can indicate that because of a certain circumstance you are not at liberty to discuss the question right now.

6. *Maintain your composure.* Some people will ask irrelevant or hostile questions. Others will use the session as a forum to state their own views. Some will attempt to sabotage your plan or your credibility. It is imperative that you remain friendly, calm, and composed in these situations. Do not argue, blame, threaten, preach, or ridicule. Do not become defensive, hostile, or attacking. You must remain confident, professional, and in charge of your emotions during a hostile question-and-answer session.

For Additional Information

Bird, Malcom. *The Complete Guide to Business and Technical Presentations*. New York: Van Nostrand Reinhold, 1990.

Harris, Todd. "The Business Week Guide to Multimedia Presentations: Create Dynamic Presentations that Inspire." *CD-ROM World* 10, No. 1 (Jan. 1995), p. 97.

Leech, Thomas. *How to Prepare, Stage, and Deliver Winning Presentations*. New York: AMACOM, 1992.

Simmons, Sylvia. *How to Be the Life of the Podium*. New York: AMACOM, 1993.

Project Management

There is growing emphasis on project management, and managers must increasingly function as project managers. There are particular skills and activities relevant to project management, which differ from the skills and activities required of functional managers. This chapter discusses the impetus for project management, the differences between project and functional management, steps in managing a project, and specific skills needed by project managers.

A *project* can be defined as an undertaking with a clear starting point and ending point. It is a one-shot task with a defined goal. The project manager oversees the whole undertaking and has responsibility for its success or failure.

Organizational Emphasis on Project Management

There are at least three factors accounting for the increasing emphasis on project management.

1. A project-management culture goes hand in hand with team-based management. As more organizations make the transition from hierarchical structures to flatter, team-oriented approaches to work, project management becomes more prevalent. In many organizations today, employees work in teams that take responsibility for planning, coordinating, controlling, and improving work. These projects typically utilize the talents of cross-functional, multidisciplinary teams.

2. Project management promotes employee involvement. Evidence shows that when employees are involved in decision

making and the implementation of change, the quality of their work improves, as does their satisfaction. Projects that once would have been done by managers themselves, or by managers delegating work to employees, now are more likely to be handled by project teams. Employees in project teams have greater input into and responsibility for the project activities and outcomes. This seems to be a more effective way to get work done.

3. Project management is best to handle the complexity of teamwork. The nature of some work requires the resources of a project team, with members drawn from different functions, disciplines, and levels of the organization. Major research and development or engineering efforts, for example, may depend on the expertise of people from a wide range of functions. The only way to effectively accomplish a complex task may be to assemble a diverse team with the oversight of a project manager. Understanding and coordinating a rapidly advancing technology may depend on the talents of project teams and project managers.

Differences Between Functional and Project Management

While there are similarities between functional and project managers, the differences are many and worth noting. Project managers differ from functional managers in their degree of control, time, flexibility, and visibility.

Project managers actually have less formal authority over project members than functional managers do over their employees. Because project team members may be borrowed from various other departments, they continue to have formal reporting relationships to their department managers. The project manager has a temporary and often voluntary relationship with employees on the project team. For example, the project manager does not have the responsibility for hiring, evaluating, rewarding, disciplining, or terminating team employees. Those responsibilities continue to rest with the functional line manager. The project manager's authority is limited in scope to the particular project. The project team member may have divided loyalties between the project and the department manager. In short, the typical manager-employee relationship does not exist with project management.

Project managers also operate in a different time frame than do functional managers. Functional managers oversee ongoing functions over time, while project managers oversee one-time efforts. The relationship between the project manager and the team members is limited in duration. From the start, it is assumed to be a temporary relationship.

Because project tasks are nonroutine, project managers may have to be more flexible than do functional managers. And team projects in an organization often are highly visible. Because employees are borrowed from their functions, a project manager is assigned, and resources are allocated to the project, the whole effort becomes well known in the organization. Top management typically has a large stake in the project. This high visibility can create performance pressure for the project manager, though it also provides greater rewards when the project is successful.

Steps in Managing a Project

The project manager must follow a number of steps, whatever the nature of the project. Careful attention to each of these steps constitutes the "how to" of managing projects.

1. *Set the project objectives.* The specific objectives of the project must be clearly defined. This sets the scope of the project as well. It is important to determine what the project seeks to accomplish and what the expected outcomes will be. The objectives and scope may be revised over time, but the goals must be delineated from the start.

2. *Develop a schedule and budget.* By attaching deadlines and costs to particular tasks within the project, the project manager builds the schedule and budget. If upper management sets a project completion date, then the schedule is determined by working backwards from the end date. A certain amount of time and cost is allocated to each task.

3. *Set the project standards.* The project manager must set standards for acceptable levels of performance. Quality levels for both human and equipment performance should be established. This provides a baseline against which actual performance is measured and deemed acceptable or adjusted to meet quality requirements.

4. *Compose the project team.* The project manager must select team members by matching task requirements to individual skills. Typically, people are selected from various functions, disciplines, and levels based on the skills they bring to the project. Certain project members may be leaders of particular tasks in the project.

5. *Initiate the project.* This phase includes a variety of activities, such as motivating and coaching team members, communicating with team members and within the organization, coordinating tasks, facilitating work, and rewarding performance.

6. *Gather data on progress.* The project manager must monitor progress. This involves assessing whether the work meets established standards, determining if the schedule is being met, and analyzing costs as they relate to budget. Various software tools are available to graphically show the relationships between tasks, the duration of tasks, and the resources allocated to and used in aspects of the project. The project manager likely will have to report progress at various points. Good data are essential to such reporting.

7. *Solve problems.* All group projects have their share of problems. Project managers must anticipate problems, be able to recognize problems, and assist the team in problem solving. Because the tasks in one-time projects are not routine, and because this particular group of people has not worked together before, unexpected difficulties are bound to arise. It is wise for project managers to consider problem solving as an inevitable aspect of project management.

8. *Close out the project.* Once the tasks of the project are finished, there needs to be a final report, which describes the completed project. The report may address such questions as: Were the objectives met at the acceptable levels of quality? What was the final cost of the project? Project close-out also should

include an assessment by the project team. It is useful for team members to discuss what they learned, what aspects of the project went well, and what could have been done differently. Such a meeting helps to put closure on the project.

Skills of Project Managers

Project managers must have good people skills. They must be good communicators, since they interact one-on-one and in groups, and they must make formal oral and written presentations. Project managers must be team builders, since employees working on a project must function as a team. Project managers must be skilled motivators and coaches. The skills of working well with people are most essential for effective project management.

Project leaders also must have analytical competencies. They must be able to analyze and schedule tasks, compare task performance to quality standards, and understand and manage the technical aspects of a project. They must be able to analyze and interpret data as they relate to monitoring the progress of the project. Project managers also must be skilled at analyzing the organization and its culture. Because they facilitate projects that span organizational boundaries, project managers must be adept at analyzing the structure, power, politics, and personalities of the organization.

While project management utilizes many of the same skills as does functional management, the unique requirements for leading organizational projects staffed by a cross-section of employees makes project management a challenging role for today's manager.

[*See also* Coaching Employees; Conflict Management; Feedback; Meetings; Motivation; Team Building; Time Management]

For Additional Information

Dinsmore, P. C. *AMA Handbook of Project Management*. New York: AMACOM, 1993.
Gannon, Alice. "Project Management: An Approach to Accomp-

lishing Things." *Records Management Quarterly,* July 1994, pp. 3–13.

Heindel, Lee E., and Vincent A. Kasten. *Vertically Integrated Project Management: An Enterprise Management Systems Approach.* New York: AMACOM, 1995.

Knutson, Joan, and Ira Bitz. (1991). *Project Management: How to Plan and Manage Successful Projects.* New York: AMACOM, 1991.

Public Relations

Public relations (PR) involves the communication of accurate information about an organization in order to enhance the image, growth, and survival of that organization. Public relations involves the sending and receiving of information with individuals and groups who affect and are affected by the organization: employees, unions, customers, distributors, the community, stockholders, the media, and the government. Simply, public relations is the function of making the organization look good to its many constituents and customers.

Public relations is a complex and vital function for any organization, large or small. To a large extent, the public relations manager or department coordinates the organization's responses to the social, political, economic, and business communities. Managers at all levels need to be aware of public relations objectives and realize that they too carry the organization's image to the public. Even recruiting and interviewing prospective employees has strong PR overtones. Progressive organizations orient their managers to the new business environment while encouraging them to make decisions and demonstrate behavior consistent with the company's image. Managers are the organization's ambassadors; they, not just the PR department or the chief executive officer (CEO), must be responsible for promoting the company's image and reputation.

The following general orientation to the field of PR and its various aspects provides information that can help an organization develop or enhance its PR function, help acquaint management with its role in PR, and help public relations specialists better understand their job responsibilities. Seven aspects of PR are discussed: media relations, community relations, customer relations, employee and labor relations, financial relations, government relations, and crisis management.

Media Relations

Public relations involves communicating to the press, handling press inquiries, preparing others in the organization to interact with the media, and working with the advertising department on ads that fulfill a public relations role. The PR manager may write and disseminate news releases or feature articles on corporate social-responsibility programs, technical or environmental achievements, positions on legislative action, employee accomplishments, or human interest items. It is important to develop an extensive and up-to-date network of media contacts. The PR manager becomes the clearinghouse for information about the organization, prepares that information for media consumption, and knows the people to whom the information should be forwarded.

The PR manager often acts as the organization's spokesperson in print and broadcast media inquiries. PR specialists appear on televised news programs, entertainment or magazine shows, or talk shows to communicate with the public about almost any aspect of their organizations. They also grant studio or taped interviews, make prepared statements for the news, or participate in call-in shows on the radio. PR specialists grant interviews to journalists and represent the organization's interests in newspaper and magazine articles. Likewise, if the company has some information of interest to all the media, the PR manager will coordinate a news conference.

Sometimes the media want access to top-level executives in the company. In that case, the PR manager may work with CEOs or other top management to prepare them for radio or television appearances. Such executive coaching is especially important when the media or public is critical of the company. The PR manager may hire an outside consultant specializing in preparing executives for media appearances.

Finally, in terms of media relations, the PR manager may be called on to coordinate institutional issues or advertising with the organization's advertising department or agency. While advertising is not a function of public relations, some types of ads fulfill a PR role. Institutional ads promote a company's image by highlighting its history, achievements, or civic contributions. Issues advertising is a type of advocacy in which the organization states its position on some controversial topic. Because these advertising vehicles involve public relations goals, the PR manager should have input into them.

Community Relations

This aspect of PR involves the cultivation of a good business-community relationship. Because organizations need the physical and human resources of communities in which they are located, they must be concerned with the health and prosperity of those communities. It is not only sound ethical practice but good business practice to be a responsible member of the community. The PR manager plays a vital role in community relations by coordinating and publicizing such organizational activities as corporate philanthropy and sponsorship, leadership in community-improvement projects, employee participation in social and civic groups, and cooperation with local government and educational institutions. In large organizations, a separate community relations specialist may coordinate these projects. The public relations manager must work closely with this person; however, the PR specialist would likely be responsible for publicizing, if not spearheading, community activities.

The business world realizes its responsibility to contribute to charitable organizations and encourages employees' charitable donations as well. Likewise, small companies and large corporations alike typically sponsor cultural, athletic, and recreational activities for the community and frequently provide funds and personnel for such community projects as neighborhood rehabilitation, child care, youth training or employment projects, and recreational programs. Many organizations encourage employees to join social and civic groups and to participate in local government. Wise organizations also make their facilities and personnel available to educational groups through company tours and speakers' bureaus. It is the job of the PR manager to apprise management of these obligations, help carry them out, and coordinate the company's information regarding all aspects of community affairs.

Customer Relations

An organization's products or services provide the direct link between the organization and the public. What a customer says about a company is probably the biggest influence on the company's image. Customers talk to friends, families, and colleagues about their interactions—positive and negative—with businesses. Customer satisfaction, then, is the foundation for effective public relations. While the PR manager is not directly responsible for customer relations, a concern for customers must be part of a PR objective. People who purchase directly from a company are not the only "customers" whom organizations must court; consumer affairs groups, dealers, distributors, retailers, contractors, and suppliers also interact with a company and shape its reputation.

While most organizations have separate customer relations or consumer affairs departments, the PR manager often must act as a liaison and help with the publicity activities of those departments. Thus it is important that the PR specialist have an understanding of customer and consumer relations.

Many organizations take an active role in educating customers about product information, health and safety concerns, and consumer rights. This may be done through owners' manuals, pamphlets, audio and videotapes, speakers, or training seminars. Likewise, progressive companies solicit customer feedback through surveys, hot lines, comments cards, and panel discussions. Two-way communication and the satisfactory handling of complaints strengthens the buyer-seller relationship, which makes the company look good and increases its profits. An effective PR manager helps others in the organization see the relationship between customer relations and public relations.

Dealers, distributors, retailers, contractors, and suppliers are a customer segment that must be informed, supported, and listened to. Frequently, organizations provide liaison personnel, brochures, sales literature, newsletters, and audio or videotapes to these groups to enhance relationships and promote the company's image.

The PR manager may be directly responsible for preparing customer-oriented news stories about new products or services; representing the company position to consumer activists; presenting statements about pending consumer-rights legislation; or communicating with the media in the event of a product recall, boycott, or liability suit. The PR specialist helps the company coordinate actions affecting consumers with overall public relations objectives.

Employee and Labor Relations

Organizations are developing a heightened sense of employees as a "public." Indeed, employees are a conduit through which organizational information reaches the larger community. The field of employee and labor relations uses knowledge of human behavior to improve the employer-employee relationship. Public relations departments can help promote the exchange of accurate information among employees, labor leaders, and management. By helping to build good employee communication, the public relations manager influences the positive image employees carry to their families, friends, and neighbors—all of whom are potential customers.

The public relations manager or the communications manager may be responsible for internal communication or may cooperate with the employee and labor relations specialist in promoting communication with employees. In either case, organizations use a variety of means to promote the exchange of internal information, including employee newsletters, magazines, handbooks, manuals, internal television programming, personal letters, meetings, and hot lines. Where many of these sources used to focus exclusively on social information such as promotions, retirements, marriages, births, and company recreational events, they now include information about substantive issues affecting the organization. Internal public relations means keeping employees informed about company plans for growth, new products or discoveries, economic news relating to the company, government regulations, employee training opportunities and benefits, key personnel changes, and company involvement in community affairs. Likewise, an employee feedback program is necessary for employee trust and satisfaction. Attitude surveys, quality circles, suggestion boxes, hot lines, and face-to-face communication give employees the chance for input. The effective exchange of information with employees provides a building block to a comprehensive public relations program.

There is another area of employee and labor relations that directly pertains to public relations: The dissemination of information during layoffs, contract negotiations, and strikes. The public relations manager may be called upon to issue statements to employees, the community, and the press during personnel cutbacks. The PR manager typically presents information about progress in labor negotiations, being careful not to jeopardize those discussions or violate legal guidelines. Finally, the public relations manager usually acts as a company spokesperson during labor strikes. So in many ways, employee and labor relations impinge on the public relations function in modern organizations.

Financial Relations

Most organizations release some information about their financial condition. Public institutions have greater responsibilities in this area than do private organizations. They must communicate with stockholders and meet legal requirements for financial disclosure set forth by the Securities and Exchange Commission. A corporation's annual meeting and annual report serve not only a financial function but a public relations one as well. While company financial officers, legal counsel, and investor relations departments handle these functions, the wise public relations manager realizes their potential as vehicles for developing positive attitudes in the financial community. The public relations specialist may also issue statements or write press releases concerning company acquisitions and mergers.

Government Relations

All businesses must be concerned with government decisions. Legislation regulates business and affects its bottom line. As a result, organizations have a role in informing legislators of their positions on issues, and they communicate with government as one of their "publics." Organizations work with industry councils or professional organizations for legislative counseling of lobbying. Lobbyists carry business information to government officials in the attempt to influence legislation. They also transmit information from government officials back to corporate executives. In essence, they act as ambassadors of goodwill, communicating an organization's image to the government and to the public at large. Although lobbying is handled by public affairs departments in organizations, the public relations manager must be aware of its impact.

The PR department may also have a role in explaining a company's need for involvement with political action committees (PACs) to employees via internal communication media. The PR department may cooperate with the employee relations and public affairs departments to educate and involve employees in government advocacy and political issues. The PR function can be instrumental in changing negative perceptions about the relationship of government and business to society. Finally, public relations specialists sometimes assist business leaders who are called on to testify at government hearings. While the public relations job does not encompass public affairs duties, it is important to realize the interrelationship between PR and government.

Crisis Management

Another aspect of public relations involves the ability to deal with the communication problems that occur during emergency situations. Types of crises organizations face include industrial accidents, product tampering, product failures, damaging rumors, boycotts, or well-publicized litigation. Any time a company receives negative publicity, the situation should be considered a crisis. A company's ability to handle a crisis and restore public confidence can affect its very survival.

The public relations department has a direct role in crisis management. Before a crisis develops, the public relations manager should develop a plan to follow in the event of an emergency. A company credo of management philosophy and social responsibility can provide a foundation. In a crisis, the public relations function may have to set up a twenty-four-hour press office; staff hot lines to handle calls from the public; and coordinate communication with the public, the media, senior management, the legal department, security, employees, the union, federal agencies, and community leaders. A crisis calls for the widespread and immediate dissemination of accurate information by the public relations department in order to preserve an organization's good image.

The Public Relations Specialist

As the diverse aspects of the field reveal, public relations specialists must have numerous skills to perform vital functions in an organization. PR managers contribute to corporate policy making, collect information to survey attitudes and reactions, communicate with various publics, coordinate communication among different groups, and prepare organizational personnel to act as company spokespersons.

PR specialists must possess numerous skills, including news writing and editing, technical writing, broadcast media production, graphic design and layout, public speaking, persuasion, group dynamics, and interpersonal communication. They must understand all the aspects of the business, be good managers, have excellent communication skills, and get along well with people.

Some large organizations with broad needs hire PR generalists who can use the services of consultant specialists in aspects of public relations, such as crisis management, financial relations, government relations, or special promotions. On the other hand, some small organizations take care of all their needs through external PR consultants or agencies. Whatever the method, it is imperative that organizations appreciate the complexity and importance of the PR function and that managers realize their role in promoting a positive image of their organization.

[*See also* Customer Service; Presentations]

For Additional Information

Berry, Jay. "Thinking the Unthinkable: Helping Clients Manage Emergencies." *Journal of Management Consulting* 8, No. 2 (Fall 1994), pp. 51–53.

Devereaux-Ferguson, Sherry. *Mastering The Public Opinion Challenge*. Burr Ridge, Ill.: Business One Irwin, 1994.

Mathews, Wilma K. "Do Unto Media as Ye Shall Do Unto Your Customers!" *Communication World* 1, No. 7 (August 1994), pp. 17–19.

Sweep, Duane, Glen T. Cameron, and RuthAn Weaver-Lariscy. "Re-thinking Constraints on Public Relations Practice." *Public Relations Review* 20, No. 4 (Winter 1994), pp. 319–31.

Quality

The concept of quality in the workplace has continued to evolve. The emphasis today seems universally strong, while the approaches are varied. On the whole, there is a progression of quality by many companies away from mere lip service to a sincere and consuming effort to improve their systems. This section examines what constitutes quality in today's business environment and how it is achieved.

What Is Quality?

Simply put, *quality* is meeting or exceeding the expectations and requirements of customers. Quality means meeting the highest standards and continually improving processes or steps to satisfy customers by empowering employees to prevent problems or errors. Quality does not mean correcting problems after they occur or allowing a certain margin of error in production or service. Many companies have embarked on the path of total quality management (TQM), which integrates all the process improvements in all functions into one interrelated, organization-wide quality system.

The Costs of Lack of Quality

In some organizations, a shortsighted and costly definition of quality has reigned. To them, quality depends on inspection after production to pinpoint defects or problems. Often this is coupled with a system of correction, so that a small rate of rejection is tolerated. Ironically, this approach promotes the absence of quality. The inspectors making a product or delivering a service decide what passes and what doesn't, not the workers. Thus, the direct producer or deliverer has no input and no commitment to improve the process or prevent further variance or defect.

An inspection or correction approach to quality is costly. Whenever work must be redone, the organization incurs unnecessary double costs: the cost to do the job the first time and the cost to redo it, with labor, materials, people, and equipment unavailable to work on other orders. Errors in production or services can result in exorbitant costs associated with warranty replacements, product liability suits, product recalls, malpractice suits, consumer actions, or lost customers. Therefore, quality truly takes root when producers and deliverers of products and services understand customer requirements and expectations, define the processes they work with, improve the relationships between internal customers and suppliers, develop and adhere to their own quality measures, and continually endeavor to improve these processes.

Emphasizing quality in production not only saves money but can also be key to survival. Customers naturally gravitate to the product or service that best meets their needs. From a customer's standpoint, quality means that the product or service does what it is supposed to do consistently, without exception. If the product or service does not provide 100 percent satisfaction, customers will turn to the competitor. In the long run, the cost of not providing quality is business failure. Organizations must meet their customer's requirements and expectations in order to survive.

The Renewed Focus on Quality— Dr. W. Edwards Deming

Managers cannot discuss quality without crediting the man responsible for sharpening the international focus on quality, the late Dr. W. Edwards Deming. Dr. Deming, a tireless educator, consultant, and crusader, began his work on the total quality systems approach by helping Japanese industry go from manufacturing laughing stock to global benchmark. The Japanese immersed themselves in the teachings of Dr. Deming, and then showed their appreciation by establishing the Deming Medal for Highest Achievement in Productivity and Quality, the ultimate Japanese business award.

In his eighth decade, Deming finally attracted the attention of corporate America. Now his structured, holistic approach to total quality, statistical process control, and employee involvement is standard fare. To understand Deming's philosophies, one must become familiar with his fourteen points.

Deming's Fourteen Points

1. *Create a constancy of purpose.* Organizations must have a clear mission, with all their actions, decisions, and practices relating directly to that mission. Constancy of purpose requires constancy of management personnel. Constancy cannot be achieved when people hold short stays in top management

2. *Adopt the new philosophy.* Practice it in a zealous and religious way throughout the organization. Instill the philosophy in every thing you do and think about it within the organization.

3. *Cease dependence on mass inspection.* A proactive, preventive approach makes more sense than a reactive, corrective philosophy. It is always cheaper to prevent problems before they happen than to try to correct them once they happen.

4. *End the practice of awarding businesss on price tag alone.* You get what you pay for! Instead, establish long-term, trusting, and accountable relationships with suppliers.

5. *Improve constantly and forever the system of production and service.* Improvement is not a one-time event.

6. *Institute modern training.* Organizations and individuals must grow. Skills can be taught internally. Continuous learning and continuous improvement are inseparable.

7. *Institute Leadership.* Quality starts at the top.

8. *Drive out fear.* Management by fear, supervision by fear, and appraisals by fear cost dearly. People become afraid to innovate, experiment, and problem-solve.

9. *Break down barriers between departments.* Customers do not want to pay for internal turf wars, or their by-product, poor quality.

10. *Eliminate empty rhetorical slogans, exhortations, and unrealistic targets for the workforce.* Slogans and unreachable goals generate worker skepticism.

11. *Eliminate numerical quotas.* Quotas are usually either inflated or too low. Replace fixed targets with ranges of acceptability. Then, with worker participation, tighten the range as improvements to processes are made. Typically, evaluation by performance, merit rating, or annual review of performance are short-term, often subjective measures. These undermine teamwork, increase turf wars, demotivate people, and build fear.

13. *Institute a vigorous program of education and retraining.* Everyone in an organization should learn the new philosophies, practices, and systems. Allow employees continuous learning opportunities. Certain jobs may become obsolete, but people can continue to learn new skills for new jobs.

14. *Take action to accomplish the transformation.* Develop an action plan and institute an organizational commitment to carrying it out.

Developing Quality

In many cases, developing quality means changing the entire culture of the organization. Creating a system-wide philosophy and an implementation plan for quality can take years. Quality is not produced just because we espouse it or reward it. However, there are some tools management can use to develop a culture of quality. In addition to Deming's fourteen points, organizations must institute all of the following over a long period of time, so that quality becomes the organizational norm, rather than the exception.

1. *Understand process variation.* Every process for every task has variation. That is, there is some deviation or variation from

the optimal or ideal for everything produced or every service delivered. The more attention paid to improving the process, the less variation there will be.

There are two types of variation, variation from *common causes* and variation from *special causes. Common cause variations* occur from differences in workers' abilities, clarity of procedures, age and capability of machinery, and so on. These usually require management intervention to fix. *Special cause variations,* on the other hand, are easier to eliminate, such as defective material from suppliers, malfunctioning machinery, and untrained workers. To conform to customers' requirements work teams must understand that variation exists and they must recognize the difference between special causes and common causes of variation.

2. *Measure variation.* Work teams must document their processes so that they know when special causes force a process *out of control.* The most recognized tool for doing this is a statistical process control (SPC) chart. An SPC chart can monitor a process to eliminate special causes and to keep the process in control when special causes arise again. Team members chart defects or gauge measurements as they produce products. They take the mean average of a batch of products made or gauges read, and plot those points on a graph, similar to the one shown. When plot points fall above the upper control limit or below the lower control limit, it is time to identify the special cause and take a problem-solving approach to putting the process back in control. In other words, it's time to eliminate the special cause. This process replaces inspection and blaming workers for problems.

For example, a quality operation in a hotel might be defined in this way: All guest rooms must be cleaned between 11 A.M. and 3 P.M.; guests must be helped by a reservation clerk within ten minutes of their arrival; room-service deliverys should be made within thirty minutes of placement of the order; and the hotel operator must answer the phone by the third ring. Each employee should chart his or her own work. If a process (answering the phone) is out of control (excessive calls answered after three rings), employees in that process meet to identify the source of the problem and find ways to correct it so that the process is once again "in control."

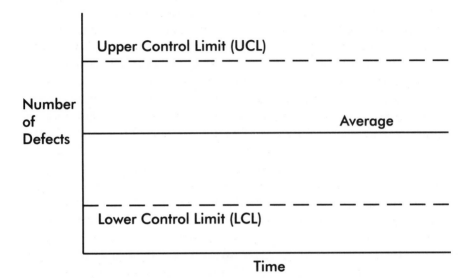

3. *Make customers the foundation for the quality system.* Identify your customers, both external and internal. For example, in an educational system, the external customers are students, their families, alumni, communities, and so forth; internal customers might be faculty, clerical, maintenance, administration, and support services. For a hospital, external customers are patients, their families, and insurance carriers; internal customers include physicians, nurses, social workers, administration, maintenance, and the business office.

Customers, whether internal or external, never ask for specific products or services. They describe their needs, then expect the supplier to come up with something to meet those needs. For example, no one ever asked for xerography; office workers did say they wanted a faster, cleaner way to make document copies. Then these customers asked for a way to stack copies. Some wanted color. Listen to your customers' needs, and develop ways to meet those needs.

External customers cannot be satisfied if internal customers have not received satisfaction from their internal suppliers. Territorial claims must be put to rest. Infighting and bickering serves only your competitors. Bring the internal customers and suppliers together to solve problems.

4. *Provide the necessary vehicles for achieving quality.* Traditional systems of quality control, already in place in many organizations, are one tool for maintaining quality. But keep in mind that quality control is just a tool, not a complete system, for achieving excellence. To be effective, quality control systems must be in place in all functions of an organization, including management.

Many companies have turned to employee problem-solving work teams, sometimes called quality circles, or Q-teams. These teams equip employees with the tools for solving problems so work can conform to acceptable quality standards. Employees who work together in the same department or function routinely meet to analyze process problems and determine solutions. They seek to reduce waste and costs, while increasing conformance to quality. Quality circles and similar programs build teamwork, improve communication, increase commitment to quality, and solve problems before they become unmanageable. They help spread the concept of quality throughout the organization.

There are many other tools for helping employees produce excellent products and services, such as process mapping, or laying out a detailed map of each process and showing how work flows from one process to another. Businesses must examine their quality standards and their existing resources. Quality control procedures, additional human resources, training and education of the workforce, and quality circles are but a few common means of promoting quality.

5. *Reward quality when it happens.* When assessments show that standards are being met, recognize and reward the achievement. Individuals or units meeting quality standards should be singled out for praise, given visibility and rewards of some type. Examples of excellence can serve as models for the entire organization. Once employees realize that company recognizes the rewards excellence, they will be motivated to excel.

6. *Coach for improvement.* Where assessments show that quality standards are not being met, management must direct its efforts at coaching for improved performance. The organization must never tolerate failure, nor should it lower standards to accommodate weakness. Individuals whose work fails to meet quality requirements should receive coaching, training, or other

assistance to improve their work. Management should examine whether there are constraints affecting employees' abilities to meet quality requirements, then remove those constraints or barriers. The organization may have to discharge employees whose work consistently fails to meet standards, despite ample assistance.

7. *Keep the quality process operating throughout the system.* Quality can never be taken for granted. The process for developing and implementing a quality culture must be ongoing if quality is to be maintained. The workplace organization is dynamic: new jobs emerge, the composition of employees changes, and new requirements develop. Organizations should continually cycle through the various steps to achieving quality so that emphasis on quality becomes perpetual.

Pitfalls in Achieving Quality— Deming's Obstacles

Many organizations have failed to institute quality because they encountered pitfalls along the way. But most organizations can achieve consistently high quality by avoiding these six pitfalls:

1. *Impatience.* Some companies hope for instant success through acclamation or affirmation of faith. They give up on quality because they do not see immediate results. Because quick turn-arounds do not occur, some managers believe that quality is impossible to achieve. Committed organizations must be prepared to spend years developing quality and never abandon the goal.

2. *Limited effort.* Some organizations assume that problem-solving techniques, new gadgets, and automation will create a transformation to a quality company. These are but small parts of a total quality change. Such a transition requires full organizational commitment to continual improvement and transformed thinking.

3. *Simplistic solutions.* Many companies attempt to use cookie-cutter solutions or follow too closely the examples of

other companies, hoping to make them fit their situation. Each company must formulate its own roadmap to quality.

4. *Half-hearted commitment.* Some companies avoid the difficult quality path under the pretext that "Our problems are different or unique." Every problem can be solved, and every process can be improved. The organization must be fully committed and prepared to spend much time, on and off the job.

5. *No top management involvement.* Starting at the bottom of the organization won't work. As with most any program, change must begin at the top. Employees must be sure that upper management is behind a program before they will embrace any change. Why should lower-level employees dedicate themselves to quality if they do not see their supervisors doing the same?

6. *Focus on inspection.* Quality improvement programs that emphasize inspection after work has been completed are doomed to failure. Thinking that after-production inspection can improve quality is short-sided and prevents organizations from finding the real causes of problems, much less how to fix these problems. The key to generating excellence is planning.

Ultimately, quality is about satisfying the customer. To do this, companies must discover what the customer wants, how the customer wants to be treated, and what it takes to thrill them. Then employees and managers must examine all their processes to ensure that the company can deliver what the customer wants, first time and every time.

[*See also* Customer Service; Team Building; Training]

For Additional Information

Rabbitt, John, and Peter Bergh. *The ISO 9000 Book: A Global Competitor's Guide to Compliance and Certification.* New York: AMACOM, 1994.

Bhote, Keki R. *World Class Quality: Using Design of Experiments to Make it Happen.* New York: AMACOM, 1991.

Brown, Mark G., Darcy Hitchcock, and Marsha Willard. *Why TQM Fails and What To Do About It.* Burr Ridge Ill.: Irwin Professional Publishing, 1994.

Deming, W. Edwards. *Out of Crisis*. Cambridge, Mass.: M.I.T. Center for Advanced Engineering Study, 1986.

Joiner, Brian L. *Fourth Generation Management: The New Business Consciousness*. New York: McGraw-Hill, 1994.

Walton, Mary. *The Deming Management Method*. New York: Perigree Publishing, 1989.

Recruiting and Selecting New Employees

Recruiting and selecting new employees are very important functions. Increasingly, organizations are coming to regard people as their most important asset. By developing appropriate hiring practices, you can avoid the costly error of hiring the wrong person for a particular job. Poor hiring decisions can cost thousands of dollars in advertising, interviewing, travel, training, and administrative expenses. Then there is the time lost in the selection process, disruption to the work unit because of a position needing to be filled, and the negative effects on productivity and morale when a new hire performs a job unsuccessfully.

Many managers erroneously believe that recruitment and selection are functions of personnel specialists and that operating managers need not be involved in the process. But there are many reasons why all managers should be skilled in recruiting and selecting new employees. In many small companies, for example, sophisticated human resource departments do not exist. Managers are expected to do their own hiring. And even in large corporations with selection specialists, the human resource staff can never know as much as departmental managers about the requirements of the position, the nature of the department, or the type of individual who could best perform the job. Only in very low-level, routine positions should managers consider leaving the whole process to the human resource specialists. In short, recruiting is an essential skill for all managers. Increasingly, some organizations empower work teams to interview and to make hiring decisions for vacancies on their teams.

Elements of the Recruitment and Selection Process

The key steps in recruiting and selecting new employees are discussed in the following sections.

Preparing a Job Description

You must be thoroughly familiar with the duties and requirements of a job before you can select the best person to perform it. In order to acquire familiarity, you must conduct a job analysis, which entails learning about the daily tasks and special assignments required of the employee. Observe the incumbent employee at work, interview the employee, administer a questionnaire about job requirements, and use written job descriptions. All of these methods will provide you with an accurate and comprehensive picture of the job.

In addition to outlining job duties, the analysis should determine other job specifications, such as education level, prior work experience, specialized abilities, and necessary personality characteristics. It is essential that these determinations not be arbitrary. For example, if the job could be done by someone without a college degree or without five years of experience, then to demand such specifications would be discriminatory. All requirements must be directly linked to job performance. The Americans with Disabilities Act (ADA) requires that job descriptions describe only *essential functions* of a job. For example, loading paper in a copier machine is not an essential function for a clerical job, since other people can do it and since the job would still exist if you removed loading paper as a job requirement.

After analyzing what the job entails, prepare a realistic and specific job description. This should include all the duties and responsibilities performed in the job, arranged in order from most often to least often performed. Some job descriptions include the percentage of daily time devoted to each specific responsibility. Other items to include are job title, reporting relationship, salary grade and range, and work schedule. These elements are especially important for job descriptions you provide to candidates.

Delineating the job specifications is an essential step that precedes the actual recruiting. By identifying the job duties, necessary skills, and important personality characteristics ahead of time, you can make more efficient use of your interviewing time and enhance your hiring decisions. This step also can reduce the number of unqualified applicants, since some people will not apply if they lack certain skills or do not want to perform certain job duties.

Selecting Recruiting Sources

There are many sources you can use to find job applicants. Some sources lend themselves to certain levels of jobs; others produce large numbers of applicants who may or may not be qualified. Common sources for recruiting job applicants include:

- *Newspaper advertising.* This method is inexpensive and produces large numbers of applicants in a very short time. But it is time-consuming because help-wanted ads can attract many unqualified applicants. Someone must then take the time to screen a potentially large number of applicants.
- *Job posting.* This entails advertising a job opening within your organization. In many companies, jobs must be made available to insiders before jobs can be advertised externally. The advantage is that you are able to hire someone who is already familiar with the company and whose performance record is known. Disadvantages include the fact that the company still has another opening to fill and that employee applicants not hired may become disgruntled.
- *Internal referrals.* Current employees recommend candidates for a job. Some organizations provide bonuses for employees whose referrals are hired. Because employees know the realities of a company, they can provide an accurate description of a job to potential applicants. On the other hand, the method can create "inbreeding," with close friends and relatives working together. Organizations using this method should combine it with other recruiting sources. Word-of-mouth alone is an insufficient recruiting practice, according to equal employment opportunity (EEO) requirements.

▪ *Campus recruiting.* Many organizations turn to college campuses for a large pool of talented applicants for entry-level professional positions. Likewise, high school and vocational schools can provide a pool of qualified applicants for secretarial or technical jobs. These sources provide, for the most part, applicants who lack work experience, however.

▪ *Employment agencies, temporary employment agencies, or executive search firms.* Using these outside sources can save a manager or personnel specialist a great deal of time, but they can be very costly to the hiring organization. In each case, the agency should take the time to learn of your staffing specifications, scout the market for qualified talent, and carefully screen applicants so that they refer only the most qualified candidates.

Executive search firms have the advantage of locating talented employees who are already employed and may be difficult to recruit through any other means. Because these recruiting sources vary in quality, you should screen them as carefully as you would any other employee or resource. Temporary employees afford you the opportunity to take an on-the-job view of their work.

▪ *Government agencies.* State or federal employment agencies can provide, at no cost to organizations, a pool of applicants for entry-level positions. Since these applicants are unemployed, they can usually start work immediately. Often, government agencies will train the employees at little or reduced cost to the employer, or the government agency may offer tax incentives to employers who hire specific types of people, such as those trying to remove themselves from government support services. Contact your local, state, or federal government for further information. Government agencies can provide qualified applicants only for limited types of jobs, however.

▪ *Professional societies and trade or business associations.* People in professional careers or skilled trades usually belong to associations affiliated with their specialty. Such associations may offer job-placement services, hold conventions where you can scout for qualified candidates, or publish job advertisements in their newsletters, magazines, or journals. This method is useful for recruiting for highly specialized positions such as engineering, law, architecture, and medicine. Also, highly motivated individuals in a particular field are most likely to be members of professional associations. The method is limited, obviously, by the type of job you need to fill.

• *Walk-in applicants.* Frequently, people will apply for jobs in a particular organization even if no openings exist. These applications can be kept on file and examined when a job opening occurs. While this recruiting method does not cost an organization, accepting large numbers of unsolicited applications can be time-consuming, especially if they are acknowledged and taken seriously.

Screening Application Materials

After the application deadline for an open position has passed, you begin to examine the application materials. In most cases, each applicant will provide a completed application form and a résumé. Depending on the position and the organization, a large number of application materials may have to be reviewed. You can solicit assistance from the personnel department or other qualified individuals to screen out the obviously unqualified applicants. In some cases, this will reduce the applicant pool substantially.

It is important that the hiring manager take the time to review the materials of all qualified candidates. While this may be time-consuming, time spent in the careful evaluation of written materials prevents unnecessary interviews and reduces the possibility of an inappropriate selection decision. You can review application materials in an unstructured fashion to determine the most preferred and least preferred candidates or develop systems for awarding points to applicants according to important job criteria, thereby rank-ordering the applicants. Whatever the method, you must screen application materials so that a limited number of top candidates emerge to be interviewed.

Naturally, the requirements of the particular job and culture of the hiring organization will dictate the criteria you use in screening applications. However, there are some standard considerations to use as you review a pool of application materials:

1. *What is the appearance of application materials?* The application form should be complete, legible, and neat. The résumé should look professional, should be easy to scan, and should be free from grammatical or spelling errors.

2. *Are there inconsistencies in information presented?* For example, are the dates of previously held jobs sequential and without interruption? If there is a gap in the work or educational history of an otherwise qualified candidate, ask the candidate for an explanation. Does it appear that the candidate was involved in activities in two widely different geographic locations during the same period? Has the candidate been obviously overqualified or underqualified for previous positions? You need not disqualify an applicant because of perceived inconsistencies in written information, however inconsistencies should alert you to seek clarification.

3. *Is there evidence of an irregular employment history?* An excessive number of job changes in a short period may indicate a problem employee. This may be confirmed if the applicant is ambiguous about the reasons for such job changes. Keep in mind, however, that some applicants have justifiable reasons for making frequent job changes. An erratic career pattern can result from company mergers or relocations, the job transfers of a spouse, changing employment trends in society, or ambitious career goals.

4. *Are there indications that the applicant is particularly well suited to your job or organization?* Perhaps the person has performed very similar duties in a previous job or has worked for an organization in a related field. Volunteer or civic activities may have helped the applicant develop relevant job skills.

The role of the manager in screening applicants is to objectively review materials to determine possible strengths and weaknesses of each applicant and to decide if that applicant should be interviewed.

Interviewing Candidates

Interviewing candidates is a key step in the selection process. This is when the majority of information about a candidate is obtained, when the candidate develops impressions about the organization, and when decisions about the match between applicant and position occur. It is important to allocate enough time to prepare for, conduct, and summarize each interview.

1. *Prepare.* You should prepare for selection interviews by reviewing job descriptions and job requirements, by familiarizing yourself with the applicant's written materials, and by preparing some standard and specific questions. Managers who are unprepared for interviews make inefficient use of interview time, present a poor image of the company, and fail to obtain pertinent information. You should develop a set of questions around certain skill categories relevant to the job.

You and your colleagues should first develop a list of defined skill categories, then prepare several questions for each skill category. Equal Employment Opportunity Commission (EEOC) guidelines prohibit questions about marital status, children, age, national origin, birthplace, religion, sex, race, ownership of a house or car, credit rating, or type of military discharge. EEOC guidelines suggest that all candidates for a job be asked the same questions, so as to avoid bias. Follow-up questions, naturally, would be different for different candidates since follow-ups are determined by the specific information needed after the candidate gives the initial response.

2. *Establish rapport.* The first step in the actual interview is to establish rapport with the candidate. This is an important ingredient in calming the applicant and in showing a positive work atmosphere. You should realize that job interviews are transactions in which each party gathers information to make a decision about the other. Both sides give and seek information to influence each other. You can establish rapport by greeting the candidate in a warm and friendly manner, by using a comfortable and private place to conduct the interview, and by describing the interviewing process. The more that you can reduce intimidating aspects of the situation and show genuine interest in the candidate, the more likely it is that you will get honest and thorough information.

3. *Ask questions.* Avoid excessive small talk, as candidates are eager to get on with the interview. It is wise to begin the actual

interview with broad, open-ended questions to get the applicant talking. For example, you can ask about daily duties at the last job. Then you can get more specific information by probing specific statements that the applicant makes. In this way, the interview resembles a conversation rather than an interrogation. Essentially, you want to converse with the interviewee in a relaxed style while obtaining specific information about previous work experience, educational background, and relevant skills. You can achieve a conversational tone by occasionally commenting on, but not evaluating, the person's remarks.

Open-ended questions are always preferable to questions that can be answered with yes or no responses. The key is to get the candidate talking, at length, in areas of interest to you. Focus the interview with prepared questions and keep it moving smoothly with well-placed follow-up questions to obtain elaboration or clarification in certain areas. Follow-up questions should elicit specific experiences and avoid general references or opinions. Beware of leading questions that cue the applicant to provide the answers you want to hear. The applicant, not the interviewer, should do the majority of the talking. You must be a careful observer and listener.

4. *Give information.* In addition to obtaining information, you must be skilled in providing thorough and accurate details to the job applicant. Here, the more candid you can be, the better. It is counterproductive to paint an unrealistic picture of the job or the organization to job candidates. Both the positive and negative features of the job should be explained.

Qualified candidates need to know the realities of a job so they can determine if the position fits their goals, lifestyle, or temperament. Some organizations arrange for potential new hires to talk with employees in similar positions or to observe part of a workday in the company. Providing an accurate rather than an attractive picture of the company will improve both the effective selection and the eventual retention of new employees.

Besides providing information about job expectations, this phase of the interview process also involves answering the interviewees' questions. Encourage the applicant to ask questions by providing enough time for dialogue, by making the interviewee feel comfortable throughout the interview, and by soliciting questions in an unintimidating manner. You can gain additional insights into candidates by the number and types of questions they ask about a job.

5. *State the next steps.* The final part of the face-to-face interview is to indicate what the next step will be. Will there be call-back interviews, reference checks, or physical exams? Should the applicant provide more information or submit a portfolio of work samples? To conclude an interview, thank the applicant. Escort the applicant out of the room and indicate how soon the decision will be made.

6. *Summarize information.* It is common for interviewers to take a few notes while the candidate talks. But note taking should be limited and unobtrusive during the interview. Then, immediately after the interview, take some time to elaborate on your notes. Your purpose is to summarize the person's answers, to record factual information, and to describe the candidate's appearance and mannerisms.

Avoid subjective evaluations. Both to make an unbiased decision and to comply with legal aspects of the selection process, you should refrain from recording opinions and unsubstantiated judgments about applicants. Personal interpretation by the interviewer can never by totally eliminated from hiring decisions, but subjective bias must be minimized as much as possible.

The postinterview summary is used as a memory aid after you have obtained information from many candidates. The manager who conducts more than a few interviews for a vacant position will find it difficult to associate information with particular candidates without the aid of detailed, objective notes on each person.

Administering Standardized Tests

Some organizations use standardized testing as part of the selection process. These may include tests of intelligence, aptitudes, skills, job information, or personality. Testing should never be the sole means of making hiring decisions, but it can be a valuable tool to provide precise, objective information you cannot obtain through other means.

If you use selection tests, they must be relevant to the job qualifications, they must be valid in measuring what they claim to measure, they must be administered and scored consistently for all applicants, and they must be administered by a qualified person. You can use selection tests initially to screen qualified applicants prior to scheduling interviews or test preferred candidates emerging from interviews to help distinguish among them. It is advisable that stardized tests be approved by legal department or company legal counsel. Whatever the method, if selection tests conform to professional and legal standards, they can provide a valuable source of additional information to employers.

Follow-up and Evaluation

Even after scrutinizing written materials, conducting and summarizing the interview, and obtaining test scores where applicable, the manager involved in selection has other tasks to perform. You should check references, verify degrees, and confirm previous employment. It is wise to check with at least three references to see if consistent evaluations of the candidates emerge. In many cases, you must be perceptive in noticing what the reference does not say about the candidate, as well as noting what comments are made. Degree verification is becoming increasingly common in the selection process and companies now exist to provide this service. The candidate's previous employers should be contacted to verify the dates of employment. Some organizations employ third-party investigators to check applicant references and to verify applicant information.

In some jobs or organizations, security clearances, physical examinations, or drug testing is performed. Certain categories of jobs require these additional screening measures and candidates may be rejected for failing them.

Once all the information from these various sources is available for candidates, it is time for you to evaluate qualifications, compare candidates, and make hiring decisions. This step should not be taken lightly. Avoid the tendency to make snap judgments, rely on personal biases, or make premature decisions. The evaluation of applicants should be systematic and as objective as possible. Some managers develop elaborate point systems for evaluating candidates. In each case, the applicant's job qualifications should be compared against job factors. You can develop lists of strengths and weaknesses for each candidate, based on factual information. The goal is not to hire the most stellar candidate, but to make the best match between a job and a candidate. Therefore, it is wise to have more than one interviewer and more than one making the hiring decision.

By carefully comparing the qualifications of the various candidates and matching them to job requirements, you can rank-order the candidates. It is important to consider several top candidates, should the most preferred candidate reject the job offer. Once your decision is made, you can make the job offer and notify applicants once the preferred candidate gives written acceptance of the offer.

[*See also* Interviewing; Turnover]

For Additional Information

Arthur, Diane. *Recruiting, Interviewing, Selecting & Orienting New Employees.* New York: AMACOM, 1991.

Yarborough, Mary Ellen. "New Variations on Recruitment and Prescreening." *HR Focus* 71, No. 10 (Oct. 1994), p. 1.

Mercer, Michael W. *Hire the Best . . . and Avoid the Rest.* New York: AMACOM, 1993.

Sexual Harassment

Managers must be aware of the issue of sexual harassment in the workplace. Equal Employment Opportunity Commission (EEOC) guidelines mandate that companies be responsible for creating a working environment free from harassment and have mechanisms for dealing with reported incidents of sexual harassment. Clearly, sexual harassment is not just an issue between two people, but an organizational issue. Because you can be held responsible when your subordinates are sexually harassed, you must know what constitutes harassment and be able to take steps to eliminate it from your organization.

What Is Sexual Harassment?

The November 1980 EEOC guidelines clarify sexual harassment as an unlawful employment practice under Section 703 of Title VII of the Civil Rights Act of 1964. The legal definition of sexual harassment is as follows:

> It is illegal for a supervisor or co-worker to engage in unwelcome sexual advances, requests for sexual favors, or verbal or physical conduct of a sexual nature. Such behavior constitutes sexual harassment whether submission is made an implicit or explicit condition of employment; whether employment decisions are based on submission to or rejection of such behavior; or whether such behavior substantially interferes with work performance or creates an intimidating, hostile, or offensive work environment.

Additionally, an employer is responsible for the behaviors of all its employees, regardless of whether those behaviors were forbidden and regardless of whether the employer knew or should have known of the occurrence of those behaviors. The employer is also responsible for the behaviors of nonemployees if the employer knew or should have known of the harassing behavior. The employer has the defense of having taken immediate and corrective action in the cases of harassment by coworkers and nonemployees.

You should examine certain aspects of the legal definition to fully understand its ramifications.

1. *Sexual harassment is unwelcome behavior.* Sexually harassing behavior differs from behavior that expresses sexual interest. Welcomed expressions of sexual interest or mutually entered sexual relationships do not constitute sexual harassment.

2. *Sexual harassment may be verbal, nonverbal, or physical.* Nonverbal harassment includes such forms of behavior as leering, offensive gestures, or whistling. Verbal harassment includes such forms of behavior as sexual innuendoes, sexual jokes, and suggestive comments. Physical harassment includes such forms of behavior as touching, pinching, and assault.

3. *Employment decisions need not be tied to the harassment.* The harasser does not need to threaten some work-related consequence in order for the behavior to be considered harassment. Obviously, making employment, promotion, or compensation decisions contingent on sexual behavior is harassment. But so are unwanted sexual behaviors with no job-related contingencies. Any unwanted sexual behavior that creates an intimidating, hostile, or offensive work environment can be considered harassment.

4. *The employer cannot claim ignorance.* The legal definition indicates that employers should know about the existence of sexual harassment in their work environments. This means that you must make sure that such behavior does not take place—you are responsible for providing a harassment-free work environment. You must be able to recognize and detect harassing behavior.

5. *You can be held accountable for the behavior of nonemployees as well as employees.* You must make sure that vendors, clients, customers, and delivery or repair personnel do not create an offensive work environment through their behavior toward organizational employees.

Why You Should Be Concerned

Evidence reveals that sexual harassment affects not only the parties involved but the entire organization. A harassed worker is likely to take more sick leave, become accident-prone, and resort to alcohol and drug abuse. An organization with sexual harassment problems faces worker stress, lower employee morale, higher rates of absenteeism and turnover, and productivity problems. In short, sexual harassment is extremely disruptive and costly.

Another vulnerability for you and your company is the possibility of a lawsuit related to instances of sexual harassment. Obviously, the harasser will be named and will be held liable for damages in successful sexual harassment litigation. But even managers who are not themselves harassers, and the company as a whole, can be liable in cases where blatant harassment was tolerated or where reported cases were handled inappropriately. As a representative of your organization, you can be implicated along with the actual persons engaging in harassing behavior.

The Nature of Sexual Harassment

Sexual harassment is a complicated issue and does not always have clear-cut boundaries. Unwanted behavior is not always distinguishable from reciprocal behavior. The same behavior may be defined as friendly by one person and as offensive by another. Experts disagree about whether the accuser should confront the accused to communicate that certain behaviors are offensive. Despite the ambiguities surrounding the issue of sexual harassment, some patterns emerge to create a typical sexual harassment scenario.

An examination of reported cases of harassment reveals that the typical complaint is filed by a female employee against a male employee. While there have been reported instances of females harassing males, females harassing females, or males harassing males, the majority of cases involve a female accuser and a male accused.

There is no clear-cut demographic profile of sexual harassment victims, but some factors seem more prevalent than others. Besides being female, targets of sexual harassment tend to be young and unmarried. Education, income, and occupation do not predict incidents of sexual harassment. Highly educated women in high-status jobs are just as likely to be harassed as are less educated holders of lower-status jobs.

Another trend, discerned from confidential surveys of employees, is the tendency for victims not to report harassment. Whether or not companies have policies and procedures for dealing with sexual harassment, nonreporting is common. Employees who have perceived themselves to be victims of sexual harassment offer several reasons for not reporting the incidents. They often feel that they will be blamed for the incident, believe that nothing will be done to stop the harassment, feel too embarrassed to report the incident, fear they will suffer personal repercussions or job reprisals from complaining, or feel guilty if the accused is hurt by the complaint.

The most common response to harassment is to leave the organization. Many victims quit their jobs without complaint once sexually harassing behavior has created a stressful work environment. In such cases, you have no way of knowing the extent of turnover from harassment in your organization. Even in instances of formal complaint or litigation, many victims opt to leave the organization. Women may quit if, after lodging a formal complaint, insufficient action is taken to stop the harassing behavior. Litigation may take so long and result in such a deteriorated employer-employee relationship that the victim feels there is no recourse except to leave the organization. In some cases, women are fired after reporting sexual harassment.

Outdated Managerial Attitude

One outdated approach to sexual harassment is that harassment does not occur in "our" company and that women who accuse men of sexual harassment are overreacting to or misinterpreting certain types of behavior. That view trivializes the subject, maintaining that allegations of sexual harassment stem from romances that have gone sour, from women taking offense at well-intentioned compliments, or from overly sensitive women employees who are not tough enough to handle a normal work environment. Managers who hold this view will dismiss reports of sexual harassment by indicating that boys will be boys, that the accuser must have behaved provocatively, that women have no sense of humor, or that no harm was intended. In short, sexual harassment is regarded as nonexistent, as an overreaction, or as a misunderstanding between two people. By perceiving harassment as an interpersonal rather than an organizational matter, managers who adhere to this school of thought either refrain from getting involved or try to protect the accused party.

Although some organizations seem to operate smoothly with this perspective, there is no way to determine the costs of absenteeism, medical benefits claims, turnover, or decreased morale or productivity resulting from unresolved incidents of sexual harassment. Such organizations and their managers clearly expose themselves to financially disastrous lawsuits, in light of contemporary EEOC guidelines.

Recommended Managerial Responses

Enlightened organizations take the view that sexually offensive behavior of any type is unprofessional and cannot be tolerated in the workplace. This position is good business practice because it reduces disruption in the workplace and eliminates legal liability. By establishing the following practices for preventing sexual harassment, you can create a safe, comfortable, and productive work environment for all employees.

1. *Establish and publicize a policy statement about sexual harassment.* Sexual harassment policy statements should communicate

the EEOC definition of harassment, provide examples of behavior constituting harassment, and explain the organizational procedure for reporting and dealing with sexual harassment complaints.

Have employees report their complaints to the immediate supervisor, to the personnel or human resources manager, to a company EEO officer, to the chief executive officer (CEO), or, where appropriate, to a union representative. Complainants must be assured confidentiality and freedom from reprisal. Policy statements may be communicated through personnel policy manuals, employee handbooks, company newsletters, bulletin boards, or memos.

2. *Establish investigative procedures.* Typically, the person responsible for EEO in an organization will follow these steps in investigating a sexual harassment complaint:

Interview, in separate sessions, the complainant and the accused. Try to ascertain, from each person's perspective, what happened, when it happened, who else might be aware of the events, the background of the incident, and each person's prior and current attitudes toward the other.

Interview witnesses. To gather documentation, you may have to talk with others who were aware of the alleged harassment. Realize that third parties will tend to take sides. Try to get the facts rather than opinions.

Act as a mediator in a meeting of the accuser and the accused. Some organizations do not take this step, either because they investigate anonymous complaints or they feel that forcing the victim to confront the accused is too traumatic or sensitive. In some cases, however, such a meeting can clarify perceptions, can show the seriousness of management's concern about harassment, and can resolve the incident.

Make an objective decision. The person investigating a sexual harassment complaint often must decide the merits of the case or must head a decision-making body. Objectivity is imperative. The decision must be based on the facts, not on personal attitudes or relationships with the people involved.

3. *Take disciplinary action.* Once a sexual harassment complaint has been judged to be accurate, some disciplinary action

should be taken. Depending on the nature and the extent of the harassment, disciplinary actions can include warnings, reprimands, suspensions, or terminations. Where the harasser is a nonemployee, verbal warnings, notification of supervisors, or discontinuation of the relationship may be warranted. Some organizations take disciplinary action against employees who knowingly file false allegations of sexual harassment or against managers who do not follow established procedures for handling reports of harassment.

4. *Educate employees about sexual harassment.* Because sexual harassment is a complicated and sensitive issue, preparing a policy statement and reporting procedures may not be sufficient. Organizations can provide training to clarify the definition of sexual harassment, to show top management support in preventing sexual harassment, to encourage employees to discuss their feelings on this issue, and to teach employees how to deal with sexually offensive behavior in the workplace. In addition, managers should be taught how to detect early signs of sexual harassment, how to intervene to prevent harassment, how to monitor their own behavior, and how to process any sexual harassment complaint that they receive from a subordinate.

[*See also* Diversity in Organizations]

For Additional Information

Kremer, J. M. D., and Marks, J. "Sexual Harassment: The Response of Management and Trade Unions." *Journal of Occupational and Organizational Psychology*, No. 65 (1992), pp. 5–15.

Wagner, Ellen J. *Sexual Harassment in the Workplace: How to Prevent, Investigate and Resolve Problems in Your Organization.* New York: AMACOM, 1992.

Weiss, Donald H. *Why Didn't I Say That?: What to Say and How to Say It in Tough Situations on the Job.* New York: AMACOM, 1994.

Stress Management

Stress is a state of physical or mental tension resulting from factors that alter the body's equilibrium, or, in other words, stress is the body's reaction to either pleasant or unpleasant stimulation. We think of stress as a reaction to negative forces or situations, but pleasant experiences or positive changes can also cause stress. Likewise, both overstimulation and understimulation can produce stress—for example, too much or too little to do on a job, or any sort of deviation from normal routine caused by factors related to the job and/or the person.

Effects of Stress

Both organizations and individuals are becoming aware of the serious consequences of stress. At the organizational level, stress can limit productivity and therefore be costly. At the personal level, it can have a variety of effects ranging from mild irritability to total disability or death. Such effects reveal the need for stress-management intervention at both levels.

Much research recently has documented the relationship of stress to certain diseases. The medical community largely agrees that cardiovascular disease, hypertension, ulcers, headaches, backaches, depression, gastrointestinal problems, allergies, sexual dysfunctions, alcohol and drug dependency, and certain forms of cancer are stress-related illnesses. Chronic stress has become a major health problem costing millions of dollars and countless lives annually.

Stress can also impair people's relationships and lifestyles. Stressed workers are more likely to be irritable, to withdraw from social situations, to engage in conflicts with others, to have emotional outbursts, and to have problems with families and friends. Stressed individuals are not the only ones to suffer; so do the peopole around them. It is difficult to estimate the extent to which work stress contributes to turbulent family relationships and divorce, but an association seems likely.

The effects of stress on the organization are numerous. Studies have documented that it leads to more workplace accidents; higher rates of absenteeism and turnover; lower group morale; labor unrest including grievances, strikes, and sabotage; and losses in productivity. The costs of such outcomes are staggering.

Extensive studies on the relationship of stress to productivity reveal that too little stress as well as too much stress impairs performance. People in boring or repetitive jobs with little challenge report feeling just as much stress as do workers in demanding, pressure-filled jobs. Moderate amounts of stress seem to result in optimum performance.

Because stress has serious consequences for the individual and the organization, both must understand the issues in stress management. Individual employees must take action to alleviate their own stress, and organizations should implement stress-management programs for their workforce. It is in the best interest of both groups to work cooperatively in managing workplace stress. Such efforts can save relationships, money, and lives. Effectively managing stress means understanding its sources, recognizing its symptoms, and utilizing strategies to reduce it.

Sources of Stress

Various factors create employee stress. Stressors can be personal (intrinsic to the individual's personality and private life), organizational (intrinsic to the job and the organization), or environmental (intrinsic to the physical surroundings and working conditions). Studies have shown that stress factors may be different for white-collar than for blue-collar employees.

Personal Sources of Stress

Personality and perception play important roles in the level of stress. Some types of people are more prone to stress than others.

Two people with similar jobs, family, and working conditions can vary in the extent to which they feel stress. Individual variations in stress tolerance and anxiety level clearly affect perceptions of stress.

Highly emotional people and those characterized as Type A personalities report high levels of stress. Type A persons exhibit extreme competitiveness, sense of urgency, aggressiveness, constant striving for achievement, impatience, perfectionism, inability to relax, desire to control, irritability, and restlessness. While many Type A individuals enjoy a great deal of job satisfaction and success, their behavior does correlate with high stress, increased incidence of coronary ailments, and workaholism.

Personal problems can contribute to stress. Psychological, financial, marital, sexual, or child-rearing problems are common types of personal stressors that can adversely affect work performance. Employers have responded by creating employee-assistance programs.

While family and friends often help alleviate stress caused by work, they can also cause stress. Troublesome relationships, communication difficulties, or illnesses of loved ones all produce stress, as do joyous events such as a wedding, the birth of a child, purchasing a home, or holiday celebrations. A myriad of personal factors can therefore produce stressed employees.

Organizational Sources of Stress

The stress of certain occupations has been found to be particularly high: police officer, firefighter, physician, dentist, farmer, miner, secretary, nurse, teacher, social worker, air traffic controller, machinist, and customer service representative. Many other occupations are stressful as well.

Work relationships are a potential source of stress. The quality of relationships with bosses, peers, and subordinates clearly affects your perception of a job as stressful or not. Stress is likely to result if you feel distrusted, threatened, hostility, or not supported in these relationships. Communication difficulties and personality clashes are a major source of workplace stress. Sometimes people like their jobs but don't like their co-workers.

Unclear or conflicting job responsibilities present another

source of organizational stress. Stressed employees often report uncertainty about what is expected of them. Many people work without job descriptions and with little awareness of the criteria by which their performance will be evaluated. Managers, for example, may be unsure of the extent of their responsibilities and the scope of their authority. A secretary may work for many managers at once who make conflicting demands.

Stress may also stem from the structure and philosophy of an organization. Organizations with strict chains of command and cumbersome rules, policies, and procedures can be very stressful places. Similarly, companies with authoritative and impersonal styles of management with little chance for employees to have input into the decisions that affect them are highly stressful. In other organizations, politics, game playing, and the lack of straight answers cause frustration. Some organizational cultures make it difficult for newcomers, women, minorities, or older workers to succeed. This category of stressors is broad and pervasive. A wide variety of issues related to organizational structure, management style, and workplace climate have been found to cause stress.

Certain issues related to career development can be sources of stress. Someone who is inadequately trained for a particular job will experience stress trying to perform it. Being overqualified for a position has its own frustrations. Many managers, especially high achievers, feel stressed when their desires for promotion are thwarted or postponed. Both stagnation in a job and eagerness in climbing the career ladder are stressors. Rapid career development through training opportunities, frequent promotions, special projects, or transfers can be quite stressful. Questions of job security inevitably produce anxiety.

Environmental Sources of Stress

Certain aspects of physical surroundings in a workplace can create stress. For example, noise, crowded conditions, uncomfortable temperatures, inappropriate lighting, uncomfortable furniture, awkward working positions, air pollution, or safety hazards contribute to worker stress. While federal regulations limit excessive noise or toxic chemicals in the workplace, many other environmental stressors go unnoticed. Working all day under flourescent lights or sitting for long periods of time at a computer terminal can produce tension, headaches, dizziness, and fatigue. Environmental features of the workplace not only create stress but also cause accidents, disability, and death. In recent years, more companies have been paying attention to environmental stressors. Indeed, a specialty area called ergonomics has emerged to examine ways to adapt the work environment to human requirements, capabilities, and needs.

Some studies have delineated different stress factors for management and nonmanagement positions. Managers are more likely to be stressed by deadlines, take-home work, responsibility for other people, competition, job instability, and the need for achievement. People in nonmanagement positions are stressed by shift work, job monotony, insufficient responsibility, social isolation, little recognition for achievement, fear of unemployment, and environmental conditions. These categories of stressors are not necessarily mutually exclusive, an individual may be affected simultaneously by personal, organizational, and environmental stressors. Obviously, coping will be more difficult for a person with a Type A behavior who has family problems and is in a highly demanding job. In fact, there seems to be a contagious effect; family problems can lead to job stress or vice versa.

Symptoms of Stress

In order to detect stress early enough to prevent serious consequences to the individual or the organization, you must be able to recognize stress symptoms. Stress manifests itself through certain feelings, behaviors, and illnesses. Chronic anger, despair, anxiety, and depression can all indicate stress. While it is inevitable that people feel some of these emotions occasionally, if they persist it may be a warning sign of stress.

Defensive or aggressive behavior can indicate stress. Stressed individuals have trouble dealing with life's little irritations and tend to have frequent emotional outbursts. Other potential stress indicators include difficulty concentrating; increased use of alcohol, caffeine, nicotine, or drugs; frequent nightmares; insomnia; loss of appetite or compulsive eating; or nervous tics. Work-related behaviors also change due to stress. For example, a decline in job performance, sudden increases in absenteeism, preoccupation with busywork, or an obsessive concern for work can all signal stress, as can the onset of typical stress-related illnesses.

Stress-Management Strategies

To be effective, a stress-management program must take a two-faceted approach. First, individuals must learn how to identify, monitor, and reduce stress in their lives. Second, the organization must revise its personal procedures, managerial styles, and physical environment to be less stressful to employees.

Individual Practices

An ongoing, dualistic approach to reducing stress will reap benefits for individuals and organizations alike. The following are some specific stress-management strategies for individuals and organizations to consider:

1. *Recognize your stress.* The first step in managing stress is to recognize its attitudinal, behavioral, and physical signs. Many highly stressed people are unaware of the messages their bodies are giving them. Be aware of individual stressors and unique symptoms of stress. On a regular basis, ask yourself what aspects of your personality, job, or private life cause you to feel stressed. Make a note of how you show the early warning signs of stress.

2. *Monitor your pace.* Periodically, you need to examine the pace of your life. Are you trying to do too much? Does your life offer too little stimulation? Remember that Type A personalities take on too many tasks and even rigidly schedule their leisure time. Setting realistic limits on work and social responsibilities is essential to stress management.

3. *Practice relaxation techniques.* Relaxation provides a temporary but important break in a period of stress. Medical approaches

to stress management typically recommend relaxation techniques such as meditation, yoga, self-hypnosis, progressive muscle relaxation, or biofeedback. Most of these techniques take just a few minutes and can be done in any quiet place at work. Each offers physiological and emotional therapy. In fact, some companies now provide relaxation or exercise breaks in lieu of coffee breaks during the workday.

4. *Develop an exercise program.* Exercise is one of the best stress-reduction strategies available. It provides cardiovascular benefits, helps control weight, boosts energy levels, and induces relaxation. The type of exercise need not be strenuous or time-consuming. The choices range from energetic options such as running or racquet sports to milder forms such as walking or gardening.

5. *Practice good nutrition.* Sound eating habits help you resist certain diseases and survive stress. A simple plan would be to moderate intake of fat, sugar, salt, calories, and caffeine and to consume recommended portions from the four basic food groups.

6. *Socialize with people other than co-workers.* For some people, work is the exclusive source of socializing. While friendships with co-workers can be enjoyable and relaxing, associating only with work colleagues can be detrimental because of the tendency to talk shop with co-workers and therefore never really escape the workplace.

7. *Develop a network of social support.* Everyone needs people who can be approached, trusted, and depended on. While family members typically fulfill this role, they do not always provide the social support necessary for coping with stress. In some cases, the family may be the source of stress. Confiding in various people—including family, friends, work associates, and professional counselors—can provide a buffer to stress.

8. *Moderate life changes.* Too much change, unexpected change, and uncontrolled change produce stress. Where possible, anticipate and pace your major life changes. Combining a promotion, the purchase of a home, and the birth of child probably will be too much to cope with all at once, no matter how positive each single event is. While we cannot control all life's changes, we can pace certain decisions with stress-management goals in mind.

9. *Practice time management.* Stress management and time management go hand in hand. People feel stressed when they lose control of their time. Setting reasonable goals, planning ahead, establishing priorities, scheduling tasks, resisting interruptions, delegating work, and avoiding perfectionism are all effective time-management techniques.

10. *Protect leisure time.* Sometimes people structure their free time as much as their workday. Hobbies and social life should not be as taxing as a job. Unstructured leisure time is more relaxing than a tightly scheduled itinerary. A little idleness each day and some larger blocks of unplanned time for spontaneous activity on the weekends is essential for relieving tension.

Organizational Practices

Because many stressors are intrinsic to the job itself or to climates in organizations, individual strategies are not sufficient for managing stress. Organizations can adopt several practices to reduce employee stress. Obviously, the best stress-management program combines both individual and organizational interventions. Some suggestions for organizations include the following:

1. *Provide stress-management training.* Organizations can teach supervisors and managers to identify signs of stress in themselves and in their subordinates. Equipping employees with stress-management skills can reduce the company's medical benefits costs and help to maintain productivity.

2. *Improve internal communication.* The more that information flows smoothly in an organization, the less anxiety and uncertainty there will be. Employees should be encouraged to communicate upward with managers, who should provide information to employees. Employees should know what is expected of them, receive regular performance feedback, and should feel free to bring problems and recommendations to the attention of supervisors. Open communication can produce better decision making as well as help to reduce stress.

3. *Clarify role expectations.* Because employees need to know their job duties, responsibilities, and authority, they should re-

ceive detailed job descriptions with explicitly stated reporting relationships. This is especially important for employees who receive assignments from several different people or groups. When an employee has more than one supervisor, strategies for resolving conflicting demands must be developed.

4. *Implement an employee assistance program.* For troubled employees, professional counseling is necessary. Some sources estimate that as much as 20 percent of a work force will have personal problems that significantly affect productivity. Providing counseling to troubled employees can be cost effective, reducing turnover and maintaining productivity.

5. *Develop people-oriented management styles.* Rigid, authoritarian management styles should give way to more flexible, democratic approaches. Employees should be treated fairly and humanely rather than like machines. Not only will people-oriented management styles reduce organizational stress, but evidence suggests that companies with democratic cultures attain higher levels of productivity. Some companies may need to begin a program of organizational development to change their management philosophy.

6. *Redesign jobs, where necessary.* You can enlarge or enrich unstimulating jobs. In cases of work overload, reduce responsibilities or delegate them to others. Periodically solicit employees' perceptions about the amount of challenge, stimulation, and fulfillment in their jobs.

7. *Provide a safe and comfortable working environment.* The Occupational Safety and Health Act mandates that working environments be free from extreme noise, toxic substances, and safety hazards. Employers can go further, however, in developing a comprehensive awareness of ergonomics. Employers should consider the relationship of spatial arrangements in the workplace to stress and productivity factors.

[*See also* Employee Assistance Programs; Time Management]

For Additional Information

Keita, Gwendolyn P. and Sauter, Steven L., eds. *Work and Well-Being: An Agenda for the 90's.* Washington, D.C.: American Psychological Association, 1992.

Rodahl, Kare. *Stress Monitoring in the Workplace.* Boca Raton: Lewis
    Publishers, 1994.
Whetten, David A. *Developing Management Skills: Managing Stress.*
    New York: HarperCollins, 1993.

Substance Abuse

The use of alcohol or drugs on the job is a problem faced by many organizations. As a result, companies increasingly are developing programs to prevent substance abuse in the workplace. Federal contractors specifically are required by the Drug-Free Workplace Act to have policies and educational programs regarding drugs. Many other organizations have developed policies, drug-testing procedures, and employee awareness programs on this issue. This chapter examines the problem of substance abuse in the workplace; discusses corporate policies, drug-testing programs, legal issues, and educational support services; and provides advice for organizations in preventing substance abuse in the workplace.

The Drug-Free Workplace Act

In 1988, Congress passed the Drug-Free Workplace Act, which requires federal contractors over $25,000 and federal grant recipients to provide and maintain a drug-free workplace. Specifically, they must have written policies, awareness programs, and disciplinary actions for illegal drug use on the job. Such policies must prohibit employees from unlawfully manufacturing, distributing, dispensing, possessing, or using controlled substances in the workplace. There must be clear consequences for employees who violate criminal drug laws while on the job. Further, such organizations must educate their employees about the dangers of illegal drug use and must explain the company policy, penalties, and counseling programs on drug use.

The Costs of Substance Abuse

While it is difficult to ascertain the extent of substance abuse in the workplace, we do know the costs to the employer when employee substance abuse is a problem. Estimates annually for lost productivity are as high as $30 billion owing to illegal drug use and $60 billion because of alcohol abuse. In addition to costs associated with lost productivity, there are the costs of increased medical expenses, workers compensation claims, and workplace crime associated with substance abuse.

Drug Testing

Surveys show disparate results on the extent to which companies test employees or potential employees for drug use. Some reports show that, on average, about one-half of all workplace organizations currently do some form of drug testing. A survey on workplace drug testing and drug abuse policies conducted by the American Management Association showed that, in 1993, almost 85 percent of firms surveyed did drug testing. Clearly, drug testing is prevalent in today's workplace.

There are various types of drug testing used by employers, including pre-employment, random, periodic, for cause, postaccident, and return to duty. Pre-employment drug testing is quite common and is typically included in a battery of screening measures employers use to evaluate the fitness and skills of prospective employees. Random drug testing is done by some organizations through unannounced testing of current employees. Periodic testing is an announced testing of current employees that is often tied to routine medical or physical exams. Drug testing for cause occurs when the employer performs an unannounced test based on suspicions of drug use. Postaccident testing occurs after a workplace accident to determine if drug use was related to the accident. The final type, return to duty testing, involves the unannounced testing of returning employees after they have had a drug-related leave from work or have participated in rehabilitation for substance abuse.

There are also various methods involved in workplace drug testing. The most popular, but most intrusive methods are physiological ones involving analysis of the employee's urine, hair, blood, or saliva. By far, urinalysis is the most common method of drug testing. In addition to psysiological measures, there are also paper-and-pencil tests that claim to measure or predict alcohol and drug use; because of the questionable nature of such tests, their use is uncommon. A final method of drug testing involves impairment measures such as hand-eye coordination tests. Increasingly, computer-based impairment measures are available to test actual performance effects of substance abuse.

Responses to Drug Testing

To fully understand the implications of workplace drug testing, it is important to take note of legal, employee, and union responses. Some states have enacted laws that limit, define, and govern procedural aspects of drug testing. Litigation has occurred on the grounds that mandatory drug testing is a violation of employees' privacy. However, the outcome of such cases has been in favor of organizational drug-testing programs.

The union response has been to ensure the rights of union representation for the employee at the time of drug testing as well as for the right of access to company drug-testing information. Further, the National Labor Relations Board has made drug testing a subject of mandatory bargaining, except for the unilateral implementation of pre-employment drug testing.

Initially, when drug testing was introduced as a workplace issue, there was employee resistance. However, when explained as a strategy to protect the health and safety of all employees as well as the livelihood of the organization, drug testing meets with less resistance. Negative reactions are reduced if the employer communicates the importance of a drug-free workplace and gives employees advance notice of testing.

Steps in Implementing a Substance Abuse Prevention Program

Drug testing is one part of a more comprehensive program for maintaining a drug-free workplace. Follow these steps to implement a complete substance-abuse program.

1. *Assess the problem.* An organization initiating a program to create a drug-free workplace should proceed carefully and obtain the advice and support from various constituencies in the organization. First, if the program is voluntary, there must be compelling reasons to develop a prevention program for substance abuse. The company should begin by assessing its risks and the extent of the problem. Are there incidents of actual or suspected substance abuse? High rates of accidents, absenteeism, medical claims, theft, and turnover may be indicators of substance abuse problems in the workforce.

2. *Seek input.* Managers, supervisors, and union leaders, as well as human resources, safety, medical, and legal experts, should be consulted in the development of a drug-free workplace program. A committee with such representatives could define the problem, draft a policy about a drug-free workplace, communicate the policy to employees, help educate employees about the dangers of substance abuse, and provide oversight regarding enforcement of a drug-free workplace.

3. *Develop a policy.* The policy should directly and simply prohibit the possession, use, sale, and distribution of drugs and alcohol on the employer's premises. It should explain the drug-testing program and the consequences to the employee for violating the policy.

4. *Communicate and implement the policy.* Employees should receive advance notice of the policy, should understand company purposes and practices regarding drug-testing, and should give their consent prior to being tested. It is imperative that the policy be applied in a nondiscriminatory manner. In cases where drug testing has been applied inconsistently or capriciously, courts have ruled in favor of employees or complainants. The results of drug testing should be confidential.

5. *Educate employees.* An effective program of substance abuse prevention cannot rest on drug testing alone. Employees and supervisors need to be educated about the personal risks of substance abuse, the effects on the organization, and the strategies for identifying substance abuse at work and making referrals to counseling or employee assistance programs.

6. *Offer employee assistance.* The organizational goal should be to rehabilitate the substance-abusing employee through the organization's employee assistance program, counseling services, or access to professional help through medical benefits.

When workplace expectations regarding a drug-free environment are clear and enforced, and drug testing is coupled with educational programs, organizations can significantly reduce incidents of substance abuse among employees.

[*See also* Disciplining Employees; Employee Assistance Programs; Terminating Employees and Downsizing; Violence in the Workplace]

For Additional Information

Arthur, Diane. *Workplace Testing.* New York: AMACOM, 1994.

Axel, Helen. *Corporate Experiences with Drug Testing Programs.* New York: The Conference Board, 1990.

Fellows, H. D. "Legal Aspects of Drug and Alcohol Testing in the Workplace." *Risk Management* 40, No. 3 (March 1993), pp. 21–27.

Oliver, B. "How to Prevent Drug Abuse in Your Workplace." *HR Magazine* 38, No. 12 (December 1993), pp. 78–82.

Sorohan, E. G. "Making Decisions About Drug Testing." *Training and Development* 48, No. 5 (May 1994), pp. 111–17.

Team Building

Because of technological advances, global competitiveness, and the realities of economic survival in an increasingly complex society, many jobs require the collaboration of people across departments or specialties. To put it simply, many heads are better than one. Team building is the process of selecting, developing, facilitating, and coaching a group to work effectively toward a common goal. It involves motivating individual members to take pride in the accomplishments of the group. Team builders must attend both to the requirements of the task (deadlines, quality, etc.) and the needs of members (fairness, managing conflict, etc.).

By cooperating to share knowledge and skills, a team can often complete work more effectively than can an individual. Teams are often intact, relatively permanent work groups; they can also be temporary groups from different ranks and departments brought together solely to complete a particular project. The former is called a *natural work team*, while we refer to the latter as a *cross-functional action team*. The most advanced forms of teams are self-directed, and they require little or no supervision and have full authority to process their work. To help permanent, temporary, and self-directed teams develop motivation, cohesiveness, and productivity, many organizations are turning to team building as an aspect of organizational development.

Objectives of Team Building

Team building helps a group function more effectively as a unit. Because of the sense of individualism and competitiveness fostered in many organizations, a work group is not automatically a team. Five or six people working on the same project does not ensure that they can work cooperatively toward a common goal. Specifically, team building enhances the morale, trust, cohesiveness, communication, and productivity of a work group.

- *Morale.* Morale is the degree of confidence a group has about its ability to get a job done. The higher the group's morale, the more motivated it is to perform well.
- *Trust.* Trust is a willingness to take risks based on a belief in others' abilities or integrity. Team members must have faith in each other if they are to function effectively as a team.
- *Cohesiveness.* Cohesiveness is the feeling of unity that holds a group together voluntarily. A cohesive group is one in which members want to belong. They feel much loyalty to the group. Cohesive groups are more productive.
- *Communication.* In order for a team to function well, members must be able to develop good interpersonal relationships, to speak openly with each other, to solve conflicts, and to confront issues.
- *Productivity.* Teams can accomplish goals that cannot be met as well by individuals. By sharing resources, skills, knowledge, and leadership, the team is greater than the talents of its separate members.

The Team-Building Process

There is no one method of team building. The objectives of morale, trust, cohesiveness, communication, and productivity can be met in a number of ways, and a wide variety of activities can help a group understand and improve its functioning. Whatever the methods, it is important that the team itself develop the ability to identify its operating problems and solve them. The five steps commonly used in team building are discussed in the following sections.

Step 1. Establishing Team Structure

Any team must operate with enough structure to empower it to tackle tough issues and solve difficult problems, while allowing the structure to be minimal enough to not stifle its creativity or its authority. This is a delicate and difficult balance to maintain. Some highly creative teams may work outside the boundaries of the organization, as did the original Apple Macintosh team. Most teams, however, require some attachment and some structure from the organization of which they are part. Although this structure differs for every company, the following is a general listing of the components for successful team structure.

- *A steering team* consists of upper management, union leaders (in a unionized company), managers, supervisors, team leaders, and other key people. Like the pilot or captain, this group philosophically sets the course for the team process and serves as a source of feedback and mid-course correction.

- *A design team* examines the whole as-is system and targets some ways to improve productivity. The design team is a cross-functional team that includes members from all levels and functions in the company. This is a team of action. It assumes supervisory, management and task responsibilities. Results may take two to three years.

- *Leaders* are important to team success. Selecting leaders and determining the appropriate type of leader is critical. The leaders must be participative. Theory X, top-down leaders do not work well with teams. Will leadership evolve? Will leadership rotate periodically? Will the team have a leader and a facilitator? What should the team call the leader?

- *Meetings* can be both essential and cumbersome. Well-facilitated, frequent meetings are a must for every type of team. Leaders must be trained to manage meeting processes and interpersonal processes. Meeting processes include such items as planning and using an agenda, managing to avoid groupthink, distributing meeting minutes, following up on assignments and securing meeting space, time, and materials. Interpersonal issues may include ensuring that all members participate, helping members to speak and prepare their presentations, resolving conflicts, and handling difficult members in meetings. Successful team meetings require significant training for all members and full organizational support.

- *Process consultants,* whether internal or external, teach, guide, assume risks, and help resolve conflicts internal to the team or with people outside the group. Because they are not actual members of the team, consultants can challenge the assumptions and behavior of team members. They can be more objective and may have a greater freedom of operation when helping the group. Consultants help teams establish norms and boundaries. They help educate team members to use various tools and charts to keep team members focused and productive. Consultants often must resuscitate teams later in the process, as the excitement and fanfare give way to tediousness. At this point, teams may stray off course. Consultants and facilitators working together may prevent such calamities.

Step 2: Collecting Information

Team building should begin with group self-assessment, which provides the starting point for team development and helps to both determine strengths and weaknesses and set goals for improvement. Information collection is necessary to diagnose problems of group functioning. Team-development needs can be determined through various data-gathering techniques, including attitude surveys, interviews of members, standardized questionnaires, role-play analysis, and observation of group discussions.

These techniques are useful in assessing a number of content areas, such as communication climate, trust, motivation, leadership ability, group consensus, group values, knowledge of team goals, and role conflicts. Needs-assessment areas and methods should be tailored to fit the team's purpose, composition, and workplace culture. Any information that sheds light on how to improve team functioning is valid. Be careful to use only objective and valid data-gathering methods in order to pinpoint real and important team problems.

Step 3: Discussing Needs

Information gathered in step 1 should be summarized and fed back to the team. The team should openly discuss and interpret trends that emerged from the needs assessment. According to the data-collection process, what are areas of team strength? In what areas does the team need improvement? It may take several meetings for the team to grasp the results of the data collection and to agree on team-development needs. These feedback sessions are essential in order for the team to establish its own goals rather than have the goals imposed externally. By participating in what can be sensitive discussions of strengths and weaknesses, the team is already on its way to self-sufficiency in problem diagnosis and solution.

Step 4: Planning Goals and Setting Technical Targets

Once issues are clarified, the team should define its goals and mission and establish some general priorities. It is essential that the team work on issues that are most important to members. By setting its own agenda, the group will be more committed to the process of team development. The group should develop a tentative schedule and action plan for meeting its goals. Consultants can be helpful here by suggesting techniques or activities through which the group can meet its goals. Organizational development or training specialists should know of exercises, films, instructional modules, or case studies to help a group develop skills necessary for effective team functioning.

Step 5: Developing Skills

The bulk of the team-building process will focus on activities to develop skills needed for high-performance teamwork. Just as an athletic team must learn plays, develop moves, and practice skills, so a work team must develop performance skills. The following are some common team process skills developed through team-building activities:

1. *An awareness of group development.* It may be fruitful for participants to realize that groups progress through predictable stages. Being able to recognize these stages can help the group deal with problems and prevent frustrations. The organizational-development literature includes activities to help a group cope

with the typical developmental phases of orientation, evaluation, and control.

The orientation phase is characterized by confusion over what roles members ought to play, the tasks to be performed, and the role of leadership. Members exchange information in order to orient themselves to the team project. During the evaluation phase, members tend to be opinionated and experience much conflict. They disagree about how to approach the task and must frequently take sides in struggles for leadership. The group may be fragmented by coalitions. In the final stage, the group begins to coalesce. Members accept influence from others and from the leader in order to achieve team objectives. The group takes on a personality and an energy of its own. Deliberations are coordinated and directed toward a common goal.

Putting a newly formed group through a case-study discussion can trigger the emergence of these typical phases. Careful processing of the discussion by an experienced group facilitator can help the group understand them. Discussing the results of self-assessment or group-assessment exercises may prove beneficial. Replaying a videotape of group sessions can provide vivid illustrations of the group's progression through the phases. By developing an awareness of this crucial aspect of group dynamics, teams can function more smoothly and more productively.

2. *Role clarification.* In achieving a group task, it helps if everyone knows his or her individual responsibility and area of authority. Even if the team has been working together for some time, there may be confusion over who is doing what and who has the right to do what. Formal job descriptions may not correspond to people's expectations of roles and rights. Sometimes supervisors and managers have difficulty giving up their traditional roles to become team members. Similarly, some team members sometimes have difficulty treating supervisors and managers as equals. If left unattended this particularly difficult issue of power switching can devastate the effectiveness of a team.

Early on, group members ought to discuss their expectations of the group's role within the organization, as well as individual members' roles within the group. What is the group's mission? Whom does the group report to? What types of power does it have? Who is the designated leader of the group? Do members agree on the division of responsibility? Do members' roles complement one another or do they conflict?

Just like members of a sports team, work-group members need to know who is playing what positions and how to play together smoothly and effectively. Role-clarification questionnaires or discussions can help members see how their performance depends on the performance of someone else. This understanding creates a strong sense of unity and loyalty within the team.

3. *Problem Solving.* Knowing how to use problem-solving tools and techniques is essential to team success. Every team member must be able to participate in using some of the following basic problem-solving tools:

- Pareto charts graphically display several problems. Each bar in the chart represents the frequency of occurrence of each problem or the cost impact of each problem. The team attempts to first tackle the greatest-costing or most-frequent problem. Pareto charts show that 80 percent of your excessive costs are caused by 20 percent of your problems.
- Flow charts or process maps diagram the many interconnected steps of a process. Flow charts show starting points, action and decision steps, and ending points, as well as unnecessary or wasted steps. Seeing the process diagrammed helps teams to eliminate or reduce steps.
- Cause and effect diagrams, sometimes called fishbone diagrams, list a defined problem at one end or at the head of the fishbone. Fin bones are labeled under type of cause (staffing, methods, measurements, materials, or machines). Possible causes are brainstormed and listed under each category, thus creating an appearance of a fishbone.
- Statistical process control (SPC) charts visualize data collected in the production or delivery of a product or service. Collected sample averages are posted as points on a control chart as the product or service is made or delivered. The chart has an upper border, called the upper control limit,

and a lower border, called the lower control limit. The SPC chart lets front-line people monitor their own quality production. When postings fall outside the control limits, work is stopped. Work teams isolate the probable causes and decide how to correct the problem.

* Brainstorming is how a group of people collect probable causes in the fishbone or cause-and-effect diagram, and how groups gather ideas on solutions to problems. Every idea is accepted and written down on a flip chart. Put-downs and idea-killers are not accepted. Some people contribute additional or clarifying information based on previous suggestions—this is called *piggybacking*. Brainstorming creates a large quantity of suggestions from which several may be combined to from a new or creative solution to a problem.

* Action plans give work-team or problem-solving teams a game plan to implement their solutions. Roles and responsibilities are assigned. Reports are required. Usually the findings and action plans are presented to management or steering teams for approval or for purposes of information and communication.

* Responsibilities charts list activities, due dates, milestones, and persons responsible so all team members know current project status and responsible members for the project or project phases.

Comprehensive training, followed by hands-on coaching, helps team members apply these tools to the real world. This expedites a thorough analysis of the technical problems the team has chosen to eliminate. The team's underlying mission is that everyone works to continuously improve everything. The Japanese call this *kaizan*.

4. *Consensus decision making.* Most decisions in the workplace are made by deferring to the views of powerful people. Consensus occurs when all members in effect say, "I can live with that decision. I don't necessarily agree with it 100 percent, but I can support it strongly."

At best, democratic decision making means that the majority

rules. When a majority decides, some people find themselves going along with, but not agreeing with, the majority. In a true teamwork approach, the group makes decisions by deliberating until everyone agrees. By taking extra time to reach consensus, more options are considered and all members have complete input. Not only does consensus decision making produce better decisions, but members feel greater commitment to the decision. The drawback of consensus decision making is that it takes longer than voting or having the leader decide. However, the quality of the decision usually is far superior, and implementation is easier, since all who participate agree to commit to the decision.

Most groups have to work at developing the skills of consensus decision making. Case-study discussions, followed by analysis of the group process, can give groups practice in decision making. Do members listen objectively to each other? Do all members have the chance to contribute? Does domination, ambivalence, or nay-saying occur? Does the group mediate its own conflicts? The goal is to systematically and patiently consider information and opinions until the best decision, not the quickest or obvious one, is reached. When a group can reach consensus, the true potential of teamwork is being utilized.

5. *Conflict resolution.* It is inevitable that a group of people working closely together will experience conflicts. If the people fail to handle these conflicts properly, the group will fall apart. By developing conflict-management skills, though, the group can realize productive outcomes from the conflict. By disagreeing openly without becoming defensive, members can see opposing viewpoints, can develop respect for each other, and can arrive at better decisions.

A team can develop its capacity to handle conflict by openly discussing the values of conflict, by removing negative consequences that typically surround conflict, by playing devil's advocate in discussions, and by encouraging skepticism and debate. Questionnaires, role-plays, and exercises can help the team develop the open communication necessary for productive conflicts. A high-performance team is characterized by members who can strongly disagree over ideas and still like and respect each other.

The team should do as many activities to develop as many specific skills as necessary. In the process of team-building activities, members may discover additional problems or needs. Skill-building areas may emerge as the team performs its organizational tasks. Because the team is developing its own capacity to diagnose and solve problems, it can channel new goals into the team-building model.

The consultant may be a valuable resource in helping the group conduct skills-building activities. The consultant can lead the group through discussions, suggest exercises, and encourage the members to analyze the process. Also, an expert in team building may be needed to teach concepts such as phase development, role clarification, consensus decision making, and conflict resolution.

6. *Evaluating results.* As an ongoing function of all types of work teams, the team should evaluate whether it is functioning effectively. Is it on task? Are its decisions and solutions of quality? Does it have high morale, trust, cohesiveness, and productivity? Are there additional areas that need improving? Evaluation should take place at several stages in the team-building effort. Initially, the team undergoes evaluation to determine needs and set goals. Also, periodically throughout the skills-building activities, the team should assess its progress. The ability to systematically assess progress is a crucial element of team development and major means by which the team becomes self-sufficient. In the workplace, most people are accustomed to being evaluated by others, but the skill of self-assessment makes people and organizations adept at change and growth.

Evaluation can take many forms. In some cases, the effects of team building can be measured by the standard workplace criteria of productivity or output. If the team is producing more units than it did before team building, then it must be performing more effectively. Less error, lower production costs, and less turnover may be signs of effective team functioning. Less tangible measures of team-building effectiveness include surveying members' attitudes and perceptions regarding team morale, trust, and cohesiveness. The team's suppliers and customers must also be asked for their feedback. The team-building cycle continues as the evaluation results feed into needs assessment and the team proceeds through the team-building model.

Characteristics of a High-Performance Team

A successful team-building effort should create a team that functions effectively based on these characteristics:

1. All members are committed to accomplishing the team goals or mission that they helped develop.
2. The team works in an environment of trust and openness.
3. Members feel they belong to the team and participate freely.
4. Diverse people with diverse experience, ideas, and opinions are valued and groupthink is eliminated.
5. Team members continually learn and self-improve. This helps the team correct itself and solve its problems.
6. All team members understand their roles and responsibilities, yet value and use each other's skills and knowledge.
7. The team uses consensus decision making.
8. Team members communicate openly and directly, and listen to one another objectively and patiently.
9. The team can handle conflict without resentment or hostility.
10. Team leaders, whether permanent or rotating, practice participative leadership.

[*See also* Conflict Management; Motivation; Quality]

For Additional Information

Butman, John *Flying Fox: A Business Adventure in Teams and Teamwork*. New York: AMACOM, 1994.

DuBrin, Andrew J. *The Breakthrough Team Player: Becoming The M.V.P. on Your Workplace Team*. New York: AMACOM, 1995.

Harrington-Mackin, Deborah. *The Team Building Tool Kit: Tips, Tactics, and Rules for Effective Workplace Teams*. New York: AMACOM, 1993.

Hitchcock, Darcy. *The Work Redesign Team Handbook: A Step-by-Step Guide to Creating Self-Directed Teams.* White Plains, N.Y.: Quality Resources, 1994.

Scholtes, Peter R. *The Team Handbook: How to Use Teams to Improve Quality.* Madison Wisc.: Joiner Associates, 1988.

Terminating Employees and Downsizing

Managers frequently regard employee termination as the least desirable aspect of their jobs. Termination is the most traumatic and disruptive event an employee faces in the workplace. Recently, organizations in every sector of employment have faced the necessary, albeit unpleasant task of reducing large numbers of their workforce in order to remain competitive. In addition, termination is costly to an organization, as well as demoralizing and anxiety-producing to colleagues who retain their jobs. Still, some companies have had to implement such downsizing or rightsizing just to survive in these economic times. For these reasons, you must be aware of the proper methods of terminating employees from a legal, psychological, and communication perspective.

Employment-at-Will Doctrine

The employment-at-will doctrine, in effect for nearly a century in the United States, allows an employer to fire an employee for any reason or for no reason at all. The doctrine is based on the rationale that if an employee has the right to quit at any time, then the employer retains the right to discharge at any time. However, unionized workers, civil service employees, and executives or professionals with employment contracts receive protection from employment-at-will dismissals. Also, federal employment statutes as well as some state laws provide exceptions to the employment-at-will doctrine. It is illegal to fire someone based on reasons of sex, race, creed, ethnic origin, age, or disability. Additionally, within the past few years, court decisions have provided further exceptions to the employment-at-will concept, and these exceptions fall into two legal categories: public-policy exceptions and implied-contract exceptions.

Public policy exceptions protect employees who blow the whistle on the company for violations of environmental, safety, or health laws; who try to start a union; who file a discrimination charge; who file a workers compensation claim; who refuse to perform criminal acts on behalf of the company; and who take time off to serve on a jury.

Implied-contract exceptions indicate that company literature, such as a policy statement in an employee manual that discusses terms and conditions of employment, may constitute an implied contract with an employee. To prevent such wrongful-discharge litigation, personnel directors should review recruiting and employment literature to eliminate statements that could be interpreted as promising job security. An employer should regard written statements in offer letters, on employment applications and contracts, in employee handbooks, and in personnel files as legal commitments to employees. Likewise, oral promises made in selection interviews, performance appraisals, and exit interviews may be binding on the employer. Such documents and verbiage should be reviewed by legal counsel before distribution to employees.

So while the employment-at-will doctrine still guides employment practices in some states, numerous exceptions have eroded the concept. You must be aware of the doctrine and its exceptions as they relate to employee termination in your state.

The Psychology of Termination

Terminating an employee is unpleasant, whether it results from one discliplinary action or is part of a massive downsizing. Many managers do not want to examine their own feelings regarding this duty. Being aware of the psychological effects of termination, though, can make the process less stressful for the manager and more humane for the discharged employee. Managers experienced in terminating employees report resentment at having to perform the task, guilt for making the wrong hiring decision or for inadequate training of the employees, compassion for the dismissed employees and their families, anger at supervisors or the organization, blame and anger toward the fired employees, and fear that they themselves may be fired someday.

The psychological effects of being fired seem to follow a predictable pattern not unlike those associated with the stages of grieving. Awareness of these effects can help discharged employees cope with the situation and can assist managers in dealing with typical employee reactions.

Terminated employees initially experience shock, disbelief, and denial. The suddenness of being ousted from an organization can be overwhelming. Employees may have difficulty comprehending the reason for termination and feel that their lives have been shattered. They may also be quite dazed, have a confused sense of identity, and feel anger toward the manager and the organization. Terminated employees may feel mistreated and want to retaliate against the company.

Some terminated individuals perceive that a mistake has been made, try to appeal the decision, or cling to a hope of being recalled. When the employee realizes the finality of the decision, depression is likely to ensue. Indeed, termination can lead to feelings of failure, bruised egos, and anxiety about financial or career consequences. There may be guilt over errors, shame with family and friends, and hopelessness about finding a new job. Finally, the employee accepts the reality of the situation, rebuilds confidence and esteem, and plunges into the task of finding new employment.

One area frequently overlooked concerns the psychological effects of termination on coworkers. Whether dismissal involves one person or many personnel, the coworkers who remain will be affected. The manager who realizes this can better deal with morale issues resulting from termination. Third parties to terminations report immediate shock and increased communication about the dismissals, relief at retaining a job coupled with the fear that "I might be next," empathy for the discharged workers, and an opinion about the fairness or unfairness of the firing based on whether the terminated persons were perceived as competent or not.

The psychological impact can be quite severe to employees, managers, and the organization. Therefore, many organizations seek the help of outplacement firms to assist terminated employees through these psychological stages and, most important, to help them find new jobs, start new businesses, or begin new careers. Outplacement services are commonly offered by external groups, though some employers create their own internal outplacement departments through Human Resources. Outplacement may help relieve employees of their negative feelings, while helping these persons focus on new beginnings. Many such outplacement services offer their clients offices, clerical assistance, and support groups, while creating a worklike atmosphere for outplacement clients to search for new jobs. Outplacement relieves managers of the stress and guilt often resulting from having to terminate employees. The company relieves itself of some of the impact of these feelings, while improving its public image during the difficult times of termination.

Conducting a Termination

There is no one way to fire an employee. Many of the decisions and methods of carrying out the task depend on the reason for termination, the status and seniority of the employee, and the organization's human resources orientation. While the fine points of conducting a termination vary from case to case, all terminations include the elements of planning, communication, and follow-up.

Planning

From a legal standpoint, careful planning is crucial and can make the difference between a dignified firing and a brutal one. You must make the decision to fire, determine the reasons for dismissal, and gather the evidence to document and explain your decision. If you have followed a system of progressive discipline with the employee, you will find this stage of the process easier and less stressful.

A progressive disciplinary system includes a series of rules and regulations regarding work behavior and performance, progressive warnings to employees who violate those rules, counseling to improve work behavior, and criteria for termination. Progressive discipline allows open and objective communication about poor performance so the employee knows that specific actions must be corrected within a certain time frame or termination will result. Under this system, the employee receives advance warning that dismissal is being considered and is less likely to perceive unfair treatment in the event of a termination. You, then, have written records to document the reasons for dismissal. In the event of litigation, these records assist in the defense that termination was fair and not abusive. Of course, the progressive disciplinary system does not apply if the termination is based on economic reasons beyond the employer's control.

Additional questions involved in planning a termination include:

- Who will communicate the termination?
- When will the employee be terminated (time of year, day of week, hour of day)?
- Will third parties be present at the termination, such as immediate supervisor, member of personnel? (It is strongly advised that more than one manager should be present for legal reasons and to help prevent violent reactions.)
- Where will the termination occur?
- How will the message be delivered?
- How will the news be communicated to the rest of the company?
- What credible and agreeable cover story (reason for separation) should be proposed?
- What severance package or outplacement assistance will be provided?
- How might the terminated employee react? How will the terminating manager handle all possible reactions?

Communication

After planning these aspects of the process, someone must communicate the decision to the employee. Careful communication is necessary to help the employee save face and cope with the news.

Consideration must be given also to the legal implications of what is said. Face-to-face communication of the dismissal is often called the exit interview. During an exit interview the employee shares improvement ideas to the manager and the organization. In addition to hearing the termination message, the employee is able to vent feelings somewhat in a focused and more constructive manner. Of course, the content of the actual message of termination depends on whether the dismissal is based on economic, organizational, or employee behavior factors.

When the termination is due to reasons beyond the employee's control, you should explain the company's problem (economic, relocation, reorganization), indicate other necessary actions already taken by the company, state the decision to release the employee, express confidence in the employee's abilities, and indicate the extent of the company's financial terms of separation (severance pay, benefits continuation). Then you must listen to the employee and allow feelings to surface. At the conclusion of the exit interview, take the employee to the personnel office to complete the necessary paperwork.

When the termination is based on incompetent performance or unacceptable behavior by the employee, you should inform the employee of the decision to terminate, minimally explain the reasons for dismissal, avoid blame by indicating there was a misfit between the organization's needs and the employee's attributes, show confidence about the employee's ability to find new employment, and explain severance and outplacement options. Again, listen patiently and deal calmly with the employee's reactions.

The exit interview should be direct and concise. It should be absolutely clear that the person has been fired and the decision is irreversible. Dwelling on past mistakes and effusive demonstrations of sympathy should be avoided. It is important that the terminator remain aloof and avoid defensiveness, whatever the reaction from the dismissed employee. Reactions can run the gamut from tears, accusations, anger, and threats, to self-pity and pleading, to disorientation to delight. When the message has been delivered, the reaction shown, the questions about severance answered, and the cover story coordinated, then the exit interview should be brought to a quick close. The final remark should refer to the employee's next step and future success.

Follow-up

The wrap-up part of termination involves the package of assistance given to the dismissed employee, a mutually agreeable cover story for prospective employers, and the dissemination of information about the termination to the rest of the company.

Some companies have specific policies regarding severance benefits. Others design severance packages to suit individual employees. Whatever the method, a severance settlement is important for helping the employee during transition to a new job. The attention given to this aspect of termination can significantly affect the morale of retained workers, as well as the overall image of the company. Most severance packages include a continuation of salary for a certain time period depending on the employee's position, length of service, and age. Typically, higher-level, older individuals with longer tenure in the organization receive larger settlement amounts. Other areas for discussion include the eligibility period for unemployment benefits and health and insurance coverage.

The manager and dismissed employee should agree on a reasonable story to tell others both inside and outside of the organization regarding the termination. The story should put both the individual and the organization in a good light, thereby protecting coworkers' morale and the employee's chances of obtaining a good position elsewhere. Prepare a draft of this story to offer the employee for approval.

The termination process is not complete until you write a summary of the exit interview and communicate information about the termination to coworkers. While all the details of the exit interview are still vivid, make a record of all that transpired.

Include all remarks exchanged, the emotional climate that prevailed, and decisions regarding severance benefits. Your accurate summary could prove invaluable should the employee decide to challenge the termination decision. Finally, provide a written announcement of the termination to coworkers, stating merely that the individual is no longer an employee of the company. Provide the effective date and indicate the process for determining a replacement. Do not discuss reasons for the termination.

Advice for Handling Terminations

Here are some additional suggestions to consider regarding the termination of employees:

1. Make sure the termination takes place in a private setting. Never conduct a dismissal over the phone, by a memo, or by a "pink slip" in the pay envelope.
2. If there is a possibility that the employee could make a case for wrongful discharge, seek advice of counsel before terminating the employee.
3. Consider whether the employee may try to retaliate against an individual or against the company. Make sure the employee cannot endanger other people, important documents, or equipment. Request the help of security if necessary.
4. Give the termination process the attention it deserves so that effective communication, dignity, and respect can prevail.
5. Owing to fears of litigation on charges of libel and slander, many experts advise against giving any recommendation (good or bad) for any former or current employee. They advise that all such requests be forwarded to Human Resources. They recommend that managers simply say that they are unable to give such information.

[*See also* Disciplining Employees; Interviewing; Violence in the Workplace]

For Additional Information

Grensing, Lin. "Downsizing: How to Do it Right." *Office Systems* 10 (May 1993), pp. 62–65.

Millman, Dorothy. "How Managers Should Handle Terminations and Layoffs." *Telemarketing Magazine* 12, No. 5 (Nov. 1993), pp. 65–67.

Pollock, Ted. "When You Have to Fire Someone." *Production* 105, No. 10 (Oct. 1993), pp. 24–26.

Weiss, Donald H. *Fair, Square and Legal: Safe Hiring, Managing and Firing Practices to Keep You and Your Company Out of Court.* New York: AMACOM, 1995.

Time Management

The skill of efficiently using time is essential for management success. Unlike other resources, time cannot be saved or accumulated. In order to achieve goals, meet deadlines, and deal with unexpected problems, you must make effective use of limited time. To be skilled in time management, you must recognize your time robbers and develop habits that protect and maximize the time you do have.

Common Time Robbers

Managers who work excessively, but merely spin their wheels with little tangible accomplishment, may be victims of three types of pitfalls: poor planning and organizational skills, external time robbers, and negative personal traits. Let us examine each category to see the specific unproductive habits that waste time.

Poor Planning and Organizational Skills

Harried managers often feel a loss of control of their workday, as well as their lives. They complain that they cannot get organized, they cannot get a handle on things, they cannot complete any one task, and they cannot prevent interruptions. Poor time managers act as if someone else controls their time and they are puppets whose strings are being pulled by others.

Clearly, other people do have legitimate claims on our time. Bosses and customers, for example, have the right to expect us to work for them, but we ultimately control whether we will respond to their requests, how we will respond, when we will respond, and how much time we will devote to their requests. Then there are all the times when we allow, if not invite, others who do not have legitimate claims on our time to take a piece of our valuable time. The first step in understanding our time-management pitfalls is to realize all the ways we give up responsibility for and control of our work time.

Another sign of poor planning and organizational skills is the lack of clear priorities. Poor managers of time hop from one project to another without successfully completing any. This is classic wheel-spinning. Managers who feel that all tasks are equally important are not efficient masters of time.

Some managers are disorganized because they do not have a system for keeping track of duties and deadlines. Work piles up on their desks, important requests become buried, they cannot find things, and they perform tasks haphazardly and inconsistently. Usually, these people waste hours searching through incomprehensible filing systems or through towering piles of paperwork to find an elusive document.

Another sign of poor planning is to let work expand to fill the available time. Ineffective time managers begin a project and work on it until the project is completed. If you have all day to do a report, the report will take all day to do. If you have a week to do the report, the report will consume your entire week. Ironically, if you allot two hours to do the report and then protect those two hours from interruption or distraction, you are likely to complete a quality report close to the two-hour deadline. By devoting unlimited time to tasks, you let the task control your time.

External Time Robbers

The majority of a manager's day is spent responding to external stimuli. For many managers, large portions of time are encumbered by mail, calls, visits, and meetings imposed by other people. Many managers have trouble protecting their time from these external interruptions.

Out of habit, you may respond to mail that is unimportant and undeserving of reply. Or you may interrupt a significant project to deal with a request that could be handled at a more appropriate time. By not limiting when you will take phone calls, you invite constant interruptions.

The same principle applies to people who drop by the office without an appointment. A manager who promotes a total open-door policy probably has to take important work home to get it done. Obviously, you need to be accessible to employees and colleagues. But this does not necessitate giving everyone immediate access to you all day! Having specified periods of the day when people are free to drop by, as well as other periods of private time, can combine approachability with effective time utilization.

You can also control, to some extent, the amount of your time consumed by meetings. Even when you are not leading the meeting, you can steer a meeting toward more productivity. By asking for an agenda, by being prepared and asking others to be prepared, and by helping the group stay on target during discussions, you can contribute to meeting effectiveness. You can also skip unnecessary meetings or ask employees to attend certain meetings in your place.

Finally, in terms of external time robbers, is the pitfall of taking on employees' problems or work. Frequently, workers bring problems to your attention and expect you to solve them. By taking on the problems or agreeing to do some part of the person's work, you have reversed the supervisor-employee role. In effect, the employee has delegated work and you have willingly accepted the delegated assignment. In most instances, when employees dump problems on you, you should guide or assist them in solving the problems themselves. This strategy not only protects your time but helps develop the employees.

Negative Personal Traits

Some time-management pitfalls relate to your personality or attitudes. For example, anxiety, indecisiveness, procrastination, perfectionism, lack of concentration, and feelings of indispensability contribute to poor time-management practices. We examine how each of these traits or attitudes undermines the effective use of time.

1. *Anxiety*. Some people spend more time worrying about certain tasks than actually doing them. Anxiety about your ability

to handle a project can sap energy and time that could be better spent on the project. Being an effective time manager requires a certain amount of confidence and risk-taking ability. Effectively using time means plunging in and completing even those dreaded assignments.

2. *Indecisiveness.* The indecisive manager shuffles paper all day while trying to decide what task should be tackled first. Or indecisiveness may manifest itself in chronic uncertainty about how to proceed on a project. By delaying the start of anything, this person appears busy but is just wasting time.

3. *Procrastination.* Some managers claim that their procrastination habits are effective because they work best under pressure. What do such people do with their time until the deadlines approach? Do they think about the task and engage in several false starts? If so, they have wasted time already. Also, procrastinators can rarely be counted on to meet deadlines. Sure, they will meet some deadlines. But the rush to do a project at the last minute inevitably means that some deadlines will be missed and some quality will be sacrificed.

4. *Perfectionism.* Perfectionists will claim that to do a project right, you must give it 100 percent. Their personal ethic will not allow them to submit work that is less than perfect. The irony is that despite such ideals, no piece of work can reach perfection. The time spent striving for the elusive ideal of perfection usually does not result in a noticeable quality difference. There comes a point of diminishing returns regarding time spent on a task and the quality of the task's outcome. Achieving excellence in your work takes a considerable amount of concentrated, well-directed time. But beyond that amount of time, only minuscule and unrecognizable improvements in quality result from additional inputs of time.

5. *Inability to concentrate.* Some people can have large blocks of uninterrupted time and still not achieve results. Daydreaming and self-imposed distractions plague these individuals. They find it difficult to focus on one task at a time. They are unable to work on a project for more than just a few minutes without losing interest or feeling the urge to take a break.

6. *Feeling you are indispensable.* They have the attitude that they must be directly involved in all work if that work is to be done correctly. These individuals cannot get caught up because they essentially are doing the jobs of several people. Managers who fall into the trap of doing it all are not effective managers.

Time Management Strategies

The following strategies will help you improve your management of time.

Eliminate Unnecessary Tasks

Some of the tasks we do each day are essential and some are unnecessary. We may not realize the unnecessary ones because we feel compelled to do them, we enjoy doing them, or we have been doing them for years. It takes an objective look at a work routine to distinguish indispensable duties from unimportant ones.

Begin by listing all work-related tasks for one day on a piece of paper. Then cross off at least two listed tasks. Do not rationalize that they all are essential. These should be eliminated altogether, not merely postponed for another day's To Do list. You may need to enlist the help of a colleague to provide objectivity in streamlining your daily routine.

One way to select items for elimination is to assess the cost versus the payoff for the task. Tasks that take a great deal of time but provide little reward should be dropped. In the majority of cases, no negative consequences result from eliminating them. It is unlikely that anyone will even notice that they were not accomplished.

It is important to use this strategy repeatedly, with the goal of increasing the number of discarded items each day. Eventually, you will learn to streamline your perceived obligations and to avoid including unnecessary tasks on To Do lists in the first place.

Set Priorities

Priority setting is essential to effective time management. Most managers, however, do not make conscious decisions about the order in which tasks are tackled. You may let daily demand determine priorities. As questions, calls, memos, or visitors grasp your attention, you respond to whatever task someone else hands you.

Some managers let past habits dictate current priorities. They may handle correspondence first every morning because they have always begun their day in that manner, not because correspondence is the top priority. Another illogical way of establishing priorities is to do favorite tasks first and put off unpleasant ones to later. The dilemma is that preferred tasks may not be the important ones and vice versa.

To begin establishing priorities, make a list of what you want to accomplish for one day. Eliminate some according to the previously discussed strategy. Then decide which ones you can delegate. For each remaining entry, label top priority tasks A, items medium in importance as B, and low priority items as C. Use the cost-versus-payoff formula for deciding As, Bs, and Cs. Obviously, tasks with approaching deadlines that were delegated to you by a boss should be top priorities. Tasks that seriously affect others, impinge on your credibility, or would result in dire consequences if ignored are likely to be high priorities. These are the things that you must get done that day. B items have moderate payoff or importance. C items have little value or importance associated with them. They are important enough to do, but not immediately.

Once you have labeled each task for priority, begin with the top-priority ones. Give them ample time and attention and as much uninterrupted time as possible. Some people intersperse an occasional B or C item as a mental break from the top-priority projects. An alternative approach to doing top-priority jobs first is to schedule these during your peak-efficiency time. Some people are mentally sluggish early in the morning and would have have the capacity to work on A items then, so they do a few Cs and switch to the top-priority tasks when they feel fully alert.

Improve Your Concentration

Being able to concentrate is a key to the effective use of time. Strive to eliminate both external and internal distractions. To create a nondistracting environment, close the door, hold phone calls, and have all necessary materials and information at hand. To free yourself of internal distractions, clear your mind of all thoughts except the particular project. Immerse yourself in the task at hand.

If you feel frequent urges to turn your attention to something else or to take a break, force your attention back to the task. Set minimum times to concentrate on the task and then reward yourself for reaching that designated goal. Over time, strive to increase the minimum periods of concentration. What may start out as fifteen-minute periods may evolve into hours of concentrated work. But there are no foolproof techniques for improving concentration. It takes motivation, will power, inner drive, and a great deal of practice.

Find Extra Time

Managers who are very busy find that they must utilize all their available time. With some analysis, you can find pieces of time throughout the day that could be put to better use. Time spent commuting to and from work could be used for planning or for problem solving. Some people listen to informational tapes or dictate while driving. Commuting time can provide an opportunity for conducting business calls. For those who use public transportation, commuting time can be spent reading, writing letters, or handling paperwork. The laptop computer helps many managers plan, write, and analyze during traditional down times or off hours of commuting and travel.

In addition to commuting time, there is waiting time. This is the time spent waiting for appointments, waiting in line to do business, or waiting for service somewhere. Wise time managers carry newspapers, paperback books, or notebooks with them to occupy such delays.

There may be other wasted time during the day. Could some long lunches be shortened to make the workday more productive? Could you reduce some social chitchat at work? The time spent getting ready in the morning could be used for planning or for preparing a talk, a letter, or a report. The point is that there is extra time during the day if you search for it and use it productively.

Distribute Your Time Effectively

It may be wise to block out certain times for particular types of tasks. This can provide a comfortable routine and maximize concentration. For example, you could set aside the same hour each day to handle correspondence or to make phone calls. Perhaps Friday afternoons could be devoted to reading professional journals. Maybe certain periods could be publicized as open-door time in which drop-in visits are encouraged. By establishing and communicating a schedule whenever possible, you protect your time and create predictability for work associates.

Schedule Relaxation Time

In trying to become a better time manager, you can easily become compulsive about every moment of the day. If this happens, you feel even more frustrated and harried. Sometimes the best use of time is to do nothing—to daydream, to look at the clouds, to meditate, to take a walk. By seizing time to relax through both planned and unplanned activity, you revitalize your mind and body. Treating yourself to a favorite relaxation technique, even under time pressures, can improve motivation, concentration, and endurance to get the work done.

[*See also* Delegation and Empowerment; Meetings]

For Additional Information

Douglass, Merrill E., and Donna N. *Manage Your Time, Your Work, Yourself.* New York: AMACOM, 1993.

Mackenzie, Alec. *The Time Trap.* New York: AMACOM, 1991.

Ramsey, Robert D. "Work Smarter and Save Time." *Supervision* 55, No. 7 (July 1994), pp. 14–16.

Stamp, Dan. "Managing Priorities." *Executive Excellence* 11, No. 1 (Jan. 1994), p. 6.

Williams, Paul B. *Getting a Project Done on Time: Managing People Time and Results.* New York: AMACOM, 1995.

Training

To effectively develop your employees you must understand the training function. You must know when, how, and where to find training for yourself, your employees, team members, and peers. From time to time, you must train your staff by yourself. Often supervisors and managers are responsible for effectively delivering on-the-job training and follow-up coaching. Managers in organizations with training departments must know how to work effectively with the in-house training staff. By understanding the functions and methods of training, as well as its benefits and drawbacks, you can make enlightened decisions about this employee-development tool.

Making Training Decisions

There is a logical five-step decision-making process that you should use to make training decisions.

Is There a Need for Training?

Usually some type of actual or anticipated problem or deficiency in the work unit leads you to consider training as a solution. A supervisor who has stormy relationships with employees may be recommended for supervision training. An organization with sexual harassment problems may use training as an intervention. Because managers rarely select training unless there is a perceived need for it, training can be selected as a reaction to a problem or as a proactive measure to prevent a problem. The more specifically you anticipate or pinpoint the need or problem, the more sound the decision-making process about training. Of course, proactive managers and companies perceive training needs to complement changes in organizational culture or to complement changes in approaches to quality.

Is Training the Best Solution?

After determining the specific problem, examine all possible solutions to decide if training is the best option. Some problems are best solved by training; others are not. For example, a manager who is effective in all areas except delegation will profit from a training session to develop delegation skills. But a supervisor who is prone to emotional outbursts may need an employee-assistance program, as opposed to a communication-training program. In some other cases, training is selected to solve a problem when a better solution would involve job enrichment, individual coaching or mentoring, discipline, or termination.

What Type of Training Is Needed?

If you determine that training is the best solution to a problem, then your next step is to identify the type of training needed. Training can be used to change attitudes, affect behavior, develop skills or technical competence, or provide information.

What Is the Most Effective Means of Delivering the Training?

Training options are enormous. The categories typically include self-instruction methods, an in-house training department, public seminars, computer-assisted training through interactive videos on the internet, video conferencing, or outside providers who train employees inside your organization. Often, the range of choices within each category is broad. A brief overview of each type will help you make appropriate training decisions.

1. *Self-instruction.* Self-paced manuals, such as user manuals for computers or electronic equipment, individual-instruction workbooks, audiocassettes, videotapes, or computer-assisted instruction are fast and inexpensive. They need not interrupt an

employee's daily work routine and can be used during free time. For certain purposes with certain people, self-instruction can be effective. There are limitations to self-instruction training methods, however. The element of human interaction, often crucial to learning, is missing. The user may feel isolated and demotivated. There is no one to check and correct mistakes. Self-instruction is therefore not always appropriate.

2. *In-house training staff.* Internal training departments provide a valuable service to managers and employees. They offer or assist in finding the training that managers need for their employees. In deciding whether internal trainers are the best option, assess the competence of the training staff. Even large training departments do not always have expertise in all training topics. Are there employees in the company who can provide the training you need? Do their schedules permit them to provide the training when you need it? Is the problem a politically sensitive one that would be handled best by an outsider? Can the internal trainer be objective regarding the problem that training should solve? Do the in-house materials and methods meet your needs? Can you work with the training staff? In-house training is not an option for all managers, because small organizations do not always have training departments.

3. *Public seminars.* Public seminars include speakers doing programs at local hotels or motels; courses sponsored by colleges, universities, and vocational schools; vendor-supplied education in conjunction with the purchase of equipment; and public programs provided by independent consultants, trade or employers associations, professional companies, or management-information companies. Public training offers much diversity in topics, facilitators, and cost. It allows your employees to meet people from other companies. Much can be learned from hearing about the experiences of other organizations. On the other hand, sensitive company information may be disclosed. Also, because public seminars must meet the needs of participants from various levels, functions, and types of organizations, the content must be general. Training from public seminars may not be applicable to the specific situation of a particular company. Most important, skills and lessons learned from public seminars may not transfer back

to your organization. The seminar may explain how to empower new hires when, perhaps, your company does not embrace the concept of empowerment or has few new hires.

4. *Outside providers who train inside your organization.* Many of the facilitators of public programs will provide training to specific organizations. They may offer the same seminar as the public version but brought to your location for a smaller number of employees, or they may create a training program unique to your needs. In the latter case, the outside provider can create the training program for someone in your company to deliver, deliver the training for you, or train someone on your staff to deliver the training in subsequent sessions after presenting the initial training session.

Outside providers who train inside your organization offer many advantages. They can tailor the training to meet your specific needs and provide objectivity and credibility. On the negative side, this type of training can be very expensive and is time-consuming for you to coordinate. Also, the trainer is still an outsider who will never know all the nuances of your organization.

How Much Can You Spend for the Training?

You must analyze the cost of training against the probable returns. The cost includes the actual training fees, training material costs, food and refreshment costs, the cost of time that trainees and trainers spend away from the job, and possible travel expenses. It is difficult to put a dollar figure on the benefits that training provides. Try to assess the tangible returns after employees participate in training. Perhaps there are measurably reduced costs, increased revenues and profits, fewer customer complaints, less signs of stress and absenteeism, fewer disputes or grievances, higher morale, better-quality products, or higher rates of productivity.

How to Select a Public Training Program

To carefully select a public training program for themselves or their employees, managers can use a number of criteria, including the following:

- *Program content.* Before selecting a public training program, you should receive a course outline that specifies objectives, content, and training formats to be used. The outline should be detailed enough so that you can identify the exact topics to be covered and the amount of attention devoted to each. Likewise, the outline should indicate how each topic will be covered—for example, through lecture, discussion, case study, audiovisual, role-play, or simulation activities. To what extent will participants work with the information or practice the skills? This may depend on how many participants are included in a session. Feel free to ask questions about the program content. In some cases, the person or organization sponsoring the program will provide sample written materials for your perusal in making a training decision.

- *Trainer's ability.* A training program, despite excellent content, is only as good as the person delivering it. Before selecting a public training program, you should feel confident about the trainer's expertise, prior organizational experience, familiarity with the topic, and platform style. Some trainers will provide sample videotapes or audiotapes of their work.

- *Evaluation system.* Evaluation may involve both the trainer's evaluation of participants and the participants' evaluation of the trainer and the program. It is helpful if participants receive from training some assessment of their own abilities or knowledge on the training topic. Some sessions will provide pretest and posttest evaluations, rating forms, or self-tests for participants. Such evaluation of participants is not possible in short programs with large numbers of participants, which are more akin to a speech than an actual training seminar.

All training programs should include a means for participants to evaluate the program. This can include a few questions on which trainees rate certain features of the program after completing the session, open-ended written or oral feedback to the trainer about program strengths and weaknesses, or follow-up evaluations after the participants are back on the job to determine how much they are applying program content. Whatever evaluation tools are used, you should solicit informal reactions or written reports from employees about the perceived value of the training. Additionally, you can observe, through relevant on-the-job measures, whether the training had an impact.

• *Participants' recommendations.* Before selecting a public training program, you should obtain a list of previous participants in similar programs. Contact these participants to obtain their perceptions of the program and ask specific questions. This is the best way to get an accurate picture of the program. Be suspicious of public program facilitators who will not disclose the names of people and organizations that have previously used their training services.

• *Price and location.* The price of public sessions can range from under $100 for a full day to several thousand dollars for a week-long program or for a nationally renowned trainer. Public training programs are held at local motels, hospitals, community centers, or educational institutions. Or they may be in posh resorts or training facilities anywhere in the world. Naturally, you will want to consider price and location in selecting a public training program.

Selecting an Outside Provider to Train Inside Your Organization

Many of the same issues of content, trainer ability, evaluation system, references from previous clients, and price apply when you choose an external provider. However, there are some criteria unique to choosing outside trainers to work within your company, such as:

• *Needs assessment.* With this type of training, you should expect the training organization to conduct a needs assessment or training audit. The trainer should distribute surveys, conduct interviews, lead focus-group discussions, or observe the dynamics of the organization. The more familiar the trainer becomes with the structure, the mission, the people, and the problems of your organization, the more effective the training will be. The pretraining phase may or may not include a fee and ranges from a few hours of work to several months of research and analysis. The nature of the needs assessment depends on the organization, the scope of the training program, and the organization's training budget.

- *The training program itself.* Do you want a standard program brought to your location so that your employees do not have to travel to a public place? Or do you want program objectives, content, and delivery formats designed to your specifications? Do you want a program delivered once to a group of employees or do you want a program that your organization can use repeatedly in the future?

- *Follow-up consultation.* You should expect more ongoing assistance from an outside provider who trains inside organizations than from public training seminars. The trainer should not disappear once the training program has been delivered. Instead, this type of training should include periodic visits from the trainer to assess the impact of the training, to monitor the progress of participants, and to offer additional coaching or training to increase effectiveness. The follow-up phase may or may not include a fee.

Working With an In-House Training Department

Managers with a full-fledged training department in their organizations are fortunate. Nevertheless, they sometimes do not realize or take full advantage of this employee-development tool. It is important to realize that internal trainers are an asset to your work unit. Managers who do not understand their role as human resources developers or who do not appreciate the benefits of training will see training as a waste of time. Some managers view training as an added luxury or as an unnecessary interruption to the work routine. In this age of business competition, information overload, technological advancements, and rapid career change, training is essential to organizations.

You can also use internal trainers to create or locate the training you need. By working closely with your training department to pinpoint training needs, to structure materials and content, and to evaluate the impact of training, you can be assured of quality training for your staff. If in-house trainers cannot provide the service you need, then you can work with them to find and evaluate quality, cost-effective programs elsewhere. In either case, good managers take advantage of the training resources within their organizations.

Advantages and Disadvantages of Training

An analysis of some of the advantages and limitations of training will present a balanced perspective for managers making training decisions. Training offers many advantages to individuals and organizations alike. It is an excellent avenue for employee development because it can improve attitudes, develop skills, and impart information. Providing employees with the opportunity for training can serve as a reward and improve their morale. Those who have participated in training usually return to work with heightened enthusiasm, as well as with ideas and suggestions for improving the work situation. Organizations with excellent reputations for providing employee training are likely to have better public relations images and recruiting opportunities. All of this translates into organizational development. The organization with an enlightened view of training usually enjoys better employee relations and higher productivity.

This is not to say that training is a panacea. One limitation is its expense. Some companies can afford no more than the most minimal of training efforts. And because the return on the investment in training is difficult to calculate, some companies cannot justify large expenditures for training. Still others simply cannot afford to take someone off of a job to send to a training program. Training can also result in employee misuse of the information gained. The employees may even take jobs with other organizations once you have paid to upgrade their knowledge or skills. Still, most companies believe that the expense of not training is far greater, and so they cannot afford *not* to train.

The Manager as Trainer

All managers face the task of training their employees, in the broadest sense of the term. In addition to knowing how to select training for employees, a manager must know how to perform the role of trainer. Managers are called on to help new hires, for example. Even if the personnel department provides general orientation training, it is the duty of the unit manager to see that the new employee learns to perform the new job correctly.

Too many managers take this task lightly. Ineffective managers typically hand new employees a manual and tell them to read it; this hardly suffices as on-the-job training. Another on-the-job training error is to tell the new hire to watch seasoned employees to learn how the job is done. But there is no guarantee that the experienced employee is doing the job correctly or can teach someone else how to do the work. In the meantime, the new hire feels like a pest and is reluctant to ask too many questions. On the other hand, some managers, like drill sergeants, dictate job procedures and command new hires to perform these tasks correctly without asking too many questions.

Rather than adopting these procedures, you must work closely with new employees to see that they develop the right work skills and attitudes. A train-the-trainer course usually helps managers who lack certain training skills or platform confidence. You will learn instructional designs and methods, as well as platform skills, to become an effective trainer and coach; both increasing requirements in a total quality environment.

You should also train in the event of employee-performance problems, when an employee's job is expanded or changed, or when you want to develop an employee for a new project or promotion. In essence, whenever you provide feedback, coach, or serve as a mentor, you are training.

In addition to directly training employees, you must provide support to employees who return to the job after attending a training seminar. It is your job to help them transfer what they have learned in the training program to the work situation. This may mean letting them try new approaches or test new ideas. It may mean removing attitudinal or structural barriers so that employees can incorporate training concepts into the daily work routine.

[*See also* Coaching Employees; Consultants; Orienting New Employees]

For Additional Information

Darling, Philip. *Training for Profit: A Guide to the Integration of Training in an Organization's Success.* New York: McGraw-Hill, 1994.

McCune, Jenny C. "On the Train Gang." *Management Review* 83, No. 10 (Oct. 1994), pp. 57–60.

Mitchell, Garry. *The Trainer's Handbook: The AMA Guide to Effective Training.* New York: AMACOM, 1992.

Morgan, Clay. "Employee Training that Works." *Supervision* 55, No. 6 (June 1994), pp. 11–13.

Pace, Larry A. "Training in Organizations: Needs Assessment, Development and Evaluation." *Personnel Psychololgy* 47, No. 2 (Summer 1994), pp. 395–97.

Turnover

Turnover can be defined as the total number of separations of employees from an organization during a given time period. Separations are both voluntary (resignations or retirements) and involuntary (terminations). Most organizations maintain turnover statistics, if only to recognize the extent to which they lose employees. Such data can also be used to calculate the costs of personnel replacement, document reasons for separation, and project future labor demands.

Positive and Negative Consequences of Turnover

Most people think that turnover is bad for a company. Indeed, organizations with high rates of turnover will probably suffer, but there are also some advantages to it. For example, when employees leave a company, they are replaced with new hires who bring new knowledge, practice, experience, and skills to the organization. Turnover can also allow for organizational renewal. With little or no change in personnel, there may be stagnation in the workplace.

While too much turnover is costly, a certain amount can save an organization money. Employees with large salaries may be replaced with less-expensive but equally qualified newcomers. Some positions may be eliminated, merged, or automated. Through turnover, an organization can rid itself of marginal performers, unmotivated workers, and people who are difficult to get along with. So turnover may provide vitality, may have financial advantages, and may serve a housecleaning function.

The potential negative effects of organizational turnover are many, however. Clearly, there are tangible and indirect costs associated with turnover. Organizations can calculate original and replacement human resources costs. Recruiting, selecting, and training new employees is costly. Exit interviews, severance benefits, and outplacement services also cost money. Temporary help may have to be hired. Then there are the costs of reduced productivity while positions remain vacant and new hires become oriented to the job and to the company.

Turnover, no matter how necessary to organizational vitality, is also disruptive. Remaining employees may have to take on more work until the separated employee is replaced. Special projects and work teams may be disrupted when turnover affects their membership. If a valuable and well-liked person leaves, group morale, cohesion, and communication can be negatively affected. Separations put companies into a temporary state of imbalance. Remaining employees find themselves preoccupied with the change and spend work time discussing the former employee and the reasons for separation. A period of anxiety and uncertainty ensues. Additional turnover can result when disgruntled employees identify with separated employees and follow their lead in leaving the organization. Turnover is especially disruptive if qualified replacements in certain job categories are difficult to find.

Organizations with high rates of turnover earn reputations as undesirable working environments. Replacing employees becomes an even more difficult and costly task. Because turnover can have a serious impact on an organization, it must be managed or controlled. Managing employee turnover involves not only being aware of the consequences of turnover but understanding the reasons for that high turnover and trying to control it.

Reasons for Turnover

A complex array of factors affect an individual's decision to voluntarily leave an organization, including personal circumstances, the job itself, the larger work environment, and the perception of alternatives.

A variety of personal reasons can precipitate the decision to resign or retire from a job. Marriage, personal illness, child rearing, family problems, the job transfer of a spouse, or the desire to relocate are common reasons for quitting a job. By having fair parental leave policies, child-care benefits, and employee counseling programs, an employer can prevent some turnover. Many personal reasons for turnover are beyond the employer's control, however.

In many cases, dissatisfaction with the job itself propels employees to quit. They may not be challenged by their jobs, they may find the work repetitive or boring, or they may not be using their knowledge or abilities adequately. Dissatisfactions with salary, benefits, work schedule, and job security are also powerful motives for leaving. The factors of turnover in which the employer has more control relate directly to selection, placement, and personnel-policy decisions made by managers.

Sometimes people like their work but have difficulty with the company itself. The larger work milieu cannot help but affect their perception of a job. Employees who are unhappy with working conditions, with supervisor and coworker relationships, with organizational policies and procedures, with company or departmental politics, and with career opportunities in the company are likely candidates for separation.

Employees may also leave because they perceive better alternatives elsewhere. They may take a similar job in a different organization as a career-development strategy. They may give few reasons for their departure other than the option that it is time to move on. Other reasons for separation are the goal of starting a new business, the desire to return to school, an interest in military or volunteer services, or the option of early retirement.

Strategies for Controlling Turnover

Managing turnover does not mean intervening just before an employee decides to quit. In order to manage employee turnover, organizations must realize that almost all managerial decisions can relate to turnover. In order to control turnover, companies must examine their recruitment, selection, and placement decisions; their performance evaluation and reward system; their salary and benefits plans; their promotion and career-development opportunities; their supervisory styles and relationships; their work environments; and their handling of special needs by certain segments of the workforce. The following sections discuss ways in which each of these organizational features affects turnover and presents strategies in each area for retaining employees.

Recruitment, Selection, and Placement

Companies may experience turnover because of hiring mistakes. If you hire the wrong person for a job, the individual will be unable to perform satisfactorily and is likely to quit or be fired. The closer the selection process can match an individual with an organization, the more successful that process will be and the more likely turnover will be reduced.

To improve the match between applicant and job, both interviewers and applicants must be more realistic and more honest. Job requirements must be clearly specified, valid and reliable selection techniques must be used, job expectations and risks must be disclosed, and significant time and resources must be devoted to the selection process. Money spent at this stage will be money saved later if turnover is reduced.

Improving the selection process also depends on effective recruiting techniques. The best person cannot be hired if few qualified individuals apply. You may need to upgrade your recruiting procedures. Do ads in newspapers, professional magazines, and journals represent the best investment of recruiting dollars? Could employment agencies, executive search firms, and placement offices associated with educational institutions increase the pool of applicants? Develop creative ways of reaching minority applicants, such as outreach programs within communities. Encourage current employees to recruit potential applicants.

The placement process is another factor of personnel selection that can ultimately affect turnover. Once an employee is placed in a work assignment, the orientation and training process must be adequate preparation for the job. Employees who start off on the wrong foot with rushed, vague, or stressful orientation periods may remain disenchanted. Some companies assume that new employees can immediately do the job or can learn the job through casual observation. Thus, they provide no systematic orientation for new hires. Orientation training should provide a realistic but supervised portrayal of actual job conditions. The new person should learn correct procedures, ask questions, and rectify mistakes.

Performance Evaluations and Reward

Many employees quit because they are unhappy with their performance reviews or because they perceive they have been passed over for a promotion. Likewise, organizations typically fire employees whose performance is consistently below expectation. Thus, the performance evaluation and reward system in an organization directly relates to its rate of turnover. Yet many performance evaluation systems are vague and subjective, leading to arbitrary decisions about workers' preformances. Inadequate performance appraisal methods can contribute to employee turnover if they fail to identify real performance problems early enough for correction or if they frustrate employees to the point of quitting.

To be effective, a performance review system should have well-defined, measurable criteria for performance for each job in the organization. Reviews should occur frequently and results be communicated directly. Most important, employees whose performance falls below standard should receive coaching until their performance improves. Identifying problems early on and coaching to solve those performance problems can make termination unnecessary.

Companies can also reduce turnover by encouraging frequent informal discussions about performance. Routine, unthreatening feedback about job-related behaviors can prevent performance problems from developing. Supervisors who routinely praise and criticize their workers' job performance support the formal performance-review system.

Because complaints about performance reviews and promotions cannot be eliminated totally, organizations should have systems for handling grievances. Impartial reviews and reconsideration of performance appraisal and promotion decisions can help reduce grievances, legal battle, and separations.

Salary and Benefits

Some employees leave jobs because they are dissatisfied with their salaries or benefits. While it is idealistic to think that employers can provide compensation packages that will completely satisfy a workforce, it is important to realize the relationship of compensation to turnover.

Organizations that want to retain valuable employees must make sure their salary ranges are competitive with industry and regional standards. Not only do employees compare their salaries and benefits to those of comparable positions in other companies, but they compare across jobs within an organization. Employees will be dissatisfied and will consider leaving if they perceive that their salaries are less than those of colleagues in similar job categories with similar experience or longevity. Perceived salary inequity within companies is a major factor affecting turnover. Organizations can intervene by making sure that salary equity exists, both externally and internally.

Organizations also must determine if their benefits are competitive and equitable. Spending more on attractive benefits plans can save turnover costs. In addition, many companies opt for flexible benefits packages that allow employees to select the benefits they need and reject unnecessary options. While this does not necessarily increase the costs to employers, it does mean offering a wider range of benefits from which employees can choose. It may represent a simple strategy for retaining certain categories of employees.

Career Development

Some employees leave their present jobs because they do not anticipate satisfying future roles in the company. High achievers especially want clear and attainable paths to career development. Organizations can implement career-development programs as a strategy for retaining valuable employees. Such programs should provide information on realistic career paths in the company; opportunities for self-assessment, education, and training for individual development; career counseling; and posting of available positions in the organization. Opportunities for personal growth and promotion can be a powerful motive for remaining with a company.

Supervisory Relationships

Another factor affecting whether an employee remains on a job is the relationship with the supervisor. Many reasons cited for voluntary separation involve supervisory problems. Conversely, a positive attachment to a supervisor can retain an employee even if other dissatisfactions arise. Employees report that they are less likely to quit a job if they have a positive personal relationship with their supervisors and if supervisors show them consideration and create supportive working environments.

It is easy to see why the relationship between supervisors and workers has such a direct bearing on turnover. Supervisors play a major role in orienting employees to their jobs; supervisors typically conduct performance reviews and recommend or withhold performance rewards; supervisors shape salary decisions; and supervisors are the people to offer praise, coaching, and career-development opportunities. They also affect most of the other factors related to employee retention or turnover, such as politics.

This means that organizations should encourage effective and satisfying supervisory relationships. Resources should be provided for supervisory-skills training. Supervisors must be encouraged to set good examples, to communicate openly and regularly, and to treat their employees fairly. Making first-line supervisors a major human resources priority can significantly impact employee turnover.

Work Environment

Certain types of work environments or climates drive people away. The work environment encompasses many elements already discussed and entails aspects that shape employees' perceptions of their jobs. People who quit their jobs because of dissatisfaction with the work environment cite these factors: mutual distrust between managers and employees, lack of communication, inconsistent policies and procedures, stress, competitiveness, unreasonable deadlines, job responsibilities interfering with personal life, and uncertainty about job security. Employers should examine whether aspects of their work environment contribute to turnover in their organization.

Special Needs

Certain segments of a workforce may have special needs that affect their ability to remain in particular jobs. Troubled employees may be fired or may quit if counseling or employee assistance programs are not available. Many organizations have found it more cost-effective to offer employee counseling than to replace employees, owing to high rates of turnover.

Organizations perceived as inhospitable to minorities may face alarming rates of turnover among minority employees. Such a trend can damage a company's reputation or result in charges of discrimination and costly litigation. Some practices to retain minority employees include recruiting minority applicants, fair employment practices that comply with the guidelines of the Equal Employment Opportunity Commission (EEOC), and mentoring or career-development strategies that meet the special needs of minorities in the workplace.

Dual-career couples, who represent an increasing proportion of the workforce, may need child-care benefits or flexible work schedules in order to remain employed. Spouse relocation assistance may be needed for a valuable employee to accept a transfer. A company wishing to retain its older employees should implement preretirement counseling or offer alternative working arrangements.

Exit Interviews

Organizations should establish procedures for exit interviews with employees who have resigned or been dismissed. There are many compelling reasons for holding an exit interview in conjunction with a resignation. By soliciting the employee's reasons for quitting, the organization can compile data on the causes of turnover. Through this information, the organization can monitor and adjust its personnel practices.

In some cases, the exit interview can be used as a vehicle to dissuade a valuable employee from leaving. Managers may not know of someone's dissatisfaction until the intention to quit is announced. They may be able to intervene to solve the employee's concerns, thereby preventing separation.

The exit interview can reduce the disgruntled employee's hostility and can serve a goodwill purpose. Organizations that provide opportunities for employees to air their feelings prior to leaving, and that take some responsibility for a person-job mismatch, have fewer vengeful people complaining about them in the community. The departing person is likely to be hired by a competitor, so it is important that the person leave on good terms.

Exit interviews in conjunction with voluntary separations ought to solicit the following information:

- Positive aspects of the job
- Negative aspects of the job
- Reasons for leaving
- Other factors contributing to dissatisfaction
- Perceptions of the relationship with supervisor
- Perceptions of the organization
- Recommendations for improvement
- Factors that could have prolonged the employment

In addition, the terms of separation must be discussed. The atmosphere should be professional and the goal should be to exchange information. The interviewer must assure the departing employee that all remarks will be held confidential and that the information can serve as a basis for correcting problems in the workplace.

No resigning employee can be forced to participate in an exit interview. However, an employee who is willing to discuss reasons for resigning should be encouraged to speak honestly, objectively, and thoroughly. The interviewer should express appreciation for the cooperation and should wish the departing employee well in future employment.

[*See also* Career Development; Feedback; Interviewing; Performance Appraisals; Politics in Organizations; Recruiting and Selecting New Employees]

For Additional Information

Dreyer, R. S. "Why Behind Turnover." *Supervision* 55, No. 11 (Nov. 1995), pp. 19–20.

Herman, Roger C. *Keeping Good People: Strategies for Solving the Dilemma of the Decade*. Cleveland: Oakland Press, 1990.

White, Gerald L. "Employee Turnover: The Hidden Drain on Profits." *HR Focus* 72, No. 1 (Jan. 1995), pp. 15–17.

Violence in the Workplace

Organizations of all types increasingly are becoming concerned about incidents of violence in the workplace. This kind of violence can be considered as any threatening behavior, verbal abuse, or physical assault occurring in a work environment. Employees and their significant others, as well as customers and strangers, can show violent behavior in a work setting. Types of this violence typically fall into four categories: (1) robbery and other commercial crimes; (2) domestic and misdirected affection cases; (3) terrorism and hate crimes; and (4) employer-directed situations.

Any workplace where money or other valuables are kept can become a target of a *robbery*. Typically the perpetrator is a stranger to the organization, though the individual can be an employee or former employee.

Domestic and misdirected affection cases are those in which domestic and intimate relationship disputes spill over into the workplace. A typical scenario involves an angry husband or boyfriend who stalks a mate to the workplace or enters the workplace in order to threaten or harm that person. In most cases, the violent individual is not an employee of the organization.

Terrorism and hate crimes often are directed at particular types of organizations by militant advocacy groups. Crimes against clinics performing abortions or against companies engaging in experiments on animals are typical examples.

In the case of *employer-directed situations*, the violence comes from an employee or former employee because of perceived injustices suffered on the job, and the violence is directed at the employer, the employer's property, managers, or fellow employees. This is the type of violence over which organizations have the most control. Most information in this chapter focuses on this last type of workplace violence.

Prevalence of Workplace Violence

While violence on the job is not a common ocurrence in most companies, it seems to be happening with increasing frequency across a spectrum of organizations. No workplace is immune from the possibility of violent behavior. A study done by Northwestern National Life Insurance projected that over 2 million employees in the United States were physically attacked in the workplace in 1992–93. The National Institute for Occupational Safety and Health reports that workplace violence is the third leading cause of death on the job. During an eighteen-month period, there were some 700 recorded cases of violence among U.S. Postal Service employees.

The Postal Service is not the only type of organization in which violence commonly occurs, however. Other organizations most at risk are those in construction, manufacturing, public sector, and law enforcement. Small retail or financial establishments such as convenience stores, service stations, and branch banks are at risk for robberies. Anyone working alone, such as a taxi driver, also is at risk. And organizations undergoing massive layoffs or terminations are in danger.

Causes of Workplace Violence

One cannot dispute that evidence of violence in our society has become more pronounced. Three factors—societal conditions, the workplace, and the violent-prone individual—have contributed to recent increases in workplace violence. Since the workplace is a microcosm of society, societal problems necessarily impinge on workplace organizations.

The increasing availability of guns, the abundant presence of violence in entertainment media, economic problems, and feelings of alienation and discrimination probably contribute to incidents of workplace violence. In addition, organizational factors contributing to workplace violence include widespread layoffs and terminations; strong dissatisfaction with the outcomes of grievance and disciplinary hearings; authoritarian management styles; and perceived unpredictability, secrecy, and invasion of privacy in an organization.

Certainly, there are some individuals whose personalities and lifestyles indicate a propensity toward violence. Individuals with histories of mental instability and/or substance abuse are likely to erupt into violence. Likewise, anyone with dysfunctional patterns of expressing anger, feelings of victimization, or a strong need for retaliation is a candidate for engaging in violent behavior. Studies have shown that typical perpetrators of workplace violence are male, loner types with low self-esteem who have a history of conflicts at work, have difficulty accepting authority, are under stress, have made previous threats at work, and have a fascination with weapons. Still, though such a profile has been developed, it is still very difficult to predict who will likely become violent and under what circumstances.

Costs of Workplace Violence

While it is difficult to put a price tag on workplace violence, any incidents can result in direct costs to employers, such as sick leave and workers compensation benefits, and negligent hiring or victims' compensation awards. Then there are indirect costs, such as high turnover, loss of productivity, and damaged public image. The Northwestern National Life Insurance study found that victims of workplace violence were significantly more likely than nonvictims to report that they were less productive, suffered from various stress-related illnesses, and wanted to change jobs. The National Safe Workplace Institute estimated that the cost to employers for workplace violence in 1992 was over $4 billion.

When we examine the range of behaviors classified as workplace violence, the prevalence of incidents, the variety of organizations at risk, and the costs to employers, it is advisable for all organizations to develop prevention mechanisms and violence-management plans.

Prevention Plans

Good organizational communication, sound human resources practices, and effective security measures contribute to prevention of violence in the workplace. It is wise to examine your organizational culture to determine the extent to which it is employee-friendly. An environment characterized by hostility between managers and employees makes incidents or workplace violence more possible. If employees feel that their rights are violated repeatedly or that they regularly are treated unfairly, they are much more likely to fight back through verbal or physical force. An employee-friendly workplace culture is characterized by open communication, respect, a sense of personal responsibility, opportunities to provide input, feelings of support, and fair dispute-resolution procedures. In such a climate, employee anger and frustration are minimal and would be unlikely to escalate into episodes of violence.

Human resources practices also can contribute to the prevention of workplace violence. It is important to have thorough pre-employment screening practices. If an employee who had a history of criminal behavior engages in violent behavior that injures either a fellow employee or a third party, then the employer is liable in a negligent hiring lawsuit.

Employers should conduct thorough reference checks on all potential employees. Many companies use waivers that release former employers from liability and authorize credit and criminal records checks. Such pre-employment screening practices reduce company liability in negligent hiring allegations.

In additional to pre-employment screening practices, organizations should have policies relating to such issues as possession of a firearm at work, substance abuse, and harassment. Violent behavior is reduced in companies that have clear policies and procedures for dealing with all types of inappropriate conduct at work.

Policies and procedures related to the termination of employees also can reduce the incidence of workplace violence. Supervisors need training on how to terminate employees in ways that are objective, respectful, and nonemotional. Supervisors need to know how to diffuse employee anger and feelings of retribution. Exit interviews and outplacement services can turn a potentially explosive situation into a professional one. By providing the services of an employee assistance program, organizations can refer violence-prone employees to counseling.

In additional to communication and human resources practices, increased security helps prevent workplace violence. Increased security is defined differently in various types of organizations. It may mean checking employee identification, installing metal detectors or security cameras, or hiring security personnel. A threat-management plan and training of supervisors to detect early warning signs of violence also constitute security measures.

A threat-management plan essentially examines areas of risk in an organization, specifies procedures for reporting and investigating aggressive and threatening behavior, delineates training needs regarding stress and conflict management, and names a threat-management team, which typically consists of individuals from top management and the human resources, legal, and security departments. Such a plan should be communicated to insurers and may contribute to lower insurance costs.

Violence-Management Plan

While all of these preventive measures likely will eliminate the occurence of violence in a company, they are not foolproof. Violence can still occur, and the organization must know how to react should a serious situation emerge. All organizations should have a violence-management plan that outlines an emergency response, designates areas of responsibility, provides for communication to employees, handles media relations, and restores public image. Areas of responsibility or oversight may include dealing with the police, ensuring employee safety during a violent situation, monitoring the emotional needs of employees, communicating with victims' families, disseminating information internally, handling press coverage, cleaning up facilities, repairing physical damage, processing medical and insurance claims, handling legal matters, informing customers of service delays, and returning the organization to normalcy.

While the need for such a plan is rare, just one instance of its use more than justifies such a planning effort. Imagine the chaos, personal trauma, financial loss, and credibility damage for an organization that has no response plan for an episode that involves physical assault, terrorism, or homicide. All organizations, regardless of type or size, should become aware of prevention strategies and response plans regarding workplace violence.

[*See also* Conflict Management; Disciplining Employees; Employee Assistance Programs; Family-Friendly Management; Listening; Substance Abuse; Terminating Employees and Downsizing]

For Additional Information

Arbetta, Lisa. "Over the Edge." *Security Management*, December 1993, p. 12.

Bensimon, Helen Frank. "Violence in the Workplace." *Training and Development*, January 1994, pp. 27–32.

Kinney, Joseph A., and Johnson, Dennis L. *Breaking Point: The Workplace Violence Epidemic and What To Do About It*. Chicago: National Safe Workplace Institute, 1993.

Labig, Charles E. *Preventing Violence in the Workplace*. New York: AMACOM, 1995.

Kurland, Orin M. "Workplace Violence." *Risk Management*, June 1993, pp. 76–77.

Index